Canyons and Ice

Canyons and Ice

The Wilderness Travels of Dick Griffith

By Kaylene Johnson

EMBER PRESS
EAGLE RIVER, ALASKA

Poem on page 249 used by permission © Lincoln Tritt

Library of Congress Control Number: 2011945736

ISBN 978-1-4675-0934-3

Editors: Anne Dubuisson Anderson
Susan Beeman Sommer
Mapmaker: Marge Mueller, Graymouse Graphics
Production and book design: Nanette Stevenson
Cover and website design: Erik Johnson, Northern Vista Enterprises

Front cover photos: Grand Canyon by Jane Wilkens; Dick Griffith by Roman Dial;
Arctic print, Dick Griffith Collection.
Title page photo: Dick in 1990 Alaska Wilderness Classic,
Nebesna to McCarthy by Barney Griffith
Epilogue photos: Kaylene Johnson

Printed in Korea by Four Colour Print Group

Distributed by Ember Press and University of Alaska Press

EMBER PRESS
P.O. Box 771054
Eagle River, AK 99577

Contents

Prologue

I MET DICK GRIFFITH AT HIS HOME in Anchorage on a sunny April evening in 2010. I'd been invited to his Sunday family dinner by a friend of his. It seemed unorthodox to attend at the invitation of someone other than the host of the meal. Yet I would soon learn that not much about Dick is orthodox. He includes many "orphans," as he calls them, at his weekly dinners.

In Eagle River, where I live, and all across the northern and interior regions of Alaska, Dick is a quiet legend. He has walked across more of the Alaskan and Canadian Arctic than any person alive—all told, more than six thousand miles. He pioneered packrafting, long before it became a popular way of traveling the backcountry. Back in 1952, he used a small rubber raft to become the first to descend the dangerous Barranca del Cobre, a remote river canyon in Mexico.

For many years, Dick completed Alaska's Crow Pass Crossing, a twenty-five mile mountain foot race through the Chugach Range. While competitors half his age collapsed at the finish, Dick turned around and headed back to the starting line to retrieve his truck. Crow Pass was just a training run for more formidable endeavors. He has run the Alaska Mountain Wilderness Classic—an extreme 150-mile, cross-country race—seventeen times and finished his last race at the age of eighty-one.

For toughness and stubborn stamina, Dick has no equal. The Alaska countryside is littered with the whipped asses of the outdoor elite. He has little patience for gear snobs or those sporting the latest in trendy equipment.

He wrote, "The only sponsor I have is Salvation Army, a place I can get clothes cheap."

Yet his narrative is more than a tough guy's raw-edged adventure. It is, above all, the story of a romance. Yes, there is the enchanting story of how he met and married his wife, Isabelle; theirs was a partnership forged in white-water fury and the call of the canyon wren. But the driving force in Dick's life has always been his tumultuous affair with the wilderness, a love-sometimes-hate relationship that nearly cost him his life on more than one occasion. His passion for solitude and travel across a wild land drew him back again and again into the Arctic. Alone and on skis, he traversed the Northwest Passage, one mile after the next, through one of the most remote and inhospitable places on earth.

At that inclusive family dinner over a steaming bowl of moose stew, Dick brought out some of the journals from his travels. He also brought out the journals of his late wife.

I opened the pages and fell headlong into a story that was both colorful and captivating. The journals and photos chronicled their early years and how a young woman was swept off her feet by a sun-kissed rafting guide. Together they rafted the Colorado River before the Glenn Canyon Dam drowned one of the most scenic places in North America. And they forged a first on the Rio Urique of the Barranca del Cobre.

Dick's later Arctic journals are a thoughtful exposition on what motivates a man to pick up his pack and travel to the hinterlands of silence. Dick's musings are also ironic and funny. Like the passage, somewhere in the mix of polar bear encounters and a fall through ocean ice, Dick writes that he is not a thrill-seeker; that he would never bungee-jump, for example.

I suggested Dick write a book about his experiences. "No," he said. He wasn't interested. He didn't want any attention or accolades.

Dick's son, Barney, spoke up. "You know this book is going to get written. Either now or later on, when you're not around. You may as well have a say in it." Barney is himself a world-class mountain runner, and has run alongside his father in many of the Mountain Classics.

Dick, who was eighty-four, thought about that for awhile. Over the next few months, we chatted and met on occasion for black coffee and pilot bread topped with peanut butter and currant jelly. He shared more of his journals and then one day he told me, "You do it."

He wanted his book authored by someone other than himself. And he wanted it written in third person. For a long time he didn't want to use his last name. For all his sometimes brusque bravado, he is basically a shy man.

To those who look only at Dick's wilderness exploits, he is a man heroically larger than life. But to read about his thoughts and dreams, his hopes and disappointments is to read the story of a man who, like all of us, is profoundly human. Here, then, is his story.

–Kaylene Johnson

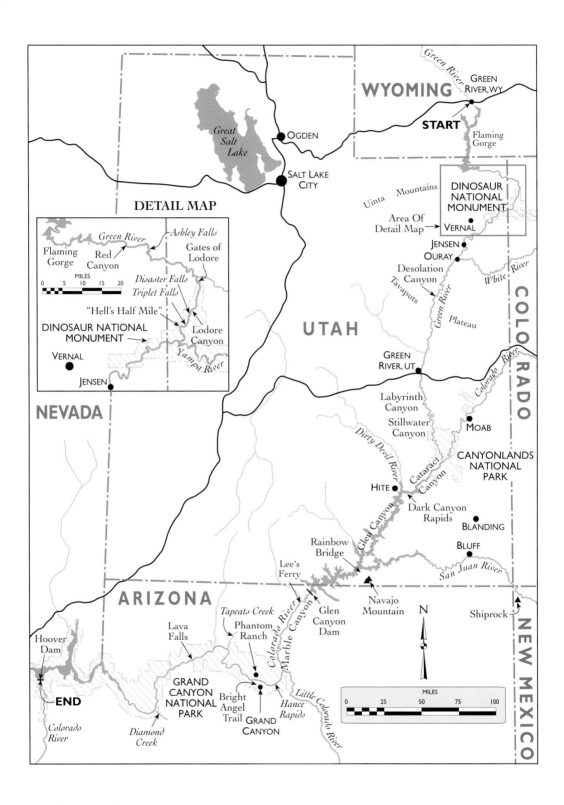

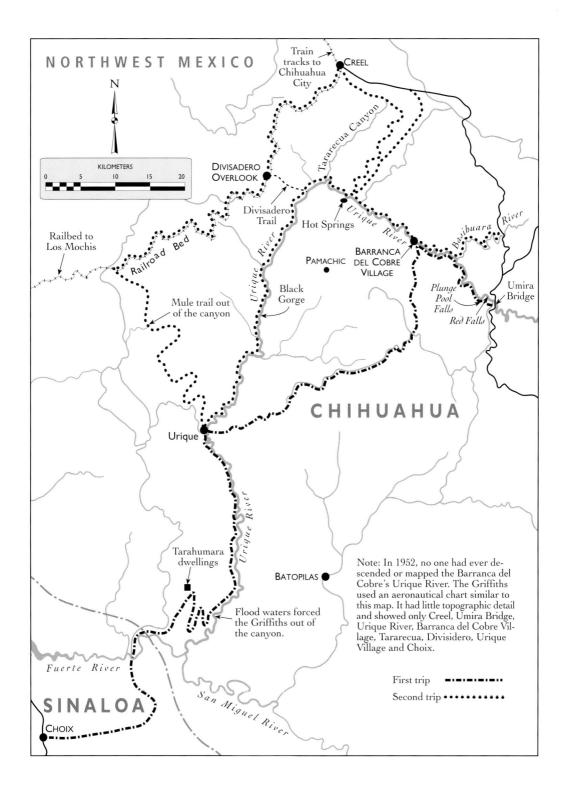

NORTHWEST MEXICO

N

KILOMETERS
0   5   10   15   20

Train tracks to Chihuahua City

CREEL

Tararecua Canyon

DIVISADERO OVERLOOK

Divisadero Trail

Hot Springs

Urique River

Bacihuara River

PAMACHIC

BARRANCA DEL COBRE VILLAGE

Umira Bridge

Plunge Pool Falls

Red Falls

Railbed to Los Mochis

Railroad Bed

Urique River

Mule trail out of the canyon

Black Gorge

CHIHUAHUA

Urique

Urique River

Tarahumara dwellings

BATOPILAS

Flood waters forced the Griffiths out of the canyon.

Note: In 1952, no one had ever descended or mapped the Barranca del Cobre's Urique River. The Griffiths used an aeronautical chart similar to this map. It had little topographic detail and showed only Creel, Umira Bridge, Urique River, Barranca del Cobre Village, Tararecua, Divisidero, Urique Village and Choix.

First trip ▬ ∙ ▬ ∙ ▬ ∙ ▬
Second trip ∙∙∙∙∙∙∙∙∙∙∙

Fuerte River

SINALOA

San Miguel River

CHOIX

Maps xi

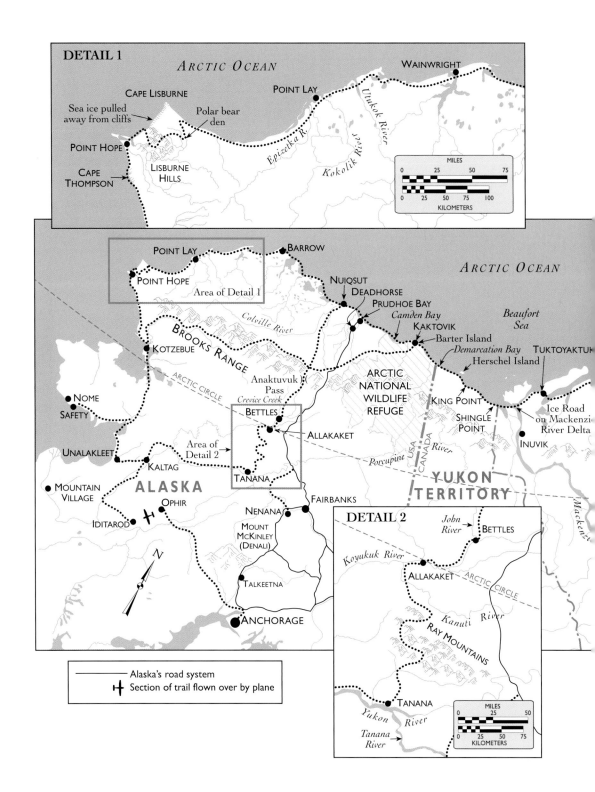

DETAIL 1

ARCTIC OCEAN

CAPE LISBURNE

WAINWRIGHT

POINT LAY

Sea ice pulled
away from cliffs

Polar bear
den

POINT HOPE

Unaleok River

CAPE
THOMPSON

LISBURNE
HILLS

Epizetka R.

Kokolik River

MILES

0   25   50   75

0   25   50   75   100

KILOMETERS

ARCTIC OCEAN

POINT LAY

BARROW

POINT HOPE

NUIQSUT

DEADHORSE

Area of Detail 1

PRUDHOE BAY

Camden Bay

Beaufort
Sea

KAKTOVIK

Colville River

Barter Island

BROOKS RANGE

Demarcation Bay

Herschel Island

TUKTOYAKTUK

KOTZEBUE

ARCTIC CIRCLE

Anaktuvuk
Pass

ARCTIC
NATIONAL
WILDLIFE
REFUGE

KING POINT

SHINGLE
POINT

Ice Road
on Mackenzi
River Delta

Crevice Creek

NOME

SAFETY

BETTLES

ALLAKAKET

Porcupine

River

USA

CANADA

INUVIK

Area of
Detail 2

YUKON
TERRITORY

UNALAKLEET

KALTAG

ALASKA

TANANA

FAIRBANKS

Mackenzi

MOUNTAIN
VILLAGE

OPHIR

NENANA

DETAIL 2

John
River

BETTLES

IDITAROD

N

MOUNT
McKINLEY
(DENALI)

Koyukuk River

ALLAKAKET

ARCTIC CIRCLE

River

TALKEETNA

Kanuti

RAY MOUNTAINS

ANCHORAGE

Alaska's road system
Section of trail flown over by plane

TANANA

Yukon

River

Tanana
River

MILES

0   25   50

0   25   50   75

KILOMETERS

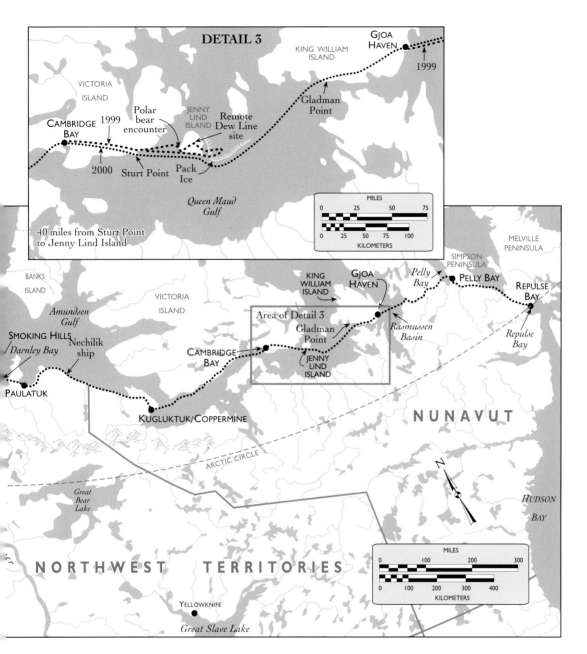

DETAIL 3

GJOA HAVEN
1999

KING WILLIAM ISLAND

VICTORIA ISLAND

Gladman Point

Polar bear encounter

JENNY LIND ISLAND

Remote Dew Line site

CAMBRIDGE BAY
1999

2000   Sturt Point   Pack Ice

Queen Maud Gulf

40 miles from Sturt Point to Jenny Lind Island

MILES
0   25   50   75

0   25   50   75   100
KILOMETERS

MELVILLE PENINSULA

BANKS ISLAND

VICTORIA ISLAND

KING WILLIAM ISLAND

GJOA HAVEN

SIMPSON PENINSULA

Pelly Bay   PELLY BAY

REPULSE BAY

Amundsen Gulf

Area of Detail 3

Gladman Point

Rasmussen Basin

Repulse Bay

SMOKING HILLS
/*Darnley Bay*   Nechilik ship

CAMBRIDGE BAY

JENNY LIND ISLAND

PAULATUK

KUGLUKTUK/COPPERMINE

N U N A V U T

ARCTIC CIRCLE

Great Bear Lake

N

HUDSON BAY

N O R T H W E S T   T E R R I T O R I E S

MILES
0   100   200   300

0   100   200   300   400
KILOMETERS

YELLOWKNIFE

Great Slave Lake

Dick Griffith's other Alaska travels include:
- Iditarod: 1,000 miles
- Glacier Bay to the mouth of the Copper River: 300 miles
- 17 wilderness races: Each 150 to 200 miles
- Chugach State Park: Untold miles in 500,000 acres

Dick Griffith's Arctic Journeys

DATES		DAYS	PLACES		AGE	MILES
Start	End		Start	End		
4-Jun-59	22-Jul-59	48	Kaktovik (Barter Island)	Anaktuvuk Pass	32	453
2-Aug-77	23-Aug-77	21	Anaktuvuk Pass	Kotzebue	49	600
22-Mar-79	7-Apr-79	16	Nuiqsut	Anaktuvuk Pass	51	200
10-Mar-80	17-Mar-80	7	Anaktuvuk Pass	Crevice Creek	52	80
7-Mar-81	29-Mar-81	22	Crevice Creek	Nenana	53	300
5-Mar-83	19-Mar-83	14	Bettles	Allakaket/Tanana	55	200
2-Mar-85	9-Mar-85	7	Tanana	Unalakleet (1st attempt)	57	60
1-Mar-86	18-Mar-86	17	Tanana	Unalakleet (2nd attempt)	58	370
14-Mar-87	15-Mar-87	1	Unalakleet	Barrow (1st attempt)	60	0
6-Mar-89	8-May-89	63	Unalakleet	Barrow (2nd attempt)	61	900
17-Nov-90	25-Nov-90	8	Anaktuvuk Pass	returned to village	62	0
1-Apr-92	2-May-92	32	Barrow	Kaktovik (Barter Island)	64	450
5-Apr-93	2-May-93	27	Kaktovik (Barter Island)	Tuktoyaktuk	65	400
13-Mar-95	11-Apr-95	29	Tuktoyaktuk	Paulatuk	67	350
26-Mar-96	6-May-96	42	Paulatuk	Coppermine/ Kugluktuk	68	475
5-Apr-97	30-Apr-97	25	Coppermine/ Kugluktuk	Cambridge Bay	69	240
29-Mar-99	21-May-99	53	Cambridge Bay	Repulse Bay	72	550
23-Apr-00	15-May-00	22	Cambridge Bay	Gjoa Haven	73	220

Canyons and Ice

Chapter 1

Drylander

*Far better is it to dare mighty things, to win glorious triumphs even though
checkered by failure than to take rank with those poor spirits who
neither enjoy much nor suffer much because they live in
the gray twilight that knows neither victory nor defeat.*
—*Theodore Roosevelt*

HIS FOOTFALL KICKED UP THE SCENT of dirt and rain. Puffy clouds sailed high in a deep blue Colorado sky. It was the summer of 1946 and Dick Griffith was nineteen years old. He carried with him only a .22 single-shot rifle and a blanket. He walked. And walked. For one hundred miles between the town of Rangely, Colorado, and its confluence with the Green River, he followed the course of the White River, whose main channel and tributaries cut a rugged trough into the high desert plains of the Colorado Plateau. One foot in front of the next, Dick breathed in sunshine, drank from clear springs and felt the breeze riffle through his wheat-colored hair. He subsisted on rabbits.

On this, his first solo trek, he had built himself a Huck Finn-type wooden raft to get down the White River. He didn't know much about boat building, navigating, or how to negotiate hazards on a swift-moving river. The first day on the water, a low cable strung across the river swept him off his raft. Sputtering to save whatever provisions he could from the capsized vessel, he watched as his rudimentary means of transportation disappeared downstream. He never saw the raft again. All that he managed to salvage were his rifle, some bullets, and a blanket. That, along with his knowledge of the wilderness, were all he now possessed to get him to his destination.

An elderly Mormon, named Bartholomew, picked Dick up as he walked a stretch of dirt road and the two of them struck a bargain. In exchange for help putting up a crop of hay, Bartholomew offered to resupply the lad with some groceries. He also agreed to drive Dick back to the rim of the canyon at the headwaters of Chandler Creek where he could continue his travels.

Dick agreed. In the evenings, after working to cut, stack, and haul hay with a team of horses, Dick went exploring for Indian ruins. Early peoples captured his imagination. He admired the way they lived and traveled on the land. He came across enough artifacts—beaded moccasins, silver bracelets, a U.S. government peace metal dated 1871—to fill a box that he shipped back home to Colorado.

The haying job took a week, after which Bartholemew and his wife drove him to the jagged edge of the canyon. A blue haze of dusk settled on the landscape as layer after layer of canyons stretched beyond the gorge and across the horizon. His hosts said their farewells. In the cool shadows of that evening, the place seemed desolate and forbidding. The wife was quite certain the boy would die out in the wilderness and begged him to reconsider his plans. Dick would not be swayed.

He descended into the canyon and followed Chandler Creek. He eventually arrived at its confluence with the Green River. There, in the middle of a scenic meadow, lay a distinctive, room-sized boulder. Ancient petroglyphs decorated the rock. Dick marveled at the notion of walking in the footsteps of the early Anasazi people. He touched the drawings and heard the sound of rapids from the nearby river—a sound oddly like the murmur of voices. There was something enchanted about this place. He wouldn't know until later how that canyon magic was soon to shape the contours of his life. He just kept placing one foot in front of the next, gazing at the wonder of an ever-changing yet enduring landscape.

When he finally reached Green River, Utah, he turned around and hitchhiked two hundred miles back home to his parents' home in Fort Collins, Colorado.

This was his very first walk-about, a harbinger of the thousands of miles he would travel through canyons and ice, across a continent and across a lifetime. What possesses a man to strike out alone across a wilderness year after year? It was a question Dick himself wondered about. Even now, whenever anyone asks him about this obsession, he never quite knows how to answer.

"Every so often," he says, "it's just time to walk."

DICK WAS BORN IN A ONE-ROOM farmhouse near Fort Collins, Colorado, in 1927 to Ray and Helen Griffith. It was the year Charles Lindbergh made the first solo nonstop flight across the Atlantic Ocean. At the age of seven, he contracted scarlet fever, an illness that would change the trajectory of his life. At eight, he moved with his parents and brother to a homestead sixteen miles west of Saratoga, Wyoming.

The Griffith homestead in Wyoming, 1944. The six-volt wind charger powered a lightbulb and radio in the house.

In 1935, the year of the move, America was in the throes of the Great Depression. Record-breaking heat had turned much of the country into a dust bowl. Unemployment was over 20 percent. Hitler had broken the Treaty of Versailles and announced the rearmament of Germany. In the midst of drought and the rumblings of war, Franklin D. Roosevelt dedicated Hoover Dam, a place that would figure prominently in Dick's future travels.

But all of that was a long way from Saratoga, a windblown, desolate area—noted even by their Chamber of Commerce as a place the pioneers gladly left behind. Dick's family eked out a living on a 320-acre parcel that bordered six thousand acres of open range. It was a place where an eight-year-old boy could explore with abandon, but only after the chores were done. While mom did the domestic work and tended the garden, Dick and his brother, Bill, helped their father care for forty head of cattle, thirty head of sheep, twenty horses, and various pigs, chickens, and other livestock. They also farmed potatoes and wheat and harvested hay. The farm work was done by old-fashioned horse-power with a team and wagon.

Dick knew how to ride and drive a team of horses even before he knew how to drive the family car. Yet by the age of ten, he was driving the Model A to school an hour each way. He and his brother carried a .30-30 carbine rifle along, because you never knew when you might come across a varmint. In those days a coyote pelt brought $10, a fortune considering that a loaf of bread cost eight cents and a gallon of gas was a dime.

As a child, Dick remembers his father always looking at the sky, checking for rain that never came. He remembers the hard physical labor of trying to make a living off the land. There was very little money, but always enough to eat—which was more than millions of Americans could say at that time. Dick shot his first antelope at the age of eleven and from then on it was his duty to put meat on the family table. That meant time outside, alone, in open country.

One of his favorite jobs was to check on cattle on the open range. Alone and on horseback, he remembers that he could travel one hundred miles before hitting a fence line. He could daydream, and think. Often, rather than ride, he ran alongside his horse—just to feel the ground under his feet. He liked the sensation of his body in motion, of covering long distances by his own power.

Ray shook his head as he watched his young son trotting alongside his horse. It would not be the only time that Dick's father was perplexed by his son's means of travel.

"My father did everything on horseback," Dick said. "No one touched his saddle horse. He was a true cowboy."

Ray actually divorced his first wife for "winding" a horse—inducing an emphysema-like condition caused by overuse of the animal. Dick himself learned the hard way about his father's intolerance for the mistreatment of animals.

On many occasions Dick's father had warned the boys to stay away from the prairie dog towns where the ground was pock-marked by holes that could break a horse's leg.

One time Dick ignored his father's warning and galloped his horse through the treacherous terrain. The horse stumbled and broke its leg.

Ray handed him a rifle with orders to shoot his own horse.

"That was a hard lesson," Dick said. On another occasion, his dog was caught in a coyote trap that Dick had set too near the homestead. The dog's legs were badly injured. Once again, Ray told his son to shoot a faithful companion.

Later on in his life, the demise of other canine companions in Alaska's wild places would cause Dick quiet dismay. "The ghosts of those dogs will always haunt me," he wrote in one of his journals.

During winter months, his father stayed on the ranch to care for the livestock while the rest of the family moved into Saratoga where his mother ran a small feed store. They lived in a small room off the back of the store.

Dick was twelve years old and each morning as he cleared the cobwebs of sleep, he warmed himself by standing next to the heat of the wood and coal-burning stove. One morning, he backed up too close to the hot stove and his pajamas caught fire. It all happened so quickly. The terrible blaze, the frantic actions of his mother, the smell of singed flesh. By the time the flames were extinguished, his back was badly burned.

Dick spent two months in painful recovery. For an active boy used to being in perpetual motion, his only solace was to read. His mother was educated as a teacher and both of his parents pressed the importance of education and reading. Now, during those endless days of healing, Dick took to reading volumes of books and every magazine he could get his hands on. His favorites were always stories of adventure and daring. One day he read an article in the *Saturday Evening Post* about a solo river trip undertaken by Buzz Holstrom from Green River, Wyoming, to the lower end of the Grand Canyon.

As the burned boy lay in bed reading about Holstrom's heroics through wild canyons, he must have imagined the cool waters of the Colorado River and what it meant to be driven by the noble pursuit of exploration. The more Dick thought about it, the more inspired he became. Inspiration grew to dogged determination that he would make that trip himself someday.

"I had to do it myself," Dick wrote. "At the tender age of twelve, I believed I could never be a real man unless I accomplished this task."

Later, Dick would also read *A Canyon Voyage* by Frederick Dellenbaugh, a narrative of General Powell's second expedition through the Grand Canyon. The account only strengthened his resolve to someday explore those rivers for himself.

Dick also read voraciously about Arctic explorers including Vilhjalmur Stefansson, Sir John Franklin and Robert Peary, who became his heroes.

In spring, after his burns had healed, Dick, his brother, and his mother returned to the ranch and to long hours helping cut, rake, and stack hay; hand pick potatoes; milk cows; and care for livestock.

"I worked with my father and brother, Bill, every day either in the fields or out on the open range with cattle and sheep." Dick said. "It was a good life on the ranch in many respects."

Even so, Dick saw how poor his family was and he saw how hard his parents struggled. He was also quick to realize that ranching meant staying in one place. And after all the adventurers he'd read about, staying put was the last thing on his mind.

"My father wanted me to take over the ranch," Dick wrote. "But I promised myself that I would never be a rancher, nor would I ever be poor."

A typical sheep wagon like the one Dick used in 1943 when he was 16 years old.

(L.R.A. Condit Papers, American Heritage Center, University of Wyoming)

For several summers, Dick herded sheep for a large operation in the Sierra Madre Mountains, not far from the Wyoming family homestead. He was tasked with moving three thousand head of sheep every few days as they grazed across the plains and mountain pastures of the region.

One summer the area between Iron Springs and Rawlin, Wyoming, was particularly dry and desolate. Due to the drought, hardly a blade of grass could be found. Without much to graze on, the sheep were hungry and restless. One night, Dick heard the sheep get up from where they were bedded and start moving out of camp. He dashed out of his tent without lacing up his boots and ran down the trail to retrieve the animals. In his rush, he stepped on a large coiled rattlesnake that was already bruised and angry from being run over by sheep. The snake lashed out and struck the side of Dick's boot, its fangs digging into the leather. Dick managed to kick the snake off with his other foot. As he inspected his boot by the light of a match, he discovered a fang embedded in the leather.

"Little things like that sometimes scared me," he wrote. He was sixteen years old.

Dick's companions were his horse, several sheep dogs, and a Mexican "tender" by the name of Placido Harmino. While Dick herded sheep, Placido cooked and moved the sheep wagon from camp to camp. Placido taught Dick Spanish and during inclement weather, offered his wagon so that Dick would not have to sleep in his leaky tent. Dick always remembered his friend's kindness, especially when he woke up one morning, feverish and aching.

"My joints were sore and my knee was too swollen to get into the saddle," Dick said. He had to climb up the spokes of the wagon wheel to mount his horse. The scarlet fever he'd had as a young boy had returned as a serious bout with rheumatic fever. Dick continued to work through the fog of an illness he didn't know he had. Eventually the symptoms subsided, but not without leaving a silent mark on Dick's health.

When Dick was a junior in high school, the family moved back to Fort Collins where Dick's father took over his grandfather's sporting goods store. Dick missed the wide open spaces.

"I gave up my horse for a bicycle. It was a hard move for me," he remembered.

The effects of the Great Depression left a deep impression on him. His brother, embittered by ranch life, left the family and was not heard from again for nearly thirty years. Dick was determined to outwork the poverty that had plagued his family. When Dick wasn't in school, he was earning a paycheck. Painfully shy, he didn't date girls or pursue friendships with other young men his age.

"I was a loner," he said, "and I was very focused when it came to making money."

Whenever possible, he looked for jobs where he could be outdoors, working for a time digging irrigation tunnels through the mountains of Colorado. He worked at a chicken hatchery and took odd jobs on the weekends to fill in the gaps. One day he was helping a friend work cattle, when they all noticed a plume of smoke rising from beyond the horizon. Dick rode his borrowed horse to investigate and met a wildland firefighting crew. The fire was nearly extinguished by then, but the crew chief, seeing Dick on horseback, hired him to ride the perimeter of the fire to put out hotspots. The forest service provided the horse and Dick spent the next several weeks in the foothills of the Colorado Rockies doing a job he thoroughly enjoyed. Once again he found himself alone in the wilderness—a place he always felt deeply at home.

Dick graduated from high school in 1945. In May of that year, Germany surrendered unconditionally. Two months later, atomic bombs were dropped on Hiroshima and Nagasaki and Japan surrendered. Even as World War II came to a close, most able-bodied young men were still eager to answer the patriotic call to serve their country. Dick was no exception.

He thought about the skills he could offer the military. His hunting experience made him an excellent shot so he went to a recruiter with the intention of becoming a sniper. Dick was confident of his physical prowess—he could outrun, outclimb, and outwork anyone. He got in line with the rest of the recruits for their perfunctory physical exam. But when the doctor pressed a cool stethoscope to Dick's chest, he shook his head.

"Son, you have a serious heart murmur," the doctor said. "You're not fit to bear arms."

Dick thought there must be some mistake. As Dick buttoned his shirt, the doctor explained that Dick's bout with scarlet and rheumatic fevers were the likely culprits of his heart condition.

The family doctor confirmed the military's diagnosis of a heart murmur and suggested that Dick's family move to Arizona. The lower elevation and dry climate would be good for him.

Dick was incredulous. The notion that he was somehow in fragile health was unfathomable. He wasn't going to be tethered by anything—not ranch life, not city life, and certainly not by some phantom medical condition.

So he took to the skies, using some of his hard-earned money for flying lessons. He would become a pilot.

When he was finally ready for his first solo flight, he was informed he would need a flight physical. Once again, his heart condition closed a door on his future.

"It was a real blow," Dick said. "I thought I was a physical specimen."

Dick lived at home for a time and went to college at the Colorado School of Mines in Golden, Colorado. "I was a lousy student," he said. He worked in his spare time.

Then one day he took a deep breath and quit his job as a roustabout on an oil rig.

It was time to take a long walk.

On that first more than one-hundred-mile walk from Rangely, Colorado, to Green River, Utah, Dick experienced wilderness skin to skin. Away from the clutter of noise and news and voices, he could think. He felt the hot sun and cool rain on his back. He heard the roar of thunder and clap of lightning overhead. In the embrace of wild places, a man could both lose himself and find himself. A young man could dream and dream big.

Dick thought about Buzz Holstrom's trip from Green River, Wyoming, to the lower end of the Grand Canyon—the one he'd read about as he lay healing from his burns. As a rancher's son, he may have been raised as a Drylander. But rivers provided passage to adventure; a way to dismiss and move beyond arbitrary or imposed limitations.

Dick would go to Arizona after all—but not in a way anyone expected.

Chapter 2

Launch

A venturesome minority will always be eager to set off on their own, and no obstacles should be placed in their path; let them take risks, for Godsakes, let them get lost, sunburnt, stranded, drowned, eaten by bears, buried alive under avalanches—that is the right and privilege of any free American.
—Edward Abbey

DICK STOOD ON THE BANKS of the San Juan River, looking at the glossy wooden boat he had built with his own hands. The year was 1948 and Dick was now twenty-one years old. Next to him stood his father, who tipped back his cowboy hat and shook his head at what Dick proposed to do. Father and son had just traveled from Fort Collins, Colorado, to Ship Rock, New Mexico, with the boat perched on top of the family Studebaker. Using a design out of a *National Geographic* magazine, it had taken Dick three months, working evenings after work, to build the ten-foot vessel. He constructed the craft of oak and marine plywood with two air compartments at each end to help keep it afloat.

Dick's plan was to start on the San Juan and join up

with the Colorado River. The route would cut across a corner of Colorado, through southern Utah, and down into Arizona as far as Lee's Ferry—a distance of approximately 250 miles.

His father must have felt a pang about Dick's upcoming adventure. Dick had been dealt some hard blows to his plans for the future, and as a father perhaps he knew this was something his son needed to do. But now, standing on the banks of the river's swift muddy waters, the whole enterprise seemed foolhardy.

"Tell you what," his father bargained. "I'll buy you a horse. If you want to go the length of the river, travel it properly and follow it on horseback."

Dick grinned but shook his head. "No thanks."

While his father looked at the sky every day to see what the weather would bring, Dick's eyes were on the horizon, wondering what lay beyond.

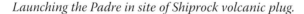

Launching the Padre in site of Shiprock volcanic plug.

Rivers would transport him from the unmoving ground to which his life had been anchored and launch him into a world he could only imagine. Dick named his boat the *Padre*. Father.

First, he had to learn how to row the damn thing.

"I thought I could drive the boat like a team of horses, pull on the left oar and go left, pull on the right and go right," he wrote. "It was a disaster—sandy waves kept flopping into the boat, I hit several submerged large cottonwood trees, couldn't get the boat to shore, couldn't get the boat away from shore."

The river swept Dick's boat downstream like a piece of flotsam, clunking against rocks and weaving drunkenly on the water. On the third day, a collision with a large tree broke the boat's oarlock, further complicating Dick's considerable difficulties.

At Bluff, Utah, Dick maneuvered the damaged boat to shore and considered his options. By now he knew he had some things to learn about being a boatman. He was fighting the current rather than harnessing its energy. With his back facing downstream as he rowed, he wasn't able to see the hazards and obstacles until there was little left to do except react. The river felt like a runaway team half the time and a disobedient sheepdog the other half.

After getting supplies in town, Dick returned to the river to discover three ten-man inflatable rafts lined up on the bank. A large group of Explorer Boy Scouts were being directed by a small, energetic man who clearly knew what he was doing.

Dick watched and then introduced himself to the boys' guide, Harry Aleson. The rafts were World War II surplus boats and Aleson planned to take the boys through the Glen Canyon on the Colorado River. He invited Dick to accompany them as long as he liked. Dick gladly took up the offer and traveled with them for a day between Bluff and Mexican Hat. Aleson, who became well-known as a pioneering river guide, took note of Dick's aptitude and work ethic. Aleson was venturing into business in commercial river tours and he eyed Dick as someone who might someday make an excellent boatman.

"Harry was a true 'river rat' and taught me everything I know," Dick wrote. The day they traveled together, Dick learned the Galloway method of rowing, facing downstream. "Now I could slow the boat down, have directional control, and spot rocks and holes ahead instead of looking over my shoulder. Without Harry's help, I wouldn't have made it very far."

Finally, Dick could kick back and enjoy the trip. While Aleson continued on his expedition with the Explorers, Dick took two weeks to explore side canyons and Indian ruins along the river between Bluff and Mexican Hat, Utah. Floating along under the sun-lit sky, he daydreamed and reflected on the beauty of the river.

"My power of expression is inadequate to explain the beauty of the canyon and the peace that prevails," Dick wrote in his 1948 journal.

His plan was to meet up with his friend Jim Gifford in Medicine Hat, but he arrived two days early. While he waited, Dick found work on a gold claim along a sandbar of the river where he dug, shoveled, wheeled, and dumped sand into a sluice. He was fed for his labor and each day the proprietor's wife baked Dick a loaf of bread on a crude wood stove.

"We did not recover enough gold to pay for the bread," Dick said.

Finally Dick's buddy arrived. They were good friends from their studies at the Colorado School of Mines. Leaving Medicine Hat, the pair quickly dropped into a canyon fifteen hundred feet deep. Steep canyon walls enveloped the river and their small boat. The shoreline had been replaced by sheer rock and the river now moved with a surging force that made its earlier current feel like a meander. There was no turning back now.

When they weren't floating the river, the two friends spent time exploring side canyons and ledges. One day they found a side canyon where they could climb out onto the plateau. The distance was farther than they anticipated and they ran out of water along the way. By the time they reached the top of the canyon, they were parched and exhausted from the heat and exertion of their climb.

"Our tongues felt like hot, dry bricks," Dick wrote. At the top of the plateau they found a puddle of brown, brackish water and drank from it thirstily. After arriving back at their camp on the river, they both became violently ill. Dick and Jim lay on their bedrolls next to the river in agony. The next day, Dick felt somewhat better, but Jim was still very ill. The wind kicked up and began whipping sand through the canyon.

San Juan Goose Necks.

"We were in a bad position; Jim could hardly move and I was too weak to row or get help," Dick wrote. "By the third day we were both much better, although Jim was weak and didn't fully recover until the end of our trip."

As they floated out of the deep canyons, they came upon towering red buttes, blue shale formations, and black petrified trees. Recovered now, Dick absorbed the mystery and appeal of the wilderness with every new bend in the river. It was easy to imagine the first explorers and their awe at the wonders of this place. As Dick and Jim entered another canyon, Dick maneuvered his boat through several rapids. Thanks to the two air compartments he'd built fore and aft, the boat stayed afloat even when temporarily swamped.

One evening, Dick and Jim found a place to camp along the river's bank and pulled the boat partially out of the water. There was no place to tie the boat so they left the rope dangling. They ate dinner, talked about the next day's travels, and laid out their blankets to sleep under the stars. During the

Lower San Juan River is now under water.

night, rainfall upstream caused the river's water to rise. Waves lapped at the unsecured boat. The river's constant nudge eventually pulled the boat back into the water where it quietly floated downstream.

When Dick and Jim woke up the next morning, the boat was nowhere to be found.

"Our faces were blank and our hearts pounded as we faced our dilemma," Dick wrote. "We had hundreds of miles to go but it might as well have been a thousand without a boat."

Although Dick had come a long way since losing his Huck Finn-type raft on that first trip in 1946, he still had some things to learn about river travel. He was learning that a small decision, a simple oversight, or a stroke of luck in either direction could alter the course—not only of an expedition—but of a life. Dick and Jim hiked downstream in silence, hoping beyond hope that somehow the boat had not traveled beyond their reach. With tremendous relief, they discovered the boat hung up by its rope on the far shore of the river. Their food, which they'd laid on top of the bulkhead, had been washed over the side. The cameras however, had been spared. The boat still held the life preservers.

The only way to retrieve the boat was to swim across the deep swift river. Jim started across but was quickly pulled under by a current that swirled between two large boulders. Jim's head bobbed up but he was pulled under again. Already weakened by his earlier illness, Jim had no strength left to fight the current. Rather than panic, he let the water sweep him downstream out of the hole. He barely had the strength to drag himself to shore.

Dick could see the boat was bobbing in the current and ready to let loose again. He climbed onto a log and paddled with his feet and hands to get to the far side of the river.

"By some lucky break the currents threw me alongside the boat," Dick said. He climbed off the log and into the vessel. "As soon as I stowed the cameras, the boat broke loose and I was able to row it to shore."

Later the two friends talked about their close call. Jim acknowledged that if the current had pulled him under a third time, he probably would have drowned.

With most of their food now gone, they hurried on, stopping at Aztec Creek on the Colorado River. From there they hiked up Forbidden Canyon, six miles to Rainbow Bridge, one of the world's largest natural bridges and a place long held sacred by Native American cultures. From the base to the top of the arch, it stood nearly 290 feet tall, and spanned 275 feet across, "a masterpiece of nature," Dick wrote. Teddy Roosevelt and Zane Grey were among early non-native travelers who made the arduous overland trek from Navajo Mountain to the foot of Rainbow Bridge.

On their hike to Rainbow Bridge, Dick and Jim shared their last bit of food—a single can of applesauce. They knew of a lodge at the base of Navajo Mountain where they could restock their provisions, but it lay another fourteen miles of rough terrain beyond the bridge. They decided that Jim, who was still ailing, would return to the boat while Dick continued on to the lodge.

Rainbow Bridge before the Glen Canyon Dam. (Note horse and rider center right.)

"I waited until dark to escape the hot desert sun," Dick wrote. He walked all night down into one canyon and up the next, over and over, gaining an elevation of almost four thousand feet over the course of the trek.

When Dick arrived at the lodge at dawn, the owners were incredulous. How had Dick found his way in the dark? Using tracking skills from his days of trapping and hunting in Wyoming, he had followed the scuff marks of steel-shoed mules across the rocks. A wrangler from the lodge offered to ferry their food by pack mule back to Rainbow Bridge. Dick gladly accepted, ate a hearty meal, and in the heat of the sun made his way back to the river.

By the time he returned to Jim and the *Padre*, he had traveled forty miles in twenty-four hours.

In the days that remained traveling the river, Dick and Jim spent time exploring side canyons for Indian ruins. At one of the pullouts, Dick spotted two intact pots lying on the bank. Jim, who later became a renowned archeologist, estimated that the beautiful red and black bowl and dipper had been crafted around AD 1100. Their trip had been a success in spite of their near-misses. And it only whetted Dick's appetite for more.

IN 2007, AT THE AGE OF EIGHTY, Dick returned to the San Juan River with his granddaughter Yarrow who was thirty-two, and her husband Tim. By then Dick had traveled thousands of river miles across the United States and Mexico and more than six thousand miles by foot, ski, and packraft across Alaska and the Canadian Arctic. He'd also trekked hundreds of miles in Ladakh and Zanskar in northern India with his daughter, Kimmer, and son, Barney.

Like all his travels, this trip with his granddaughter had its challenges and hazards. And as usual, Dick held little regard for the rules. The threesome did not have a permit to float the river.

"The big trick was to sneak out of Mexican Hat and get in the canyon as quick as possible before we were detected," Dick wrote.

Not only did they not have a permit—the notion of which would have seemed silly back in 1948—but Yarrow and Tim had never traveled in a packraft or a river boat. On this their maiden voyage, Dick assured them the river was mellow without significant rapids.

As it turns out, things change over the course of fifty-seven years. Just around the first bend and three hundred yards from their launch, they discovered a churning cauldron of muddy water. The rapids were too big for their small crafts. Dick flipped out of his boat first. Then Yarrow. Tim managed to maneuver to the far bank. Dick and Yarrow, in cold water and clinging to their packrafts, swam to shore.

Dick was shaken. "My only grandchild survived easily; I—being eighty—just made it to a sandy beach."

It was a dubious start to their adventure. "We so wanted to get into the canyon undetected," Dick wrote. But they had to stop, dry out, and get reorganized. They did manage to stay under the radar. Once they continued on their way, Dick said, "It didn't take long for the kids to become experts at handling the five-pound packrafts."

They spent three days on the San Juan, which had changed dramatically since Dick's early days on the river. Rapids had appeared in new places and others were gone—the Navajo Dam and Glenn Canyon Dam had changed its course forever. "The river had ceased to exist as I knew it," Dick said.

After three days on the San Juan and upon reaching the mouth of Grand Gulch, eighty-year-old Dick, Yarrow, and Tim packed up their rafts, and over the course of nine days, hiked along the river and in and out of side canyons to the highway—nearly sixty miles—exploring and investigating Indian artifacts, pictographs, and petroglyphs along the way.

In a 1992 outdoors column for the *Anchorage Daily News*, Craig Medred wrote, "The hair might be all white now, the skin heavily weathered, but inside that old chest still beats the heart of a lion."

Launching his little wooden boat into the muddy waters of the San Juan in 1948 was the first river trip in a life spent proving that desire and spirit can trump even a damaged heart. To hell with doctors, or rules, or at times, even common sense. A whole world awaited discovery. Over and over Dick would chase adventure and fall in love with the wild places that he traveled. Along the way, as it turns out, he would also fall in love with a woman.

Chapter 3

Isabelle

The new moon is slender and delicately curved. Silent, brooding,
blue-black cliffs silhouette against the sky. It's that old canyon magic.
—Isabelle Galo Griffith

SHE WAS A BEAUTIFUL WOMAN with striking green eyes, chestnut brown hair, and energy as effervescent as it was charming. In 1949, Isabelle Galo decided to spend some of her earnings from her job as a medical technician in Milwaukee to join Harry Aleson on a float down the San Juan River. Isabelle wasn't the first young woman to sign on for Aleson's river tours. Trendy girls from the East Coast often came west looking for adventure.

Aleson had launched his river tour business using surplus World War II inflatable boats and had hired Dick as a boatman and cook. During 1949 and 1950, Dick made four trips with Aleson from Bluff, Utah, to Lee's Ferry, Arizona.

Dick had always been self-conscious and ill at ease with girls. At the age of twenty-two, he had never dated. Besides, he said, "Girls cost too much money and they took too much time."

Whatever Dick's notions about girls, the young women on Aleson's boat tours invariably took note of the bronzed, shirtless boatman and drew him out of his shy silence.

"They all wanted to cut my hair," Dick said. So he let them. "My hair was pretty short by the end of those trips."

Once the ladies had him talking, he was not above bragging a bit. He talked about a river trip that he was planning with Jim Gifford—a twelve-hundred-mile odyssey that would retrace the journey of Major John Wesley Powell in 1869 from Green River, Wyoming, to the lower end of the Grand Canyon at Lake Mead. To date, less than sixty people had ever completed the trip. Many boats and lives had been lost along the way.

Isabelle listened raptly to Dick's plans. The daughter of Hungarian immigrants, she lived with her mother and stepfather over their tavern on a Milwaukee street corner. Her biological father had been shot and killed by police during Prohibition when she was just a toddler. Adventuresome and strong-willed, Isabelle had no qualms about traveling alone. She had met Aleson on a canoe trip in the Boundary Waters of Minnesota and agreed to join this tour from Bluff, Utah, through the Glenn Canyon. She loved the canyons they were now traveling and she was drawn to the young man with big dreams.

Dick explained how he and Jim planned to make their trip the cheapest expedition ever put together—because, in short, they had no money. Although they planned to live off the land by hunting, they still needed another boat. And supplies. And a pickup truck to take it all to the river.

Aleson's tour group, in four rafts, was floating down the river one hot day, when Isabelle decided to go for a dip. She had only just learned to swim and planned to stay near the boats as they meandered downstream. The wind suddenly came up, catching the boats like sails. Isabelle was caught by the current and swept downstream. Not a strong swimmer, she was clearly in trouble.

Dick tried to muscle his raft to her rescue but the wind was blowing in the wrong direction. So he dove into the water and swam out to Isabelle, keeping her afloat until another boatman could maneuver a raft alongside them. Isabelle hung onto the raft while Dick climbed on board. Then he reached down, grabbed her by her arms and began pulling her over the slippery rubber tube. As she came up out of the water, her swimming top slid off. Dick was so stunned and embarrassed, that he dropped her back into the river.

Someone threw her a towel and eventually a covered-up Isabelle and a red-faced Dick were safely in the boat together. Everyone dissolved into

Isabelle Galo, circa 1936.

laughter. And Isabelle looked upon her rescuer with both respect—and mirth.

As they continued down the river over the coming days, Isabelle thought it over. What an adventure it would be to accompany Dick and his buddy, Jim, on their trip to retrace Powell's expedition. She had money—enough that she was using some of her paychecks as bookmarkers. So she made Dick a proposition. She would buy them their boat, a truck, their gear, and food with one stipulation—that they take her along on the trip.

"We weren't being mercenary, just practical," Dick wrote, "Iz was a beautiful woman. But there was no romantic interest." In the end, they condescended to taking her with them.

They would begin at Green River, Wyoming, and take Dick's wooden boat, the *Padre*. It took one of Isabelle's bookmarker paychecks to buy an additional surplus inflatable raft. Another paycheck bought the pickup truck, and half of one more to purchase oars, food, and equipment.

Isabelle chronicled her observations about her trip with "the boys" in daily journals and through letters home to her parents, Dick's parents, and to her good friend in Milwaukee, Henrietta Marcott. Their trip began July 8, 1949, at Green River, Wyoming, and Isabelle's diary sang with the pleasure of discovering scenic wonders around every bend.

"This is what I've been waiting for—canyon country," she wrote. "There's nothing like it in the whole world. You look at it silently and can barely believe what you see."

There were miles of lazy river laughter as the threesome traveled downstream. Dick and Jim argued endlessly about everything—campsites, distance, time. "It's funnier than the dickens," Isabelle wrote.

Dick and Jim hunted geese along the way, shooting birds for their dinner and sparring over which of them was the better shot. Dick did most of the cooking using a Dutch oven—a cast iron cooking pot with a tight-fitting lid. He baked bread almost every day over the coals.

"That Dick sure can cook," Isabelle said. "He rubbed the goose inside and out with butter and salt, tucked in a few onions and covered it tightly in the Dutch oven. The smell of goose, pine, and cedar was overwhelming.

Ashley Falls is now under the waters of Flaming Gorge Dam.

Jim threatened to bite a chunk out of Dick's leg if the goose wasn't done soon. Such contentment."

Dick wore a red bandana tied around his head, with a couple of goose feathers tucked on the side. In the evenings, around the warm embers of their fire, Dick played a flute and Jim played the harmonica. They slept under starry skies.

"Isabelle Galo of Milwaukee was a dude if there ever was one," Dick said, commenting on her lack of wilderness experience. "Yet the canyon country held such a fascination for her that it was not long before she was rowing the boats, shooting our pistols, and cooking bread and fresh meat in our Dutch oven. The three of us made perfect companions; each of us had our special duties for the day."

Isabelle mentioned the misery of poison ivy and the abundance of mosquitoes. Dick agreed that the Uinta Basin is matched only by Alaska for mosquitoes per square inch of flesh. Isabelle also expressed her trepidation at the rapids. When they approached the roar of white water, they would secure their boats and then hike or climb to see what lay ahead. After studying the rapid, they could either run the white water, or opt to "line" the boats by tying them to a rope and walking on shore as their boats floated downstream past the falls. Often, at Dick's insistence, Isabelle walked the bank while Dick and Jim rode the white water. It was a common practice in the day—lightening the load was considered safer. The rapids may have been scary, but so was the climbing. Isabelle followed "the boys" up and over boulders and cliffs—all of which challenged her deep fear of heights.

The trio had been on the river for a week when they floated into Brown's Park, a placid section of the Green River. Halfway across, they spotted the spectacular Gates of Lodore where the Green River cuts its way through the Uinta Mountains, making a gorge several thousand feet deep. Everyone knew that exciting whitewater lay ahead.

First rapids in Lodore Canyon.

As their only guide, Dick had brought along a copy of Frederick Dellenbaugh's *A Canyon Voyage: The Narrative of the Second Powell Expedition*, a book first published in 1871. Dick knew that beyond the Gates of Lodore, one of Powell's boats had been crushed to pieces and three men nearly lost. The wreck had cost them two thousand pounds of gear and one third of the expedition's food supply. Powell had aptly named this dangerous portion of the twenty-one-mile-long Lodore Canyon "Disaster Falls."

With Dick and Isabelle in the inflatable and Jim at the oars on the wooden *Padre*, they scouted and then shot several rapids before deciding to stop early for the day. Dick wanted to organize their gear and lash down what they could for the following day's adventure.

The next day, as they rowed through one stretch of whitewater after the next, they came upon a spectacular and thunderous roar of water. Dick got out the camera. "At that distance we could see there were no rocks to dodge, so we omitted our customary procedure of stopping and looking over the rapids." Dick and Isabelle went first while Jim followed.

When they got around the bend, Dick realized their mistake. They were headed over a water fall but it was too late to pull to shore. He searched frantically for a place to slide off the falls and found a narrow channel. Jim bore too far to the right.

"The little red boat plunged down into the boiling water, shot straight up into the air, then tipped backwards end over end," Dick wrote. "Jim was thrown from the boat into thrashing undercurrents without a life preserver. I tried to reach him, but my boat was swept into a different channel."

Jim managed to grab hold of the capsized boat as it barreled downstream into bigger rapids. Again and again, the wooden boat slammed against boulders and then rolled over them. Jim hung on for his life.

"I prayed then as I never prayed before, because the river had him and only God could help now," Isabelle wrote later. "The rapids were endless."

As Dick and Isabelle watched the catastrophe unfold, Jim and the boat swept past them and disappeared. They followed in their inflatable raft, frantically scanning the water and bank for signs of Jim and the boat.

They discovered Jim lying on the bank. The splintered *Padre* was wedged on a rock in midstream—broken nearly in half by the rage of water against rock. Relief surged through them to find their friend alive. Somehow, miraculously, Jim had kept from being dashed between the boat and the rocks. The waters were calmer here and Dick maneuvered the inflatable boat to shore.

The *Padre* was destroyed. If any supplies were to be salvaged, Dick would have to rescue the remains of his boat. He swam out, fighting the

Recovering wrecked boat below Disaster Falls.

strong current and lashed a rope to the fractured hull. From shore he pulled on the rope from different angles, trying to break it free of the rock. The boat finally dislodged and he was able to pull it back to the bank.

"We lost all our food staples—flour, sugar, salt, raisins, eggs, bacon— the medicine kit, Jim's jacket, $20 sunglasses. Both boys' boots, Jim's pants and Stetson, geology pick (which the boys say they lose every year), $20 of unexposed film, rifle, bullets, and fishing equipment were all gone," Isabelle reported. "All I lost were a pair of scissors and the Ex-lax."

The wrecked Padre.

That evening a slow drizzling rain set in. The three friends camped under an overhanging rock ledge. The rain created waterfalls that poured over the red canyon walls turning them purple. Along with the drumming rain, they could hear the incessant pounding of more rapids several hundred feet downstream. The place felt dismal and eerie. All three of them were shaken by their close call and the loss of the *Padre*. Their banter that night was strained. Isabelle cooked dinner while Dick and Jim looked at Dellenbaugh's book and checked the landmarks near camp. Suddenly a realization began to dawn on Dick.

"Jim, do you think it's possible that we ran Disaster Falls?" The idea seemed too fantastic. At first Jim scoffed, but they quickly bent their heads over the book, which offered descriptions but no maps of the canyon.

"We checked and double checked and reluctantly concluded that we had wrecked our wooden boat in Disaster Falls, at almost the exact spot where Major Powell had lost one of his boats eighty years before," Dick wrote.

The next morning the sun came out and they all piled into the inflatable raft. Their spirits had improved but they proceeded with caution. They maneuvered through Triplet Falls and in the afternoon came to a long stretch of quiet water. Downstream, they could hear the roar of another major rapid. Dick had decided they would portage Hell's Half Mile, the most feared half-mile on the river. They were unloading gear for the portage when Jim began to tease Dick about whether or not he had the courage to run the rapid. It didn't take much for their earlier caution to disappear. Dick took up the challenge. Isabelle wanted to go too, but Dick refused.

"I begged to ride along, but Dick said 'I wouldn't let Jesus Christ through this rapid,'" Isabelle wrote later.

Dick trembled as he pulled the raft into the water. It was always like this, the trepidation just before a challenging run. And this one would be the toughest yet. The seething water was punctuated with rocks and deep swirling holes.

"All the water gathered up from both sides and plunged through a narrow opening. On the edges were large blocks of rock that had tons of water crashing into them," Dick wrote.

As the boat slipped in among the boulders, Dick's fear gave way to exhilaration.

"I made it through the rocks but when I came out into the opening, I dropped into a large hole. The boat kicked and bucked, and the pots and pans in the bow rattled. At the same time a huge wave dropped into the boat filling it and practically drowning me. To make matters worse, [one of] my oar[s] snapped like a stick," he said.

As Jim and Isabelle watched, Dick grabbed another oar and whooped. At the bottom of the rapid, wet and grinning, he maneuvered the raft to shore. Dick had just joined the ranks of only a handful of people to date who had ever successfully shot the rapids of Hell's Half Mile.

Dick, Isabelle, and Jim continued out of Lodore Canyon and into tamer waters. Their camaraderie never wavered. Dick called Jim "Hound-dog" because he liked to sit in the shade while Dick cooked dinner. Jim called Dick a Moqui Indian with feathers for brains. And they both called Isabelle "Mighty Mouse."

One day Jim and Isabelle decided it was high time that Dick's shirt got washed. Jim distracted Dick while Isabelle snatched the shirt and ran down the beach. Dick discovered their plot and caught Isabelle in a flying tackle. Jim came to the rescue and while Isabelle spit sand, Jim managed to get the shirt into hot soapy water.

Several days later Isabelle wrote, "The darndest things make us helpless with laughter." Dick had heard somewhere that swishing prickly pear cactus through muddy river water would clear up the water. Between handling the cactus, trying to make bread that evening, and licking the sticky stuff off his fingers, Dick had successfully embedded tiny spines of a cactus in his tongue. "We howled with laughter as I painstakingly pulled them out with a pair of tweezers," Isabelle wrote.

The teasing banter, the sunshine, and heart-stopping rapids solidified their friendships. It also drove deeper the attraction Isabelle felt for Dick. He could read a surging river the way a man might read a wild horse, anticipating

Desolation Canyon.

its unbridled movements, yet still able to ride its unruly course. With each passing day, the hot sun bleached his hair lighter and his broad shoulders grew more bronzed. Isabelle's admiration for Dick was giving way to something more.

Near the confluence of Green River and Chandler Creek, Dick remembered from his first walkabout from Rangely, Colorado, the large boulder inscribed with petroglyphs. While Jim went hunting for Indian artifacts, Dick and Isabelle hiked to the rock and sat in its cool shadow. The boulder sat perched in the middle of a flat meadow as if it had been placed there by a thoughtful giant. Although the river was some distance away, Dick and Isabelle clearly heard the enchanting sound of water tumbling over rocks. It was a sacred place, that boulder, a place with almost mystical energy. Dick was convinced if they listened long enough, they would hear the voices of the Anasazi and ancient Navajo.

After weeks of sharing the scent of wood smoke and starlight, after miles of traveling the deep fissure between earth and sky—Isabelle wrapped her arms around the untamed boatman. Their kiss swept Dick up into a current as powerful as any whitewater he'd ever known. He knew this could change his life, knew it could disrupt his nomadic plans for adventure. But in that moment, he didn't care. What the ancients were singing that day was a song about love.

Chapter 4

Standdown

The very fact that she's a girl and people talk makes things complicated.
—Dick Griffith

WHEN DICK, ISABELLE, AND JIM ARRIVED at Green River, Utah, in 1949, Jim had a letter waiting for him at the post office. His mother was ill and she requested that he return home immediately. They were crestfallen. Dick and Isabelle couldn't help but wonder if Jim's mother's illness didn't coincide with their letters home about his close call at Disaster Falls. Jim bought his ticket and took the next bus out of town.

Dick told Isabelle she should go home too. The rapids at Cataract Canyon were too dangerous, he said. She was a poor swimmer. Besides, people would talk, knowing a single woman was traveling alone with a man.

Isabelle was incredulous. Of course she would continue on their trek. She hadn't cared what anyone thought before she signed on—why should she care now? She wasn't about to come this far simply to quit. Besides, if Cataract Canyon was so dangerous, Dick shouldn't try it alone. They would take the rapids together.

"No," Dick said.

Isabelle insisted. She went with Dick to town to buy supplies. Dick bought only enough food for himself. Isabelle had only $10 left, but instead of buying a bus ticket, she bought groceries for the trip, starting with a dozen cans of milk.

"Iz, I'm telling you," Dick said. "It's no use. You're wasting your money."

She bought tomatoes.

"Please Iz. You can't. I've made up my mind."

She bought eggs.

After the store keeper loaded the food in the truck and took it down to the river, Isabelle slipped behind some trees and put on her river clothes—a dirty shirt, stained shorts, and beat-up old shoes. Then she threw her duffel bags in the boat and sat on top of them.

For two hours they argued. Then she pleaded.

"Dick, don't leave me here. You just can't go down that river alone," Isabelle said.

"You can't go. Please, Iz."

Dick was worried about the responsibility of taking Isabelle through the most difficult rapids of the trip. "Cataract Canyon is no place for a girl," he said. Between 1909 and 1912, at least seven men had perished in that one short section of the rapids, a stretch known as the "Graveyard of the Colorado." If something happened to him or they lost the boat, he knew she wouldn't be able to scale up two-thousand-foot canyon walls and cross miles of desert to safety.

Isabelle sat on her duffels and refused to budge. They argued and finally Dick exploded. He stormed onto the boat with the intent of throwing her off. But Isabelle quickly slipped over the side of the raft, into the water, and hung on.

"Trying to lift me into the boat was like hoisting a five hundred pound bag of cement out of a hole," Isabelle wrote.

Dick grabbed Isabelle's duffels and threw them to shore. Then he sat down in the shade of a large rock and glared.

"I'll never understand women," Dick muttered.

After another hour of fruitless argument, they were getting nowhere. Dick clearly would not change his mind. Isabelle finally let Dick pull her out of the water. He offered her the remaining few dollars in his pocket but she angrily refused. Then she watched from shore as he rowed down the river without her—in a boat purchased with her paycheck.

She had four dollars left but could not abide the thought of waiting around for the 9:00 p.m. bus. She shipped her duffels back to Milwaukee, wired home to pick up more money in Denver, and then took to the highway, thumbing for a ride. That night she spent $2 on a room in Thompson and got up early the next day to continue hitchhiking. At Palisade, she got her first glimpse of the Colorado River.

"I scrambled down the bank and gazed at the passing water feeling forlorn, lost, and discouraged," she wrote. She wanted to be on the river, not on her way home to Wisconsin.

Her next ride was with two outdoor enthusiasts who were fascinated by her story. Throughout their journey, Isabelle and Dick had written home with accounts of their adventure. Their parents relayed that information to local newspapers and now many people knew about the adventures of these young river travelers. The two men encouraged Isabelle not to give up and to join up with Dick downstream in Hite, Utah.

Following Dick and meeting him downstream of Cataract Canyon hadn't even occurred to Isabelle. But the more she talked with them and worked out the details—the more convinced she was that it would work. By the time they got to Eagle, Colorado, Isabelle had made up her mind. The men bought her dinner, gave her $10, and she headed back 130 miles to Grand Junction. There, Isabelle checked in with the newspaper editor, who also encouraged her. She made arrangements to stay at a motel, then called Henrietta asking her to forward money and return the duffels she'd just shipped home to Milwaukee.

"No more doubts or hesitations," she wrote. "I had been spitting and clawing empty air like a cat held helplessly by the scruff of the neck…but now my stubbornness was in full swing and I was ready for definite action."

Meanwhile, Dick traveled alone but he could not erase the image of Isabelle standing on the bank while he rowed her boat downstream.

"She just knew she could win me over, but she lost, and I am the one who really suffers. I broke my promise to her and I am about the loneliest person," Dick wrote in his journal.

The river had grown smooth as molasses. The air shimmered with relentless heat. Dick passed Crystal Geyser, but now these new discoveries held less appeal—he had no one to share them with. The first night after leaving Isabelle, rather than make camp, he slept on the boat. He didn't bother to eat. His energy waned. When he finally did eat, the food only reminded him that everything of worth, including his food and boat, belonged to Isabelle. He owned nothing more than his river clothes, a flute, and $3.83.

"I used to take pride in the fact that I was a loner and could do anything by myself. I now know that my life is due to a drastic change," Dick wrote. He could feel his plans for life as a single, nomadic traveler slipping away. "She, Iz, is a tough one."

Late one day he climbed out of the river's meandering bed to watch the sunset. For miles and miles he saw a vast scorching desert being cooled by evening rains. The sky had never looked more beautiful as it fired pinnacles and spirals of rock with intense color. And he couldn't remember ever feeling so deeply alone.

Back at the boat, he baked bread and ate. Then he pulled out his flute and filled the canyon with the haunting echoes of shadow and song.

As the Green River sank deeper into the strata of the Colorado Plateau, Dick contemplated the rapids ahead. Three miles past the confluence of the Green and Colorado rivers lay wild stretches of white water. From Dellenbaugh's book, he knew he might need to portage—but was it possible to do alone with a 450-pound raft?

The night before the big drops, Dick set up camp and then hiked high to overlook the next day's challenge. At the top of the canyon, miles of boulders created a rock garden of house-size stones, caves, and narrow passageways. From the canyon's rim wall, Dick could see the LaSal Mountains to the east. He focused his attention back on the river. He would need to plan carefully and be cautious especially in the forty-mile rollercoaster of Cataract Canyon. When he returned to camp it was nearly dark. He slept restlessly, tossing and turning as whitewater roared through his dreams.

The next morning he lashed down spare oars, the gun, his bedroll, and flute. He studied the river again, checking each rapid by walking down and

Lower end of Cataract Canyon.

back again memorizing each rock and swirl of the current. He stood on the bank and threw logs into the water, noting when the log was pulled under and then watching to see where the river spit it back out.

Time after time, when his fifteen-foot boat slid over the smooth tongue of a hole, Dick felt as if he were diving to the bottom of the river. He gripped the oars to hang on, hoping he wouldn't be swept overboard or that the boat wouldn't capsize. Waves crashed over the top of him as he struggled to maintain control. Each time, Dick rowed to shore and bailed out the water before venturing farther down the river. The first day in Cataract Canyon, he made just nine miles.

That night to settle his nerves he went looking for fossils. He cooked dinner and played his flute. He woke up sleep-walking along the sandstone rocks, looking for Isabelle and Jim. "I couldn't understand why they weren't on the sandbar with me."

The next day, on August 11, 1949, the water grew even more furious. The flow of the river at that point was roughly twenty thousand cubic feet per second. Dick crawled over boulders to scout out the river and discovered sudden drops and waterfalls. Boulders and churning holes were strung all across the river. He knew these were places more safely traversed by lining the boat downstream or by portaging it altogether. But between the weight of the boat and the force of the river, he also knew he could manage neither on his own. His only choice was to run the rapids. One rapid in Cataract Canyon, with its folds of water and churning whirlpools, made Dick shudder.

"This rapid scared me more than any other rapid I had run before," Dick said. "I would have backed out right then and there, but the only way out was down the river."

He rowed within thirty feet of the drop off and positioned the boat. His mouth was dry. His heart pounded. He aimed for a narrow five-foot opening that would take him between two boat-eating holes. His boat plunged down the falls and shot through the strip exactly as he'd planned. Dick was elated. "It was the most beautiful run of all my river experience," he wrote.

The night brought its shadows however, and as he set up camp, the dark narrow canyon felt ominous. "I was dwarfed by its immenseness and silenced by the power of the rapids." Ahead lay Dark Canyon Rapids, the last rapids in Cataract Canyon. People had died there. Dick's nerves were frayed.

He spent the evening intently walking the river to map his route. One more day and he would be on his way to the more manageable waters of the Glen Canyon. Deep in thought, he looked up and was stunned to see a young man standing on the rocks.

Too startled to speak at first and each wary of the other, they finally introduced themselves. The young man turned out to be Jon Lindberg, the son of Charles Lindberg, whose first solo trans-Atlantic flight took place the year Dick was born. Jon was one of a group of Explorer Scouts who had hiked in from the rim through Dark Canyon. As Dick was scouting downstream, Jon was exploring upstream. After chatting, the pair climbed into Dick's raft and floated downstream to the Explorer group's camp. It turned out the boys were short on food but thanks to Isabelle's rations, Dick had plenty to spare. He was happy to part with it. He also skinned and cooked a rattlesnake that the boys had killed. Their leader, Kenny Ross, who was himself a boatman, wondered how Dick had managed more than forty miles of rapids in Cataract Canyon by himself—especially in an inflatable boat.

Rubber rafts were only just emerging as a boat of choice in the world of river runners and Dick was only the third party ever to run Cataract Canyon in an inflatable boat. Eleven years earlier, in 1938, Amos Berg and Buzz Holstrom—author of the article Dick had read as a boy—made the trip between Green River and the lower end of the Grand Canyon in a commercial inflatable; two years earlier, in 1947, Harry Aleson and Georgia White had also run Cataract Canyon in an inflatable. Dick's solo run helped prove the worthiness of the craft. Following Dick's lead, Boy Scout leader Kenny Ross and Jon Lindbergh also ran Cataract Canyon with an inflatable craft later that summer.

The dark shadows of the evening dissolved in the company of good conversation, a campfire, and a delicious meal. The next day, Dick invited Jon to run the Dark Canyon Rapids with him, and while the others watched from shore, they easily shot the churning water. Then, Dick said goodbye to

Dick and Jon Lindberg running Dark Canyon Rapids.

his new friends and headed toward Glen Canyon, Dirty Devil River, and out of the canyon's shadows.

While Dick assumed Isabelle was safely on her way home to Milwaukee, she was instead hitchhiking her way to Blanding, Utah.

"The dangers of the Green and Colorado rivers are like a wading pond compared to the uncertainties and hazards of the U.S. highway," she noted.

Hite was still ninety miles away and she went from one gas station to the next asking if any truckers were heading that direction.

Aaron Porter, who was in Blanding to have his truck repaired, agreed to drive her to his family ranch in Hite once the repair was finished. The fix took most of the day and Isabelle was impatient. As she sat in a café waiting, she wrote in her diary and watched as people came and went.

"A bunch of tourists burst through the door in noisy enthusiasm," she wrote. "It's amazing the weird sizes and shapes these Levi jeans can adjust to. Most entertaining. I'm critical because I've been exposed to perfection." Perfection was presumably wrapped up in her feelings for Dick.

Porter's truck wasn't finished until 7:00 p.m. but they set out anyway down the bumpy, two-tire track road. It took them all night to travel ninety miles. Arriving for breakfast, Isabelle was charmed to meet the rest of the family. The food from the family's garden and orchards was sumptuous and they offered friendship as amply as they offered the bounty of their table. "They treated me just swell. It's a little embarrassing to have people be so grand. There's so little one can do in return," she said.

Isabelle's plans to hike upstream to meet Dick were dashed when she learned that sheer walls of rock went straight down to the water, leaving no shore on which to walk. She met a surveyor doing work on the Dirty Devil River, which flowed into the Colorado River. He offered to ferry her upriver the next day, to a sandbar where she could camp and wait for Dick. If Dick didn't show, he would be passing through the following week and could pick her up again.

Isabelle gladly took the offer. She was getting closer now. She set up camp on the river where she and the surveyor had agreed to meet the next day. The setting sun blazed red on the sheer cliffs across from her campfire. To the faint roar of rapids, she watched the first stars appear in the sky. Isabelle Galo had come a long way from a pub owner's daughter in Milwaukee. Earlier in the summer—a lifetime ago it seemed—she had started this journey as a tourist. Now here she was, camping solo on the Colorado River, not only growing confident in the wilderness, but inexplicably drawn to it. The moon cast silver shadows on the sandbar. As she closed her eyes to sleep, she thought about the boatman who had introduced her to the thrill of whitewater and the beauty of deep canyons.

The next day, Isabelle broke camp, loaded her duffels into the surveyor's boat, and headed upstream toward Dirty Devil River. As they motored around a bend in the river, Isabelle saw a sight that took her breath away.

"There floating lightly on the dirty Colorado waters was a black rubber boat manned by a man clad only in shorts and a red bandana tied around his head," she said. "His skin was burned so dark he looked like an Indian. It was Dick."

Their timing could not have been better. After eleven days of solo adventure for each of them, they were back together.

Dick's journal entry on that day, August 14, 1949, does not disclose how he felt about this unexpected surprise.

"I met Iz," was all he had to say about that.

In later years, he laughed about that meeting on the river.

"She stalked me," he said. "Never have I seen a girl with such perseverance."

AT THAT POINT, DICK AND ISABELLE were both out of money.

"I have no more book markers, so we're out of funds," Isabelle said. The Porter family invited them to stay long enough to earn what they needed to continue their trip. Dick put up hay using a team of horses—a job he knew well from his days in Wyoming. He also helped the older son, Farnum, hand dig a well for a neighbor. Isabelle picked fruit from the family's orchard and they feasted heartily on sun-ripened cantaloupe, peaches, fresh cream, and generous portions of home cooking. Isabelle noted that Dick was regaining the weight he'd lost.

Dick Griffith, age 22, 1949. The town of Hite, Utah is now under the waters of Lake Powell.

Ten days later they returned to the river. This time Farnum, seventeen, was tasked with going along as a chaperone. Once again, they were a team of three, happily floating downriver toward Boulder (Hoover) Dam, Nevada.

Dick, Isabelle, and Farnum floated through deep gorges, past fortress cliffs and chiseled red rock that within a matter of a few years would be under water. In the 1950s, the nation was in a mood to build dams to supply the West Coast's ever-thirstier demand for electricity. Completed in 1963, the Glen Canyon Dam created Lake Powell, covering thousands of acres of wilderness, hundreds of side canyons, two hundred miles of river, and more than three thousand Indian ruins.

"Foothills rise gently like pulled taffy into higher, violet-tinted rocks, then jagged red cliffs. Finally in the background, Navajo Mountain looms silent, black, and forbidding," Isabelle wrote. Words could not come close to capturing what they were seeing. The photos they took revealed only slivered glimpses of a vast and soon-to-vanish landscape.

The six-mile hike to Rainbow Bridge was daunting for Isabelle. She struggled to keep up with Dick and Farnum and they weren't inclined to wait for her. For all her frustration, the reward at the end of the trail was stunning. They spent the night on a sandy beach near a water fall that cascaded into a clear deep pool. The next day they headed back to the river to continue their journey.

Through sundrenched days and star-strewn nights, Dick and Isabelle once again cloaked themselves in canyon magic. Dick chuckled remembering those final days of their trip saying only, "It's a good thing Farnum was a sound sleeper."

Hidden Passage.

At the end of a 900-mile float from Green River to Lee's Ferry.

During the summer of 1949, only four boating parties attempted to float the Colorado River through the Grand Canyon. Although Dick had hoped to make the entire trip from Green River, Wyoming, through the Grand Canyon and on to Boulder (Hoover) Dam, they made it only as far as Lee's Ferry, Arizona—three hundred miles short of their destination. Time had run out and Dick, who was working on a degree in geology, had to return to college. They vowed to return and someday finish their trip.

It was not the only vow they made. On August 30, 1950, exactly one year after completing their nine-hundred-mile adventure, Dick and Isabelle were married.

Chapter 5

Canyons and Character

We have an unknown distance yet to run, an unknown river to explore.
What falls there are, we know not; what rocks beset the channel, we know not;
what walls ride over the river; we know not.
Ah well! we may conjecture many things.
—Major John Wesley Powell

DICK WAS DETERMINED TO RETRACE Major Wesley Powell's 1869 route of discovery from Green River, Wyoming, through the Grand Canyon on to Boulder (Hoover) Dam, Arizona. Prior to 1950, less than 110 people had ever traversed the Grand Canyon. The summer of 1951—two years after their first attempt—Dick and Isabelle found a willing partner in Johnny Schlump who could afford to buy a boat and spend an entire summer on the water.

They launched two ten-man military surplus inflatable boats from Green River, Wyoming, on July 1. Dick and Isabelle had been married for almost a year. By now, the Green River and northern portion of the Colorado River were growing as familiar to Dick as a temperamental old friend. He looked forward to getting even more acquainted as they discovered the Grand Canyon for the first time.

They floated quickly through Flaming Gorge and the eighty-mile Red Canyon. Carved by water, wind, and time, the canyon's strata laid out a chronology of the Earth's history from two billion to 250 million years ago. Bit by bit, water sliced into the great Colorado Plateau, carrying sediment seventeen hundred miles into the Sea of Cortez in the Gulf of California. All that sediment acted as a giant rasp, grinding against the terrain and cutting the canyons ever deeper. The fissures of earth left behind created great caverns, slotted canyons, and pillared formations—places of wonder and awe.

The waters of the Green and Colorado rivers ran a chocolate brown. Choked by silt, they had been described as "too thick to drink and too thin to plow." For drinking water, Dick, Isabelle, and Johnny let river water sit in a bucket until some of the sediment settled to the bottom. They often stopped at clear springs and streams from side canyons to drink and bathe. In all of Dick's travels over time, he never once treated or filtered his water.

Isabelle and Johnny Schlump in camp.

They often saw wildlife—bighorn sheep, deer, geese, even wild burros. From the willows they heard the bird calls of Bell's vireos. Sweetest of all was the liquid call of the canyon wren, a plaintive cry that both Dick and Isabelle noted in their journals.

Gates of Lodore.

"The canyons of course are the same as they were two years ago, only this time with about five feet more water, which makes the rapids rough," Dick wrote.

Johnny had no river experience before this trip, but he learned quickly from Dick. "Johnny is going to make a good boatman," Dick wrote. "He understands water, and above all things, he is careful."

Disaster Falls, where they had earlier wrecked Dick's wooden boat, *Padre*, was thrilling but easily managed this time.

Triplet Falls proved otherwise.

They had stopped and looked it over and Dick had plotted their descent. But somehow he missed his entry and wasn't able to pull away from the canyon wall as he'd planned. The boat dropped straight down into the churning rapids. As it swung around the curve, the river pulled the boat into a seething hole. The entire front end went under water and wouldn't shake loose. The boat shuddered as Dick furiously plied his oars in the white whorl of foam. A tremendous surge of water hit the boat, sweeping Dick, Isabelle, and their gear overboard. Isabelle caught hold of a ring on the boat and held on. Dick struggled to the surface but came up underneath the boat. He managed to reach up and around to catch hold of the boat's rope rail. Their boat continued to buck and shake as Dick pulled himself back into the besieged vessel. Isabelle tried to keep her head above the crashing waves. As Dick strained at the oars, the river finally released the boat, flinging them back into the current.

Dick and Isabelle in Crystal Rapids in later years.
(photo by Janice Tower)

Dick pulled Isabelle back on board and into the waterlogged boat. They chased after the gear that had shot downstream without them, recovering their duffel bags and extra oars—everything except a hat and bar of soap. They were bailing water out of the boat when Johnny came through and met them on the beach. He had missed the excitement.

They all breathed deeply and took a moment to take stock. The incident proved to Isabelle that she could keep her head, even in grim circumstances. And it gave Dick pause to consider Hell's Half Mile that lay ahead.

Dick didn't like that rapid. He remembered it from the last time—angry waters beginning with a cyclone hole and nine others just like it stacked up beyond the first. He'd managed it on a dare last time but today, after barely getting out of Triplet Falls, he wasn't in the mood.

Isabelle described Hell's Half Mile in strong language, "That monstrous raging torrent gone completely mad and berserk and roaring like a gigantic demon straight from hell ... It was like looking death in the eyes."

Dick decided they would line the boats along the edge through the churning waters of the boulder field. Although he'd considered it on previous trips, he'd never actually lined a boat before. He supposed there was no place like Hell's Half Mile to learn.

They lashed everything securely into the raft and tied long ropes, one to the bow and one to the stern. The idea was to walk along the shore while easing the boat downriver. Johnny would hold onto one rope, Dick the other. It quickly became clear this would be much harder than it looked. The raging water grabbed the loaded-down raft, forcing it into the main current. Dick quickly tried snubbing the boat on a rock. This only served to catch the boat up short and water surged into the raft. Quickly, they loosened the line and the six-foot-wide boat crashed into a pile of rocks, jamming between two boulders. The river swept over the top, carrying their air mattresses downstream. But their gear was the least of their worries.

"I could have cried to see her twisted and torn and ground against the rocks," Isabelle remembered.

Dick and Johnny secured the ropes on shore to look the situation over. They decided to loosen the stern line and pull from the front—maybe between their pulling and the forceful surge of water from behind, the boat

Hell's Half Mile. Inexperience almost lost the boat.

would come loose. As they heaved on the rope, the advantage of an inflatable raft became obvious. The boat drew herself up, folded inward into a V and squeezed between the massive rocks. As soon as the raft broke loose, Johnny and Dick heaved with all their might to bring her to shore. By then the boat, filled as it was with water and gear, weighed more than one thousand pounds.

They had learned their lesson. When it came time to line Johnny's boat through Hell's Half Mile, they unloaded the boat first. A lighter boat would be easier to maneuver. That meant carrying their food and gear downstream below the rapids, a job that took hours as they picked their way over rocks and boulders along the shore. This time, when they lined Johnny's boat, Dick was careful to allow the raft to keep moving forward. The weight of the boat was now more manageable and this time they got it past the rapids with relative ease.

The deeper into the canyons they traveled, the higher the temperatures soared. The sun beat down relentlessly and the rubber boats grew too hot to touch. At one point Dick's thermometer read 110 degrees. One evening at camp, Dick and Johnny decided to build some shade for their rafts. They cut slender willows, trimmed off the branches and leaves, and lashed together a curved framework. They covered the framework with blankets and secured it to the boats.

"The boats look like glorified sheep wagons, but it sure did the trick," Isabelle wrote. "[They] gave us shade and heavenly relief from the heat and brilliant sun."

At Jensen, Utah, they stopped to resupply their expedition. Bus Hatch, a well-known boatman, picked them up and drove them ten miles to his home in Vernal, Utah, where they enjoyed a home cooked meal. Bus knew of Dick and Isabelle's travels by the accounts he read in local newspapers. Hatch became a legend in his own right for his exploration of the Green River—and his sons later followed in his wake by becoming boatmen and river guides. Dick couldn't know then, that some forty years later, he would meet Bus's son, Ted Hatch, as he made an outlaw run on the Colorado River.

Back on the river, and in the evenings' cool canyon shadows, Dick, Isabelle, and Johnny would built a fire, cook dinner, and drink tea. After the meal, if there were no rapids below, Dick would swim across the river and back—a habit that made Isabelle and Johnny uneasy.

One month after they had launched their trip, they spent a day traversing three successive rapids so wild that Dick insisted Isabelle watch from shore—with a camera. It aggravated her that she was often the designated photographer. She liked whitewater as much as anyone. But she was a poor swimmer, and Dick felt more comfortable giving her this role as he and Johnny ran the rapids.

Travel through the forty-mile Cataract Canyon was a serious challenge. A flash flood upriver had raised the level of the water by five feet. On August 1, 1951, the river was running at approximately fourteen thousand cubic feet per second. They took what Dick called "the chicken route" along the edge of the river, which involved more rocks but less holes and standing waves.

One of forty rapids in Cataract Canyon. Many of these now lay under Lake Powell.

The difficulty lay in maneuvering through the rocks without getting wrapped around or hung up on the boulders.

Just below Dark Canyon rapids a stone wall was inscribed with the names of previous pioneering river runners. To the names etched in stone, Johnny added "Griffiths & Schlump." Dick wasn't so sure that was a good idea. Some of those names had come to dubious ends.

First, there was the 1889 Brown-Stanton Expedition, passing through twenty years after Major John Wesley Powell, with a crew of eleven. Three men, including Brown, were drowned, and five abandoned the trip.

Also inscribed were the names of the Kolb Brothers—Emery and Ellsworth. They had traveled from Green River, Wyoming on to the Colorado River, all the way to Needles, California in 1911. One of the brothers was currently at the South Rim ranger station giving talks about their treks. (Years later, when Emery died at age ninety-five in 1976, an unexplained skeleton with a hole in its skull was discovered in a canvas boat in the attic of his garage.)

And then there were the Hydes, Glenn and Bessie, honeymooners who disappeared in the lower Grand Canyon in 1928—a mystery that to this day generates speculation of murder.

Norm and Doris Nevills were also inscribed in the rock. Dick had met Norm during his 1948 trip with Jim. Norm never thought inflatables would amount to much. In the log book at Rainbow Bridge in '48, Dick had made acerbic remarks that called Norm Nevill's bragging into question. Now the couple was dead, killed just two years earlier in a small airplane crash.

Another name on the rock was Buzz Holmstrom—the author of the article that Dick had read in *Life* magazine as a boy. He died of an apparent suicide shortly after his trip with Amos Berg from Green River, Wyoming, to the lower end of the Grand Canyon.

Finally, and less foreboding, was the name of Dick's former employer, Harry Aleson. Dick was happy to associate their names with that of his friend.

Lower end of Glen Canyon at the Arizona/Utah border.

Glen Canyon Hole-in-the-Rock where 250 Mormon settlers, 83 wagons, and 1000 head of livestock crossed in 1880.

As they threaded the canyons, the threesome decided to stop and camp at the confluence of the Colorado and San Juan rivers. This was thought to be a sacred place where two Navajo deities met to create the children of rain and clouds and that night, the gods conceived a spectacle.

"A fury of a thousand storms broke over our heads," Isabelle wrote.

Wind and rain swept through the canyon while thunder crashed and lightning struck the far side of the river. A duffel bag tumbled into the river. The heavy lid to the Dutch oven went flying. Dick, Isabelle, and Johnny ducked under an overhang as wave after wave of rain drenched their camp.

Storms were not uncommon on the river, especially after mid-July during the rainy season. The falling rain loosened rocks from their beds and brought them tumbling down sheer canyon walls. So along with the crack and rumble of thunder came the crash of boulders falling into the river.

Dick stepped out into the fury as lightning lit up the canyon walls. He shouted an epithet at the maelstrom, his voice mocking the storm's ferocity. In the next instant, lightning and thunder bellowed back. He was young and strong and sure of himself. He could challenge the wilderness with a young man's swagger. This was one of many lover's quarrels that Dick would have with the wilderness over the years—fist-shaking moments of tempest and wrath. The roar of the storm forced Dick to duck back under the overhang. Years later, in the relentless and deep cold of the Arctic, the haunting indifference of the natural world would force him to face his own mortality—but tonight the wild weather was exhilarating.

DICK, ISABELLE, AND JOHNNY ENTERED the Grand Canyon on August 14, 1951. At this point the river was flowing at 12,900 cubic feet per second. In the new territory ahead lay a multitude of challenging rapids including Lava Falls.

Navajo Mountain.

Marble Canyon.

Rapids in the Grand Canyon are rated differently than those of other rivers. Other rivers are rated one to five, with five being the most extreme with potentially fatal consequences for mistakes. The Grand Canyon rapids are rated one to ten, to accommodate a wider variety of variance depending on the river flow.

Isabelle rated the river according to the items that Dick portaged to safety below the falls. If he carried his flute, camera, and film around the rapids for safekeeping, she knew to strap her life vest a little more snugly. Or she walked.

At Lee's Ferry, the threesome took a short break from the river. Like their trip in '49, Dick and Isabelle had taken care to write letters home, describing their adventures. These were reported in their hometown newspapers and on their route along the way. When they arrived at Lee's Ferry, they were met by well-known boatman Stu Campbell, who had heard of their travels. He drove them seven miles to Marble Canyon Lodge, gave them groceries, and after a steak dinner took them back to the river. The next day he delivered their mail.

Several days later, and deeper into the canyon, they looked up to find a cable car that ran one thousand feet from the floor to a wide ledge of the canyon above them. On the ledge was a camp belonging to a crew of sixteen men doing exploratory work for a proposed dam in Marble Canyon. The crew invited Dick, Isabelle, and Johnny to dinner, an offer they gladly accepted. Isabelle, wildly afraid of heights, clutched the railing of the cable car with white knuckles as they ascended to the crew's camp at the top of the red wall limestone.

Isabelle described their meal in sumptuous detail, "Roast pork, roast beef, spaghetti ... buttered sweet corn ... spinach, green beans, cottage cheese, biscuits, peaches, ice tea, milk, coffee, and cherry pie."

Later, in 1968, the Marble Canyon Dam project would be shut down with officials yielding to the protests of the Sierra Club. The group was determined to save the Grand Canyon after conceding the Glen Canyon in a political compromise that allowed for the building of the Glen Canyon Dam.

While Dick and Isabelle were aware and also wary of the country's "dam fever," their more immediate concerns were for the rapids ahead. Dick took none of them for granted. They ran across a monument alongside the wrecked boat of pioneer boatman Bert Loper, who had died on the river two years earlier. And at President Harding Rapid they passed the grave of fifteen-year-old David Quigley, a Mormon who drowned on a church outing earlier that summer.

Gravesite of Mormon youth, David Quigley, at Harding Rapids.

Bert Loper's wrecked boat.

They also ran Hance and Sockdolager Rapids on their way to Bright Angel Creek. Then they parked their boats and hiked the nine-mile trail out to the famous South Rim of the Grand Canyon. At this point the canyon was one mile deep. The trail was the most famous of the Grand Canyon, with tourists traveling up and down on foot and by mule.

"People! Five thousand a day average," Isabelle wrote of the crowds. 'We see so few people on the river that we get friendly as puppies and will stop to talk with anyone."

Today, in 2012, the South Rim has nearly five million visitors a year with over thirty thousand people who run the river every season.

Emery Kolb, whose name was etched on the stone below Dark Canyon Rapids, was showing a film to visitors about his and Ellsworth's 1911 exploration of the canyon. The Kolb brothers were the first to record their adventures on the river with a movie camera. Emery ran the movie daily at their photo studio from 1915 until his death in 1976, making it the longest-running movie in history.

Dick, Isabelle, and Johnny checked in at the South Rim Village park headquarters, bought their supplies, and ate. From here, maps of the canyon were available. As they headed back down to the river, they came across mule trains carrying tourists.

"Oh, you are the ones with the rubber boats?"

The tourists recognized the threesome and inundated them with questions. Dick teased the saddle-sore travelers and asked if they would trade in their mules for two slightly used boats.

Back on the river, their travels were often washed with rain. One afternoon, in a drizzle, they decided to seek shelter for the night under an

A bucket boat with primitive oarlocks and flimsy oars.

The cave has since fallen in.

overhanging rock shelf upstream from Upset Rapid. The overhang was two hundred feet long, thirty feet deep, and twenty feet high, providing a perfect refuge complete with firewood and a sandy floor. As the rain fell, the water rose. Several times Dick and Johnny retied the boats to higher rocks. Suddenly, toward evening they heard a tumultuous roar. They ran to the edge of their cave and looked.

"There, high up against the skyline were two waterfalls directly above the end of our cave," Isabelle wrote. "We ducked back in and a second later a torrent of water poured into the river over the spot we were standing on."

They slept restlessly as the waterfalls poured through the night. The rain continued and on August 29, Isabelle wrote, "Tomorrow is our first anniversary. Dick and I will make our first year together but if it doesn't stop raining, I can't promise more."

Everyone was getting testy. In Dick's journal notes, he summoned the legend of Bessie and Glen Hyde, the newlyweds famous for their disappearance on the Colorado River in 1928. Under the strain of their current situation Dick wrote, "We were newlyweds, but my wife did not shoot me."

Finally the sun emerged and just in time for the trio to prepare for Lava Falls, the rapids they had heard so much about—the ones they'd been anticipating the entire trip.

A roar that Isabelle described as the sound "like ten express trains" announced the impending falls. Stretching the width of the river, Lava Falls is rated an X at all levels of water. Between massive rocks, roiling waves, and deep holes it took only one look for Johnny to announce, "We line her." Dick agreed.

It took six hours to portage the 450 pound boat.

They unloaded the boats and carried their food and gear over and around the rocks past the rapids. The sun beat down and sweat trickled off their brown bodies. Dick was quiet and thoughtful throughout the hours it took them to portage gear around the raging falls. It was hard work that didn't leave much energy for conversation. Besides, Dick was thinking as he watched the river. At one point he sat down to rest in the shade of a rock and tamarisk.

Isabelle looked at her husband and her hand flew to her mouth. All she could whisper was "*Dick.*"

Next to Dick, lay a coiled rattlesnake, its eyes glittering. The sound of rushing water drowned the sound of its rattle.

Dick's face never changed expression as he slowly eased up and away from the snake. As it uncoiled and tried to slither away, Dick grabbed a rock and killed it. Whitewater wasn't the only source of excitement on the river.

Throughout the day, Dick continued to study the rapids. Once all the gear was moved beyond the falls, Dick and Johnny attached ropes on the first boat and eased it downstream. At times they had to lift and turn it between boulders, slipping it through sideways. Isabelle took photos as they went. When it was time to line the second boat, Dick looked at Isabelle and Johnny and made a startling announcement.

"You know," he said, "I'm going to run her."

After the rattlesnake incident, he was feeling lucky.

Johnny and Isabelle were dumbstruck. After initially looking at Lava Falls their decision to line the boats had been unanimous. Yet they both knew that once Dick made up his mind about something there would be no arguing about it. Johnny was skeptical and asked Isabelle what she thought.

"I know Dick and I know his confidence," she wrote. "I answered that I thought he could make it."

Johnny prepared his own boat and got a tow rope ready since there was a good chance Dick would need to be rescued. Isabelle set up the cameras. Only a handful of river trips to date had ever attempted to run Lava Falls, and none of them in a rubber boat.

Dick wrote, "The entry is the tough part … You cannot see the rapids until you pour over the tongue … The trick is to be in the exact spot when you

First run of Lava Falls in an inflatable boat, 1951.

peel over the top. There is no maneuvering from side to side once you get in the rapid. To go between the two large rocks I had to be perfectly lined up. I was! I went through the rapid without incident much to the amazement of those standing on shore. They thought I would be killed dead."

Dick became the first person ever to run Lava Falls in an inflatable raft.

In the coming days, they continued on through the remaining rapids. At Separation Canyon they saw a plaque in memory of three men who left the Powell expedition in 1869. By the time the expedition reached this point, they had only a musty bit of flour, a few dried apples, and a small amount of coffee for their remaining travels. Powell's men had portaged Lava Falls and the rapids ahead looked just as ominous. At this point, three men decided to walk out—and they were never seen again. At first it was assumed that Indians had killed them. More recent research revealed the three men were likely killed by Mormon settlers who mistook them for U.S. government agents with whom they were feuding.

The Colorado River—that great sculptor of canyons and character—eventually widened into the flat waters of Mead Lake. Ahead lay ninety miles of calm water before Dick, Isabelle, and Johnny reached their destination of Boulder (Hoover) Dam. Now they had no river to propel them, so they rowed one mile after the next, averaging ten miles a day. Sometimes the wind blew them backward. Other times they flew across the water using a sail Dick made from driftwood and canvas. Sometimes they traveled at night when the wind and waters were calmer. One morning as Dick played his flute, the coyotes in nearby hills answered. Soon their journey would come to an end and they would be back to everyday life where their adventures would became both memory and motivation for the next trip.

The final hazard of the last miles of their odyssey turned out to be a scorpion. They were camping on the banks of the lake when Dick felt something crawling up his back. He slapped it away but as he did, it lashed out and stung him. A wretched night ensued as pain shot up and down Dick's legs, back, and head. The next morning, still feeling terrible, he decided that a day

Crossing Lake Mead.

End of a 1200-mile journey.

of rowing would fix him right up. So they launched the boats and rowed ten hours to their next campsite.

As Dick, Isabelle, and Johnny neared Boulder Bay at Hemingway Harbor, recreational boaters in the Hoover Dam area approached, offering food and beer and congratulating them on their achievement. They accepted a tow for the last several miles and when they arrived, newspaper reporters and fans gathered around.

It took Dick, Isabelle, and Johnny sixty-nine days to make the twelve-hundred-mile journey from Green River, Wyoming, to Boulder (Hoover) Dam, Nevada. According to historian Otis "Dock" Marston, Dick, Isabelle, and Johnny were the 144th, 145th, and 146th individuals to have made the traverse from Lee's Ferry to the Grand Wash Cliffs at the end of Grand Canyon.

Dick and Isabelle may have finished one long trek but they were nowhere near finished with their canyon explorations.

On their next adventure they would become the first to descend a place as yet unmapped in the world.

Chapter 6
Barranca del Cobre

We often hear drums a thousand feet above us on a ledge.
And still we haven't seen a single Indian.
It is kind of like a western movie. We are surrounded.
—Dick Griffith

IN THE SEPTEMBER 25, 1950, issue of *Life* magazine were photos of a place as stunning in scope and beauty as the Grand Canyon. Hidden in the Sierra Madre Occidental Mountains of northwestern Mexico lay a mysterious canyon, the Barranca del Cobre (Copper Canyon). No one knew the depth or the length of this remarkable canyon. The photos depicted deep gorges, exotic plants, and colorful birds. It also captured glimpses of the Tarahumara people who lived on the terraced cliffs of the canyon. And there, in ink, were the words that set Dick and Isabelle on a new course of adventure.

"No man is known ever to have traversed the canyon from end to end."

Air Force Lieutenant Colonel Bill Matthews read the article and knew that if anyone could make that trip, it would be Dick Griffith. The Barranca del Cobre had become the Holy Grail of boatmen, a wilderness uncharted. Matthews had caught the river rafting bug as a client of Norm Nevilles—a commercial boatmen and rival of Dick's boss, Harry Aleson. Matthews knew about Dick and Isabelle's Grand Canyon adventures through various newspaper accounts. So Matthews tracked Dick down and offered him wages as a guide in an attempt make the first successful descent of the Barranca del Cobre.

Tarahumara Indians.

They set out on February 8, 1952, to drive to Creel, Mexico. The party was made up of five people. Dick, Isabelle, Lieutenant Colonel Bill Matthews, Sergeant Johnny Wlodarski, and once again, Dick's college friend Jim Gifford, an archeology student interested in learning more about the native Tarahumara people.

First they had to get to the Urique River, which itself was a challenge. The Mexican roads were too much for Dick's Pontiac sedan. The car hit a rock on the rough road, punching a hole through the flywheel housing.

"The noise was worse than the damage," Dick noted. But it was obvious the car wasn't going to make it to Creel. Outside La Juanta, they all piled into Jim's truck, which was already overloaded with their gear. No signs marked the way along the dusty road; they stopped at every village to ask directions.

"At one village Bill jumped out and spilled out a string of Spanish to a Mexican," Dick wrote. "The Mexican answered him promptly saying 'Me no speak English.' So much for our Spanish!"

They finally arrived in Creel and rented a room from a Chinese innkeeper. Isabelle noted how gracious the innkeeper was—and that he had three beautiful daughters. The tab for the whole group including rooms and meals came to just $7.

That night, they lay awake anticipating the adventure that lay ahead. Unlike their trips down the Green and Colorado rivers, there likely would be no place to leave the river, resupply their rations, or send letters home. No one had ever mapped this canyon. Their only guide was an Air Force chart of the area. With no contours and a scale of only 1¼ inches for every ten miles, it revealed few details for their canyon descent. The hazards were unknown; they weren't sure it was even possible to float the river from one end of the canyon to the other.

They arrived at the Umira Bridge the next morning, eager to see the Urique River. The hundred-foot gorge revealed sparkling blue water tumbling over rocks and boulders. Scenic yes, but the river itself was very low. That meant even if floating conditions improved, traversing the canyon would still require many portages.

Dick immediately knew this required a big change in plans. He ordered all their gear unloaded from the truck, unpacked, and spread out on the ground.

"Then he ruthlessly put aside about half of our equipment to be sent back with the truck," Isabelle wrote. "Our 450-pound, rapid-running neoprene boat wasn't even unloaded. Back went the life preservers, surplus clothing, and a good part of the food. Jim and I protested vigorously, because we thought the river might become more floatable lower down. Dick was firm—he didn't give an inch."

As the truck drove away from the bridge, leaving the expedition party, Isabelle experienced a momentary feeling of panic. "There went our last contact with civilization," she wrote.

Even with their gear cut by half, they still had the weight of two seven-man inflatable surplus boats at sixty pounds each, three ten-gallon cans of food, six duffel bags, sleeping bags, air mattresses and tarps, seven cameras, paddles, two guns, jackets, and medicine.

By the trip's end, nearly all of it would be abandoned.

After making their way down the steep embankment to the water, they were surprised to discover that unlike the Grand Canyon, the water was icy cold. They slept in the gorge under the bridge, a cold clear night, and the next day, put their boats in the water.

"The canyon is magnificent," Isabelle wrote. "Sheer towering walls with trees clinging everywhere, rugged terraced rock climbing straight up, clear, sparkling water … We had a splendid run—for about a hundred yards. Then the river was choked and blocked by monstrous boulders as big as houses."

Everyone looked at each other with apprehension. How far and often would the river be blocked by boulders like this? As the men ferried the gear and tried lifting the boats over boulders, Isabelle scouted the river ahead. Downstream, massive rocks continued to plug the river and she began to hear the faint roar of rapids. She hiked to see exactly what the river was going to dish out next. What she saw stunned her. The river suddenly disappeared into a chute carved through the rock. On the other side, water plunged down a twenty-foot waterfall.

This wasn't going to be easy. They named the place Red Rock Falls and had to portage the rest of the gear and lower their boats down with ropes. It took all of the first day for their party to travel just two miles.

The next day the Urique River continued to present boulder after boulder and at one point the canyon walls dropped into the river on both sides. The river tumbled into one pool and then over a twenty-five-foot drop into a second pool. They called this Plunge Pool Falls. Lowering their boats and gear over the whitewater took hours. By the end of the second day, they had traveled only one short gooseneck bend in the river—less than half a mile.

That night around the campfire, they discussed the situation. Matthews and Wlodarski had to be back by March 15 or they would be AWOL—absent-without-leave—from their military commitments. Jim had to be back by March 10 or lose his semester's credits. At the rate they were going, they wondered if they would make it through the canyon in time. And at some point, it might become impossible to walk back out.

The next day they were able to glide a half mile through deep pools of green water between nearly sheer cliffs. Just as they thought things might be looking up, great house-size boulders once again blocked their way. After

Portaging around the falls.

another two-hundred-yard portage, Dick decided it was time again to lighten their load.

"Every one of us threw something away," Dick wrote. "Jim abandoned his sleeping bag, archeology equipment, clothes, and soap. Bill and Johnny both unloaded clothes. I threw away two blankets, my gold pan, and clothes. Isabelle was sitting on top of a huge boulder and protested loudly and vigorously when she saw the blankets go. We piled everything on top of a huge boulder hoping the Indians would find it."

That night, after hours of grueling work, they made camp only one and a half miles beyond the previous night's camp.

"One mile yesterday and three miles the day before isn't much," Dick reflected. "We work very hard and our labors seem barely worth the effort. This canyon is so large and difficult to traverse that I can't see any way to get down it with boats. One could walk, but many places require swimming to cross."

One of many long portages.

As they struggled downstream, they occasionally looked up to the vague feeling of being watched. They saw footprints in the sand but not the people who had left them. They often heard the ghostly sound of drums echoing through the canyon. It was an eerie feeling. The Tarahumara remained out of sight. These shy people were known as indefatigable runners, with stamina enough to run deer to exhaustion.

The next day, they portaged around masses of gargantuan boulders that filled the canyon floor. "The river wound in and out, going under the boulders, dropping off into crazy waterfalls, forming deep, silent, gloomy pools where the waterfalls shouted and screamed," Isabelle said. "The sun never reaches down into this devil's cellar."

As they descended into the canyon the nights grew colder and without their extra blankets, they had to curl closer to the campfire. By the eighth day of the trip, they had traveled only ten miles. They had also reached the quitting point of two men from El Paso, Texas. A year or two earlier, Paul Reed and Frank Lynch had painted *El Paso City Limits* on a rock and abandoned their expedition.

What had begun for Dick as an intriguing job to guide the Colonel had now turned into a consuming desire.

"Now that I have touched the fringes I'm becoming fanatical about this area—I've got to have it all," he wrote.

These sentiments were not shared by his employer, however. On February 16, the Colonel, his Sergeant, and Jim Gifford decided to quit. They did not believe there was time to complete the trip before the Air Force would come looking for them. And Jim needed to get back to school.

Dick looked at Isabelle. "I'm walking through," he said. He wasn't about to quit.

Isabelle knew Dick would have no qualms about going on without her. Later in life, as a white-haired volunteer guide on back country trips in Alaska, he was once fired for this propensity to forge ahead without his charges.

Isabelle didn't hesitate. She would go, too.

Once again the group had to reorganize their gear and pare down. Except for cameras, sleeping bags, air mattresses, some food, and Dick's gun, everything was left behind. The boats, much of the food, clothes, and air mattresses were all put in a pile for the still elusive Tarahumaras to take as they wished. Then the party shook hands and wished each other well as Dick and Isabelle headed downstream and the other men headed out of the canyon.

Dick and Isabelle were on their own now and without a boat. That day they made four miles. The terrain was daunting, as they climbed over and around boulders and skirted steep rocky walls.

"What I dreaded finally happened today," Isabelle wrote. Canyon walls plunged hundreds of feet straight down into the water. The only way through was to swim or to climb the surrounding cliffs. Isabelle looked at the sheer walls and trembled. She had never gotten over her fear of heights.

"I'll swim," she said, even though she was a poor swimmer.

"Might be a waterfall below," Dick said quietly. So Isabelle followed Dick along a narrow ledge up the sheer wall only to discover that this too was impassible. As they carefully inched their way back to where they started, Isabelle sang, whistled, looked at the sky—anything to keep from looking down.

Back at the river—no further along for their efforts—they called it a day. And Dick considered what to do.

In the morning he built a raft. He gathered five logs and tied them together with his belt, shoe strings, fishing line, and twine. He put the air mattress across the logs and then balanced their gear on top. Dick and Isabelle stripped to their underwear, piled their clothes on top of the raft, and slipped into the icy water. Hanging onto the raft, they kick-paddled across the river.

This became their means to cross deep, otherwise impassable sections of the canyon. After each crossing, Dick disassembled the raft, saving the shoestring and any other line for the next raft he would have to build.

Dick would build at least four different driftwood rafts and their progress downstream was painstakingly slow. Isabelle found it difficult to climb high cliffs to skirt around impassible areas of the river. In one instance she wrote, "Dick scouted the right side of the river. He found the beginning of a trail marked with a long pole. It climbed up into the sky and over the cliff. I started gamely enough. But about a third of the way up, as the trail got steep and edged near drops of two hundred feet straight down, I sat and quietly went into hysterics. Dick patted me on the shoulder and tried to comfort me. I wailed all the louder. Gradually I relaxed, wiped away the tears and started again."

Between the deep water, sheer cliffs and slow progress, their supplies were dwindling. The Tarahumara Indians—with whom Dick had hoped to barter for food—remained elusive and out of sight. Dick came to a disappointing conclusion. That evening he wrote, "We will be out of food in a few days." The question was which direction was the best way out of the canyon?

The next day involved more cliff climbing and Isabelle wrote, "I'm glad I had my hysteria yesterday because today there is no time."

Dick had decided they would climb to the rim of the canyon, traverse some miles along the top where the going would presumably be easier, and then drop back down to the river. But there was no water for drinking higher up and they had only a single canteen between them. It took most of the day

A raft made of driftwood.

to reach only three-quarters of the way to the top of the canyon. By then they were out of water. So they returned to the river.

Dick built yet another raft for the long deep stretch of water ahead. This swim would be the longest yet, more than two hundred yards. Since Isabelle didn't swim well—especially not for long distances in frigid water—Dick built a bigger raft using seven logs, a rickety boat big enough to carry Isabelle and their gear.

With Isabelle kneeling on the air mattress holding the camera and gear, Dick kicked his legs to propel the tottering raft forward. He blew hard from exertion and the cold. By the time they reached the other side, Dick was hypothermic.

With teeth chattering, he said, "Iz, make a fire, quick!" He was shaking too hard to strike a match.

Isabelle scrambled to gather wood and light the fire. Then she heated up milk for Dick to drink. They built up the fire, crawled into sleeping bags and slept.

Their distance for the day's extraordinary effort was only one-half mile.

DICK KNEW FROM THE AIR FORCE chart that there was a mine farther downstream. Just beyond the La Purisima Mine lay the village of Barranca del Cobre. He hoped that here they would meet up with people who knew of a trail to get out of the canyon.

Hiking along the rocky shore toward the village, they were met by Mexicans and Tarahumara Indians who gathered around them wondering where they had come from. The couple seemed to have appeared from nowhere.

In halting Spanish and by putting sticks together and balancing a stone to look like a raft, Dick explained how they had traversed the river. The villagers shook their heads in amazement.

As for trails out of the canyon, they learned that there were two. One was to Creel where they had started, a day's walk away. The other traveled overland sixty-five miles to Urique. Rather than go back to Creel, they decided to make the longer cross-country trek. By the time they reached Urique they hoped the canyon's rivers would be more navigable and they could buy another boat. With a boat they could float to San Blas and then on to Choix, the original destination of the expedition party. Although they would miss a section of the river canyon, one way or another they would finish the trip where they had first intended.

For five pesos a day, a Tarahumara guide offered to carry a pack for them. They resupplied their provisions from the villagers, buying dried meat, beans, flour, and oatmeal.

The village of Barrance del Cobre.

Villagers urged the couple to stay a day before their trek, inviting them into their homes for food and hospitality. The entire village saw them off. Jose, their guide, carried a sixty-pound pack and Dick carried the rest of their gear on his back. Isabelle carried only a water canteen. Even so, she was hard-pressed to keep up.

Jose traveled at a steady trot wearing nothing on his feet except tire-soled sandals called huaraches. Dick and Isabelle marveled at his stamina; so this was the Tarahumara way, a slow steady pull uphill and then a steady trot that ate up the miles on the flats and downhill. Up and down they climbed, across the Sierra Madre mountains. By the end of the first day out of the village, Isabelle could barely lift one foot after the other. They had not even stopped for lunch.

"As I dragged my shoes off, I counted a blister on every toe. Dick had a hole in his heel from a nail that had poked through his boot. But he is another Tarahumara. Never complains," Isabelle wrote. "It was the most severe, exhausting physical exertion I've ever experienced. We made about thirty miles over rough terrain from sunup to sundown with no long breaks."

The next day they told Jose to go on ahead; he traveled too fast for Isabelle. They would meet up again later in Urique. They continued across the mountains and then once again dropped down into the Urique River canyon. By now the river had widened and was navigable by boat. Having traveled through canyon depths reaching almost six thousand feet—as deep as the Grand Canyon—and having traveled many of those miles on foot, they looked forward to buying a boat and getting back on the water. Several bends in the

Urique Village.

A Tarahumara dwelling 3000 feet above the Urique River.

river later and three weeks after their expedition had begun they arrived in the town of Urique.

Dick and Isabelle were sorely disappointed to learn there were no boats in Urique. Everyone assured them they would find one farther downstream at the confluence of the Fuerte River.

So they set off by foot down the trail where once again they crossed and re-crossed the river, climbing over boulders and rugged terrain. Jose continued to travel with them along with a little white dog they called Perro. The dog was another mouth to feed and they eventually gave him away to a passerby. To their dismay, they later learned that the dog had likely become someone's family meal.

They passed by Tarahumara houses with roofs of thatched palm leaves. They learned the native handshake, a whisper light touching of fingertips, a gesture that Dick found fitting for these shy people.

People always seemed to materialize right around meal time to share the Griffiths' food. One day, a man exchanged a freshly caught catfish for some fishing hooks and line that Dick had in his pack. Early the next morning, while it was still dark, the man and a woman arrived with warm tortillas for sale.

Tarahumara hut.

It had begun to rain, and the Griffiths found shelter in caves and rock over-hangs. The rising water began to erase the trail and the locals recommended that they travel overland across the mountains to reach the Fuerte River.

"Looks like Dick is going to make a mountain climber out of me yet, darn it," Isabelle wrote. "It is such terrific work dog-trotting over these mountains up and down for fifteen miles a day."

The flooded Urique River wiped out the trail.

When they reached the Fuerte River, they were once again disappointed to find no boats. They looked longingly at the strong wide current. People they met assured them they would find boats downstream in the village of San Francisco.

When they arrived, it was hardly a village—just a couple of households. And they learned San Francisco had no boats either.

"Shucks, I don't think these people ever saw a boat in their lives," Isabelle wrote with exasperation. A man in San Francisco suggested they hike thirty miles over the mountains to Choix. From there truck roads would take them to El Fuerte and on to San Blas where they could catch the train.

So once again they trekked cross-country. It took Dick and Isabelle ten days to travel from Urique to Choix. They arrived on March 8, 1952, to the cold pleasure of a frosty beer and sweet soda pop. By that time, Isabelle's boots had fallen apart. Dick had given his boots as a parting gift to Jose, and now sported threadbare tennis shoes. Husband and wife were both bronzed and lean from their travels.

"[Dick's] so skinny that he could tote a watermelon in the sag in the seats of his pants," Isabelle wrote.

Hiking through the Barranca del Cobre—then trekking up and over the Sierra Madre Mountains—Dick and Isabelle still managed to arrive in Choix one day before their original party of five had planned to finish the expedition.

By the time Dick and Isabelle were through, they had hiked more than three hundred miles.

At the end of the trip, Dick's obsession with the Barranca del Cobre had only intensified. They had left the canyon between the village of Barranca del Cobre and the town of Urique unexplored. He was determined to come back and travel the section they had missed.

Just two weeks after leaving Mexico, Dick and Isabelle returned. Dick was determined that this time they would succeed. And one thing was certain: Dick would not be building rafts with driftwood and shoelaces.

Isabelle's boots after 300 miles of hiking.

Chapter 7

In the Land of Foot Runners

He [Dick] has a disconcerting habit of whistling when things go wrong.
—Isabelle Galo Griffith

DURING THE RAINY SEASON, the richly textured landscape of the Barranca del Cobre shimmers green. Here the pines, junipers, and oaks of the plateau give way to the opulent greens of acacia and mimosa trees. As they descended into the Mexican canyons, Dick and Isabelle found cactuses, kapok trees, and stands of cane on the slopes. Deep on the canyon floor, they would discover tropical parrots flying among fig and palm trees.

The Barranca del Cobre is part of the Rio Fuerte drainage, which includes four other major canyons including Batopilas, Sinforosa, Chinipas, and Septentrion. During the dry season, colors in the canyons grow brown and red, with desert varnish staining the canyon walls. Unlike the sedimentary layers of the canyons on the Colorado River, the geology of the Barranca del Cobre region is igneous—formed from volcanic activity. In a region where altitudes range from near sea level to an average high plateau of eight thousand to ten thousand feet, several of these canyons reach depths of nearly sixty-six hundred feet—greater than the deepest point in the Grand Canyon at fifty-five hundred feet.

The Griffiths arrived in Chihuahua, Mexico, on March 31, 1952. This time they would enlist the help of the people who knew the Barranca del

Cobre best—the Tarahumara Indians. Since the arrival of the Spanish in the 1600s, the Tarahumara had been brutalized in a series of wars, forced into slave labor, and oppressed by missionary zeal. The canyons provided safe harbor from intrusion by the outside world and allowed them to preserve their traditional agrarian and subsistence lifestyle. In the summer they lived in cooler, higher altitudes. In the winter they migrated to the warmth of the canyon bottoms.

Dick and Isabelle were surprised, then, to discover Tarahumara women and children begging in the streets of Chihuahua. This was in sharp contrast to the self-reliant people they'd encountered earlier along the Rio Urique. They learned that a three-year drought had forced many of these reticent people out of the canyons and into more populated areas where they bartered beautiful blankets and colorful woven belts in exchange for food. Once their wares were gone, there was nothing left but to beg. The morning after their arrival in Chihuahua, Dick and Isabelle bought one hundred bread rolls and passed them out among families living in camps along the riverbed.

Hungry Tarahumara migrated to Mexican cities for food.

After catching a train to Creel, Dick and Isabelle enlisted the help of Father Manuel Martinez, a Catholic priest—who spoke English, Spanish, and Tarahumara—to find men who could help transport their food and gear through the Barranca del Cobre's Urique River canyon. Three men were chosen: Luis, Patricio, and Bonito Juarez. The two younger men, Luis and Patricio, wore modern clothing—jeans, shirts, and straw hats for protection from the sun; but the elder Bonito sported traditional Tarahumara garb—a white shirt and a white loin cloth, with a bright red kerchief tied around his head.

After asking what their helpers liked to eat, Dick and Isabelle bought: twenty-two pounds of flour, twenty-two pounds of sugar, ten pounds of rice, twenty-two pounds of beans, seven pounds of cheese, five pounds of coffee and thirteen pounds of dried meat. The tab for 120 pounds of food came to $17 dollars. It was enough to feed five people for two weeks—or so they thought.

This time they started their trip near the village of Baseborachic, about thirty miles from Creel, down a steep winding road into the canyon. As they descended, the cooler semi-arid uplands gave way to the humid, subtropical climate of the canyon bottoms.

"It's a primitive beauty, untouched and natural with a wealth of trees, flowers, and birds. There's an exotic combination of pine, maple, cactus, and orchids," Isabelle wrote.

After shouldering their packs they began working their way to the river. They weren't on the trail for long when—in spite of the drought—rainclouds gathered and they had to seek shelter from a thunderstorm.

"There seems to be a conspiracy in the heavens to always rain on the outdoor adventurer on his first day on the trail," Isabelle wrote.

The next day they reached the Urique River near the place where the original party had split up on their earlier trip. This was familiar territory to the Griffiths. When they reached the first impassable gorge, Dick stopped and unpacked the most important piece of gear for the journey—a bright yellow inflatable boat.

The small Air Force survival raft was built to be used for downed military pilots in World War II. It weighed fifteen pounds compared to the sixty pounds of the larger inflatables they had used on their earlier attempt. This one could be inflated only when it was needed and then folded up and stashed in a pack. The idea was to trek through the canyon and use the raft where necessary to ferry gear and people through the otherwise impassible waters between sheer canyon walls.

The yellow raft was the kind of boat that would someday become known as a "packraft." As Dick inflated the boat, their Tarahumara porters looked on incredulously.

"Bonito's eyes nearly bugged out as he watched in amazement," Isabelle wrote. "Dick tied the rope to the boat and then stepped in it gingerly while

First documented use of a packraft, 1952.

it tilted and bobbed like a cork. I played out the rope while he paddled with his hands, guiding the boat to a point about 150 feet below. There he tied the other end of the rope and pulled the boat back hand-over-hand."

Dick ferried four duffel bags, one by one, across the water. Then Isabelle sat on his lap while he padded her to the other side.

"Our Indians eyed the boat dubiously and were not too happy over the prospect of their first boat ride, but they got in without a murmur," Isabelle wrote. "We were happily surprised and ever so relieved because the Indians don't like the river and even hate to get their feet wet."

Their first crossing in the boat now made walking back upriver impossible. They were committed. But Dick and Isabelle worried about their companions.

"They are doing a difficult job carrying fifty-pound packs through the canyon with no trails for five pesos a day (approximately sixty cents). We feel guilty about that even though we are paying them more than the daily wage of two or three pesos a day," Isabelle wrote. "We give them all they can eat to try to make up for it."

Luis had not even brought a blanket and the three took off their huarache sandals to hop from boulder to boulder along the river. It pained Isabelle to watch.

"Traveling under such difficulties, following no trail, progressing slowly with heavy packs may seem senseless and silly to them," she worried. "The language barrier makes it almost impossible to explain to them that it is a great challenge for us to explore a region where white man has not poked around much yet."

It wasn't long, however, before their business arrangement with their hired hands developed into an easy companionship, in part, due to the Tarahumaras' emerging respect for Dick and Isabelle. On one occasion, the elder Bonito discovered a beehive one hundred feet high on the canyon cliff. Hoping for honey, he tried throwing rocks to knock it off its perch. When that didn't work, he began scrambling up the cliff wall to retrieve it. Dick quickly followed behind and helped nab the hive even as the bees swarmed. They did not find honey, but Dick was quickly proving that not only could he paddle a boat, he could also climb and hike and travel with ease alongside a people known for their stamina. The Tarahumara called themselves Raramuri—the Foot Runners. Running was not just a means of transportation for the Indians, but great sport between villages. Festivals included contests of endurance including *Rarjiparo*, a race to kick a small, hand-carved wooden ball for up to forty hours at a stretch.

The group reached the section of the river with the deep, four-hundred-foot channel where Dick had crossed earlier by kick-paddling nearly to the point of hypothermia. Here he was happy to inflate the little yellow boat. This time he would ferry their gear in relative comfort—no swimming, just a four-hour job of ferrying gear and people across.

"Dick lays on his back in the boat and we set on top of him," Isabelle wrote. "His arms hang over the side so he can paddle."

Although she grew braver all the time, Isabelle still had trouble traversing heights. On one river crossing, she had to jump between two boulders with whitewater rushing through the ten-foot drop below.

"Dick leaped across easily. The others stopped and refused to move ... I braced myself for the leap, hesitated, and was lost," Isabelle wrote.

Dick shouted, "Jump Iz, don't wait to get up the nerve because it never comes. Just jump!"

She gathered her courage and leapt—after which, she noted, Bonito, Luis, and Patricio followed. "By a man's code they could do nothing else but leap too."

Evenings brought a meal-making ritual. The Tarahumaras took turns making the tortillas while the rest of them sorted and cleaned the beans. One day Isabelle dropped several on the ground and she was chagrined when she later discovered Bonito carefully picking up each bean, washing it, and adding it to the pot. It was a reminder of the slim margins by which the people of the canyon had learned to live. Resourcefulness was key to survival not just on an expedition, but to the Tarahumara people's daily way of living.

One evening while Bonito, Luis, and Patricio lingered by the fire, Dick and Isabelle found a broad sandbar one hundred yards from camp and unrolled their sleeping bags for the night.

"We'd both fallen asleep when I woke abruptly to the sound that turns blood to ice when one is in a deep, rocky canyon," she wrote. "A rock slide!" She bolted out of the sleeping bag, dashed to a nearby boulder and covered her arms over her head. When the crash of hurtling rocks subsided, the air was dense with the cloud of pulverized rock.

Dick called out, "Iz are you all right?"

Shaky, they gathered their sleeping bags and moved back to the camp fire. In daylight the next morning, they inspected the rock slide. A refrigerator-sized rock lay just shy of the place they had been sleeping. Any one of many lesser rocks that had tumbled down the cliffs could have killed them.

Beyond the village of Barranca del Cobre, the Griffiths were now entering new territory. Here the canyon grew narrow and dark and the river crossings grew increasingly challenging.

"The boulders made everything weird, forming deep dark caves ... At times I was lost in a maze of dark, narrow passages between boulders," Isabelle wrote. When they finally emerged into sunshine, they found a clear spring that formed a series of pools alongside the river. It turned out to be a hot spring and they decided to camp there.

"Dick got out a bar of soap and had himself a grand time taking a hot bath, singing lustily all the while," Isabelle wrote. As they set up camp on the other side of the river, Bonito informed them that this was the last place to leave the canyon for Creel.

After just seven days, they had already burned through most of the groceries that were supposed to last for two weeks. So the decision was made that Dick, Bonito, Patricio, and Luis would leave the next day to get more food in Creel. Isabelle would stay behind. They weren't sure how long the journey would take—maybe four to six days.

Later on, Dick good-naturedly remarked that this marked the end of the honeymoon. "We'd only been married eighteen months," he said. "Then I left her."

Typical Tarahumara cave dwelling.

Isabelle wrote eloquently of her time alone in the canyon. Admittedly, the first night alone was unnerving. "Sometimes I thought I heard whistling, or the distant, muted rumbling of a rockslide. But the chirping of the night birds was real and comforting," she wrote. For Dick and his companions, the distance between the canyon and Creel turned out to be thirty-five miles over lung-busting terrain.

"The climbing was very hard," he wrote. "Like all Tarahumara trails in the canyon it was mostly vertical cliffs."

Almost to the rim.

Distances along the entire river system were deceptive. From one point to another in a straight line might be a few miles, but by river and mountain trail, distances were easily three and four times as much. Dick, Bonito, Luis, and Patricio climbed four thousand feet out of the canyon, one of the deepest and most scenic sections of the Barranca del Cobre. Once they reached the plateau, Dick joined the Tarahumara in their ruthless trot across the wilderness. Up and down mesas and valleys, across rugged territory, they ran.

"Hour after hour we moved silently, always at a relentless pace," Dick wrote. They ran for several hours past dark and then stopped only because they began to lose their way. They made a fire and tried to rest, but snow began to fall. Here at higher elevations, temperatures often fell below freezing. While Isabelle likely slept on top of her sleeping bag in the tropical canyon floor, the men spent a miserable night huddled around a fire. By dawn, two inches of snow lay on the ground. At daylight the four men once again began to run.

Perhaps Dick's early years as a boy, running alongside his horse on the Wyoming ranch, helped prepare him for the rigors of this trek. Or maybe it was the thought of Isabelle, alone in the wilderness that motivated his feet to keep moving. It was the kind of physical test that Dick relished and he was gratified to have the stamina to keep up with the Foot Runners.

When they reached Creel, Dick purchased twenty-five pounds of dried meat, thirty pounds of flour, twenty pounds of beans, and twenty pounds of

Creel, Mexico.

Easter Sunday.

brown-sugar candy. The next day, Easter Sunday, with full packs they began running back to the canyon.

Just before the rim, Bonito met up with a friend and Dick gladly took the half-hour break to rest. As he rested, across the canyon on a high plateau, he saw the ancient village of Pamachic. As he considered the maze of unexplored wilderness here and in the canyons, he promised himself to return someday. Specifically, he decided he wanted to see Pamachic.

"Descending to the Urique River was almost as hard as climbing out," Dick said. "Many times we walked on narrow ledges, and in places the rock was grooved for footholds," he wrote. All while carrying heavy packs.

Meanwhile, Isabelle grew eager for Dick's return. At one point a shepherdess dressed all in white, came to the springs with her herd of goats. Isabelle, eager for companionship, approached the girl.

"*Buenos dias*!" Isabelle said. She knew Tarahumara women were painfully shy. Yet she was surprised and dismayed when the girl quickly brandished a shiny, twelve-inch knife and then hurried away with her herd.

Descending the canyon to return to Isabelle.

Crestfallen and lonely, Isabelle wrote, "I love the wilderness and the outdoors, the fresh unspoiled beauty of a wild, rugged country like the Barranca del Cobre. But beauty shared is twice as beautiful."

By then two days had passed. The men had left on Good Friday and it was now Easter Sunday. She yearned to hear the Russian Easter Overture. Growing up Hungarian in a Catholic home, Isabelle had always loved classical music.

"This is the strangest place I have ever been on Easter," she wrote. As the sun set, she built a smoke fire to ward off the *moscas* (flies). She was just settling in to read for the evening when a brusque voice broke the silence.

"Hey there, why haven't you gathered any wood? Where's our supper? Lazy good-for-nothing woman! All you do is read!"

It was Dick, gaunt and grinning. The men had traveled seventy miles round trip in forty-eight hours.

IN THE COMING DAYS, THEY MADE their way past the big bend of the Urique River where they saw spectacular waterfalls tumbling down the sides of the canyon. For a time past the falls, the walking grew easier. Past the Rio Tararecua, the landscape opened up enough for cattle and horses to reach the water.

"The canyon is not as dangerous as we were led to believe by others. There are no Apaches, Mexican bandits, or jaguars," Dick wrote. "During the rainy season (summer months) the canyon would be impassable because of rocks falling and the great volume of water plunging through such a narrow passage. We have witnessed what a small rainfall does; all the water from the plateau pours into the canyon unimpeded. One could be trapped within several hours, unable to move downstream or upstream and faced with rapidly rising water."

Even in good conditions, their canyon trek was still a long way from the comforts of home. Isabelle noted that the flour Dick had brought from Creel was teaming with boll weevils with their numbers increasing daily.

"I try to pick them out but it is hopeless," Isabelle wrote. "They quickly quit squirming when we place the tortillas on the hot coals."

As the canyon passage narrowed, they found themselves traversing boulders twenty to thirty feet in diameter, often leaping from rock to rock. At one point the trail led to a sheer cliff where the edges for walking were just inches wide.

"We can do one of three things when we come to a sheer cliff," Isabelle wrote. "Sneak around near the water's edge, climb a catwalk high on top, or use the boat. All three invariably happen each day."

The canyon grew dark as the walls pressed together in the narrowest section so far. This was an area that the Griffiths' called "Black Gorge" and that is known today as "The Narrows." The boulders that choked the canyon now were like a jumble of dark planets—immense and forbidding.

Black Gorge.

"It was a spooky place with the wind wailing like a malignant spirit resentful of our intrusion," Isabelle wrote.

Even the sky grew menacing, with the threat of rain. They hurried through this section, knowing that a thundershower could quickly fill the gorge with churning whitewater. The kind of water that would devour a little yellow raft.

After negotiating through the obstacle course, the landscape grew less perilous and they stopped to camp for the night.

Isabelle noted the emerging friendship between Dick and the Tarahumara men.

"The Indians admire and like Dick. He's a good mountain climber, has a pair of long, strong legs, and is afraid of no obstacle. He usually takes the

Dick and Bonito, best of friends.

initiative in climbing over high, narrow, difficult places and ferrying everyone across in the rubber boat. He's one of those rare people who show an utter disregard for personal comfort … He endears himself to the men by always trying to learn their language, and they love his clowning antics and fearlessness on the trail."

As Dick read each evening, Bonito rose from his place by the fire, carefully filled a cup of water, and then gravely presented it to Dick. Each time Bonito's face lit up as Dick responded in Tarahumara, "Thank you."

"It's a little ceremony I never tire of watching," Isabelle wrote.

At night, a pot of beans simmered on the campfire. Sometimes Isabelle would wake to see Bonito adding more water to the pot.

"He'd stand silhouetted by the fire, lost in thought. I wonder what he was thinking," she wrote. "Their future is so uncertain; dressed in rags, not enough to eat, no work, no crops because of the drought. Yet they are cheerful, laugh easily and don't complain. When we were eating beans

Patricio sadly said they ate very little beans (at home) because they were so expensive (about 9 cents a pound). Our friends can eat hearty for a little while anyway. We make huge quantities of food yet they always scrape the bottom of the pot."

THE CANYON REMAINED A NARROW obstacle course. Rain showers brought falling rocks that tumbled from their loosened beds down the canyon walls. The canyon travelers often sought caves for shelter and camped early. It wasn't far now to Urique, and on the last day they decided to keep moving, leaving the shelter of a cave to traverse the slippery slant of wet rocks. The going was tough and at one point, Isabelle lost her footing. She grabbed hold of a branch but slowly felt her grip give way. Just as she was sure she would drop into the boulder-strewn river below, Luis thrust his stick in front of her. She grabbed it and managed to regain her balance.

At another point, Luis too lost his footing. Both feet flipped out from under him and he landed hard on his rear end. Finally, the canyon walls flattened out to rolling hills. Boulders from the river disappeared. And the sun began to shine.

"The rain eased and the clouds became thinner and thinner until they were like a gossamer veil. Bits of blue sky peeked through. Suddenly our canyon was flooded with light," Isabelle wrote. "Behind us lay the deep, narrow canyon. Ahead of us the cliffs flattened out to gentle rolling hills ... We followed a well-worn path into Urique."

Arriving in Urique on April 19, 1952, the Griffiths finished their trip just in time. Rains were quickly filling the canyon with floodwaters, making it impossible to travel. Their little yellow boat had saved them days of climbing around otherwise impassable stretches of water. Thirty years later, Dick would use a packraft to compete in the two-hundred-mile Alaska Mountain Wilderness Classic, earning him the distinction of the "Grandfather of Packrafting."

Dick, Isabelle, and their companions still had to return eighty miles to Creel and so once again they walked the rugged terrain of the Sierra Madre Mountains. This time they followed well-worn mule trails and an unused rail bed as they traveled north. When they arrived in Divisadero,

A lunch stop on the way back to Creel.

the trail opened to a grand specter of the Barranca del Cobre. They sat perched on the canyon's edge for some time, absorbing the scene. Canyon after canyon spread out below them. Just days before, they had been trekking the depths of that earth's great rift, exploring the precipitous path of the Rio Urique.

Dick was ambivalant about leaving. Here were all the things he loved— wilderness, unexplored country, and the great satisfaction of traveling on one's own power. That was the thing about wilderness travel—it always left you hungry for more.

DICK AND ISABELLE, WITH THEIR COMPANIONS, had made the first descent of the Barranca del Cobre. The only recognition they received was in a short article dated April 27, 1952, in *The El Paso Times*: "Pair from Colorado Walks Entire Length of the Barranca."

Dick shrugs when talking about this achievement. He did not make the trip for recognition—rather it was a personal quest to finish what he'd started as he explored virgin territory. Yet later, when others laid claim to the feat of a first descent, Dick's friend Roman Dial would set the record straight.

Dick conceded, "Human kind remembers only the first who succeed. Who was the second man to reach the North Pole, the South Pole or to climb Everest?

Dick would one day attempt to return to Pamachic, the village he'd seen from across the canyon during their food run to Creel. But the subsequent trek would prove even more dangerous than their first descent of the Barranca del Cobre.

In 1987, when Dick was sixty years old, he took his elderly mother on a tour that included a train trip to the area. Helen had always wondered about her son's exploits and this was an opportunity for her to see a bit of what he had experienced. The Copper Canyon railroad is considered one of the world's most scenic rail trips. Construction on the 410-mile rail line began in 1881, but was not completed until 1961, almost a decade after the Griffiths had passed through.

Divisadero overlook.

The tour stopped in Creel. Dick, who had packed photos from their earlier trip, went looking for some of the people he'd known some thirty-five years earlier. He learned the Chinese innkeeper with the three daughters had been cruelly murdered by bandits. Father Martinez had passed away. A storekeeper informed Dick that Bonito had been dead now for many years but that his family was doing fine. The storekeeper then opened up his credit book and showed Dick that Bonito's family owned a debt of about $20. Dick got out his wallet and paid it. He left the photo of his friend for the storekeeper to give to Bonito's family.

"For years I harbored a guilt," Dick wrote, "We paid each of the three Indians sixty cents a day for risking their life."

Dick and his mother continued by train to the rim of Mexico's Copper Canyon at Divisadero. Dick was disheartened to find that sidewalks and a guardrail were now in the very place where they had once sat overlooking a pristine wilderness. And he remembered his promise to one day visit the village of Pamachic.

He accompanied his mother to Los Mochis and then "turned her loose" with the rest of the tour group so that he could return to the canyon.

"I was never into tours," he said.

He returned to Divisadero, hopped the guard rail, and headed into the chasm.

Locals had warned Dick not to go into the canyon without a local guide. Travel through this country was dangerous. Marijuana and opium poppy—from which heroin is made—were now grown on the hillsides. As Dick worked his way toward the canyon floor, a "ghetto blaster" seemed to be blaring from inside every Tarahumara dwelling.

"No longer do you hear the clear notes of the bamboo flutes or the resonate boom, boom of the drums," he lamented. Many of the creeks were now choked with garbage.

He passed several surly, armed men. What was once a magical place, was now something else altogether. He camped that night at the Urique River and the next morning began climbing up toward Pamachic. Halfway up the slope toward his destination, Dick stopped to boil water for drinking. Before long, two men approached his camp with pistols. Dick greeted them and tried a few Tarahumara words that he remembered. The men said nothing. When they saw Dick's camera, they glanced at each other. Then one of the men picked up a large rock and smashed it.

"I had to stay cool," Dick wrote. "They had guns. I didn't."

They then dumped the contents of Dick's pack and discovered the photos he had taken in 1952 of Bonito, Luis, and Patricio in the canyon country. The photos seemed to calm the men. They took none of Dick's belongings and left.

Dick was lucky to be alive. Reflecting back on his years of trekking, he would come to say that given the choice between luck and skill, he would always choose luck.

Convinced now he needed to get out of the canyons as quickly as possible, he spent the next day trying to stay out of sight as he made his way back. On his second night in the canyon, a group of eight men built a fire several hundred yards downhill from where Dick had sought refuge under a rock ledge. They appeared intoxicated and had weapons. Their party grew raucous and they began firing the guns. Suddenly two of them discovered Dick's trail and began following it—away from Dick. They had picked up the trail going down into the canyon. Dick tried to sleep but was again awakened, this time by the orange glow of a torch. Two men in loin cloths were tracking him and heading toward his cave.

They were too close for him to slip away unnoticed. He scooted as far back into the cave as he could and lay still. As he held his breath, they followed the crisscross of Dick's tracks, and eventually passed by him undetected.

At first light, he made a dash to the rim.

Dick was heartsick about what had happened to the Barranca del Cobre. The canyon's labyrinth, which had once provided refuge to a reclusive and dignified people, now sheltered illicit crops and violent *narcotraficantes*. Local Tarahumara Indians either cooperated or they and their families were subjected to torture, rape, and murder. The drug trade began in the mid-1960s when the completion of the railroad opened the area; which also happened to coincide with America's increasing demand for mind-altering substances. By the time Dick returned in 1987 the drug culture was firmly entrenched.

Dick was also disappointed he had not made it to his destination. "I now know I can do *anything* I want to," Dick said. "I can't do *everything* I want to. There is a limit when you are dealing with space and time."

As always, rules, limits, and guardrails held little sway in Dick's life. At age sixty, he had jumped the railing at the canyon rim to pursue a destination that proved elusive. Yet the coming years would prove that there was still a whole lot of *everything* left to explore.

Chapter 8

Call of the Arctic

The continual nervous strain of a hand-to-mouth existence, where there is not even the shelter of a poorhouse in case of failure, has a telling and cumulative effect ... This is a hard country for a hungry man."
—*Vilhjalmur Stefansson*

THE CRAVING FOR A LONG WALK began to gnaw on him. It was 1959 and it had been seven years since Dick and Isabelle's first descent of the Barranca del Cobre. Dick had finished school at the University of Wyoming in Laramie with a geology degree that he later called "worthless." To save money as Dick finished college, they lived as house parents at an orphanage. From Laramie they moved to Poplar, Montana, where Dick worked for a seismograph company looking for oil. Isabelle worked as a medical technician in an Indian hospital.

In Poplar, Isabelle gave birth to the Griffith's firstborn daughter who died at birth. It was a sad time in their lives and Dick felt a change of scene would be good for both of them. Isabelle agreed. So on a spring day in 1954, he and Isabelle loaded up their pickup and headed north.

The Territory of Alaska encompassed a wilderness landscape that for Dick offered both solace and sustenance. He had never forgotten the explorers he'd read about as a boy: Stefansson, Amundsen, Peary. And of course there were Jack London's tales of hardship and adventure. Alaska was famous for its fish and game and at the time, Dick was an avid hunter and fishermen—a pastime that, in later years, he relinquished.

They arrived in Anchorage where Dick soon took a job as a gandy dancer on the Alaska Railroad, a physically demanding job of maintaining track along the line between the seaport town of Seward and the interior of Alaska at Fairbanks. In the next several years Isabelle and Dick had two more children, a daughter, Kimmer, and son, Barney. Dick changed jobs to work for the Corps of Engineers, testing soils around the state. His travels around Alaska whetted his appetite for adventure.

Roads were nearly non-existent in Alaska at that time—just a couple of strands on the map. The rest of Alaska was accessible only by airplane or boat. Flying over vast stretches of wilderness, Dick saw firsthand the expanse of the Arctic. The great coastal plains, immense mountain ranges, and sprawling river deltas all sparked his imagination.

Dick was getting restless.

Kimmer was four and Barney was two in 1959 when Dick announced his plans to walk from Kaktovik to Anaktuvuk Pass, a distance of nearly five hundred miles. Isabelle was neither surprised, nor did she object. She knew her husband's resolve and she knew his skills in the wilderness. As she wrote before his descent of Lava Falls, "Dick has faith in his skill and I have faith in Dick." Dick used all of his vacation days and the remaining time off he took without pay.

Kaktovik lies on the northern tip of Barter Island, just off the northern coast of Alaska. At the time it was home to about thirty families of Inupiat Eskimos. Anaktuvuk Pass lay 453 miles to the southwest, tucked in the heart of Alaska's northernmost mountains, the formidable Brooks Range.

Dick described the range as he saw it from his airplane seat. "From the air, row after row of mountains stretches as far as the eye can see to the west and to the east. The immensity is mind-boggling. North of the Brooks Range the Arctic Coastal Plain is flat as a pancake but equally as immense."

As the plane landed in Kaktovik, he felt that familiar tightening in the gut, a dry-mouthed apprehension mixed with eager anticipation at what he had set out to do. Dick arrived in Kaktovik on June 4, 1959, a week before his friend, Eugene "Hungry" Horning, was to join him. Dick would eventually

Flying over the Brooks Range.

travel solo across the Far North, in part because it was difficult to find anyone with the time or desire to make the long traverses across such an austere
landscape.

"I knew nothing about Arctic travel and would have to live off the land
by killing animals because I lack the resources to provide for costly re-supply
points," he wrote. "No one would find me in such a large expanse of land if
I failed to reach the pass. Furthermore, no one knew which way I would go
because I did not know myself."

In the week before Hungry arrived, Dick—with the help of a local resident—built a dogsled and made dogsled harnesses and packs. He bought two
dogs for $40, one he called "Whitie" and the other "Blackie." He noted that
the Inupiat did not treat sled dogs as pets.

"They play a strictly utilitarian role in the harsh boom-and-bust life cycle of the Arctic. In times of plenty the dogs feast. In times of hardship they are fed to each other or eaten by the villagers," he wrote.

He bought a third dog that he called "Pup." The dogs fought incessantly. First the two older dogs against each other. Then, when "Pup" joined the group, the two older dogs teamed up against the youngster. He tried hooking the dogs up to the sled and went out onto the sea ice for a test run, but the dogs fought constantly.

Back in Kaktovik, Dick befriended the villagers, playing volleyball with them every night on the bluff overlooking the sea ice. They played into the wee hours of the morning. Dick described the Arctic daylight: "The sun never sets—it just rolls around the sky like a goldfish in a round bowl."

Dog team coming into Kaktovik, Alaska.

Village of Kaktovik.

The weather grew warmer and it began to rain. Suddenly the sea ice became a lake of water as snowmelt and rain ran over the top of the ice. The soft, melting ice conditions would make it difficult to cross the two-mile distance between the Island and the mainland's coast. Hungry was due in on June 12 and Dick, who was packed and ready, decided to leave immediately on Hungry's arrival—before traveling conditions grew worse.

Frigid ankle-deep water deepened to icy, knee-deep slush as Dick and Hungry and the three dogs tried to make it across the sea ice. Hungry's feet grew cold and the dogs struggled to pull the sled through the freezing mire. The dog sled, made to travel on top of snow, quickly bogged down and broke apart.

They abandoned the sled and Dick sent Hungry back to the island's shore to build a fire while he ferried most of their gear and equipment across in the two-man inflatable boat he'd packed along for river crossings. Already he could see they had too much to carry so he went through their equipment and threw away mostly food. They intended to live off the land as much as possible. One thing he kept was the canteen that Isabelle had filled with wine. In the tent that night, the wine warmed their dampened spirits.

Even with minimal food for the trip, their gear weighed in at 140 pounds. The dogs each carried twenty pounds while Hungry and Dick each carried forty pounds. Their rations included:

50 lb. of food (dried milk, tea, dried soup, rice, sugar, salt, and chocolate)
15 lb. guns (.30-06 rifle, over under .22, and a .410 gauge shotgun)
15 lb. ammunition
15 lb. footgear and extra clothing
15 lb. sleeping bags and air mattresses
15 lb. two-man inflatable boat
15 lb. Army surplus two-man tent

The next day they trudged from the Island to the mainland with frigid water so deep that the dogs had to swim at times. Fog, mist, and a cold wind blew off the Arctic Ocean. Once they reached the mainland, they walked several more miles in search of caribou to feed the dogs. But they found none and that night the dogs had to go without.

Cold wind and fog continued to roll in from the Arctic Ocean. All reference points were hidden and their maps weren't much help. On the third day into their trip, Dick shot a caribou so thin it hardly had enough meat to feed the dogs. They set up camp next to a large river, one they couldn't identify.

"Sometimes the [maps] only tell us that we're lost," Dick wrote.

The tundra spread out treeless before them. It took them an hour to gather enough twigs to fuel a small fire—enough to boil the heart, tongue, and liver of the caribou. It was difficult to set up camp in the wind. They had no suitable stakes to pound into the frozen ground and their gear was soaked. The dogs continued to fight and Dick came to the realization that the dogs had been a big mistake.

"Blackie and Whitie keep trying to kill the Pup ... The dogs chase the caribou, leaving gear and packs scattered on the tundra. It takes a lot of energy and time just to kill enough game for them," Dick noted. Even so, Dick grew attached to the dogs—they provided amusement and company.

After crossing the flooded Akootoaktuk River, they came to the calving grounds where thousands of caribou migrated each year. The animals were on the move in every direction; the skin of the earth itself seemed to be rippling. As the caribou traveled, the tendons in their ankles clicked with each step, like the tick of time across the tundra. For centuries these animals had traveled to this particular place in springtime to calve. Their well-worn paths etched furrows into the ground, some of them several feet deep. As the men tried to sleep, they heard the clicking of hundreds of caribou hooves passing right outside their tent.

Hungry's Achilles tendon grew painful walking through miles of tussocks. Also known as hummocks, these mushroom-shaped mounds of grassy vegetation surrounded by seeping water were the equivalent of walking on beach balls. They were unavoidable and some of them were as tall as twenty inches.

"There's no graceful way to get through them. Step on one and it bends over, dumping the hiker. Step between them, taking high steps, and their overhanging caps grab your foot. Walking through miles of tussocks is exhausting, painful, irritating and dull. It's even worse for the dogs because their packs constantly hang up which requires us to free them," Dick wrote.

By June 23, eleven days into the trek, Hungry could barely walk. When they reached the Naval Arctic Research Science Camp on Lake Peters, Hungry was forced to abandon the trip and wait for the next plane out—a ride which would not arrive for more than three weeks.

Dick didn't mind. He was just getting warmed up. With the first day's jitters gone, he was feeling stronger every day, and he'd established a routine for setting up, breaking camp, and traveling. Besides, even though they were more trouble than help, he had the dogs for company.

Dick repaired some equipment and reduced his weight by cutting the two-man tent down and sewing it into a "very miserable one-man tent." Then he studied the maps for a route to Anaktuvuk Pass, a distance he estimated was another 340 miles.

When Dick left the scientists' camp, his first priority was to feed the dogs. He fished at Lake Schrader, hooking into a twenty-inch trout and several other fish before a torrential downpour forced him to take shelter. In less than two weeks, this Arctic trip had spanned three seasons. He'd begun from Kaktovik in late winter when the sea ice was still frozen. Water overflow on ocean ice announced a fleeting spring; and now summer announced itself with the arrival of mosquitoes.

Penetrating row upon row of mountains.

"Today the mosquitoes stumbled out of the tundra in full force and they're driving the dogs crazy. Ten days ago the Arctic tundra was brown and barren. Now the hills and plains are lush with greenery such as flowers, grass, and green willows," he wrote.

The need to feed the dogs grew pressing. Moving into the mountains, they'd moved away from the caribou herds. Dick followed sheep trails but found nothing. Not even the Arctic's plump game bird, the ptarmigan, was anywhere to be found.

On June 27, 1959—his thirty-second birthday—Dick wrote "I searched for caribou all day but found none, no ptarmigan, no fish, no rabbits, no squirrels, nothing. I camped on a gravel bar, a slight breeze kept the number of mosquitoes down. I had soup and cocoa and fed the dogs some soup although it does very little for them nutritionally."

The next day the dogs did not want to leave camp. They were footsore and weak from hunger. Dick followed Ikiakpuk Creek looking for game but found nothing but old tracks.

"Toward evening the dogs had their noses in the air, and I knew they smelled caribou. About 30 minutes later I ran into fresh caribou tracks crossing overflow ice. I followed them and spotted a large bull caribou about 400 yards away, too far for a clean kill. I tied the three dogs because the bull was watching us, then sneaked around to the side and dropped the bull while he was still staring at the dogs," Dick wrote.

One of many caribou kills.

The animal had half an inch of back fat—badly needed by both Dick and the dogs. Finally they could eat their fill. In general, the dogs had eaten far more than Dick had expected. They could each easily consume the hindquarter of a caribou—a good thirty pounds of meat. But they were working hard, carrying their packs, and traveling many difficult miles over the aggravating terrain of hummocks.

The dogs weren't the only ones that were hungry. As Dick and the dogs moved into the mountains Dick noted, "I'm still making about ten miles a day but don't know how long I can keep it up. I expend twenty miles of energy to go through ten miles of hummocks."

Dick set traps to catch parka squirrels. He shared what he caught with the dogs.

They were trekking cross-country when Pup disappeared. Not only was the dog missing, he'd vanished with the pack that carried Dick's tent, cooking pots, and the .30-06 ammunition. Dick used the rifle scope to scan the countryside. He shot the gun in the air, hoping the signal would call the dog in. No luck. Dick starting tracking and eventually discovered Pup in a gully not far from camp, eating a dried up caribou hide.

Clouds of mosquitoes tormented Dick and the dogs. Dick took refuge in the tent at the end of the day and at night he spent time trying to sew it tighter to make it mosquito-proof.

Whitie and mosquitos.

"I can escape their wrath by retiring to my tent ... the [mosquitoes] constantly pelt it which sounds like a downpour of sleet," he wrote. The dogs, however, could not escape the onslaught and spent the night pacing and shaking the chains around their necks. It seemed as if they were all slowly being eaten alive. Blackie had open sores on his eyebrows where mosquitoes had relentlessly chewed on him.

Hunting for sheep.

The dearth of animals to hunt in the mountains forced Dick and the dogs back out onto the coastal plain to look for food. They were all growing weak with hunger and Pup continued to lag behind. After twenty miles of travel, Dick finally spotted a bull moose in the distance. He worried that if the dogs saw a meal on the hoof, they might take chase. So he went back to get Pup. By the time he had the dogs in hand, the moose had left the area. He tied Blackie and Whitie, but left Pup untied figuring the dog was too worn down to leave his companions. Then he went looking for the bull. It was late in the evening when Dick returned to the dogs empty handed. Once again Pup had disappeared—along with the tent and cooking pots. Dick was furious with Pup and with himself for not restraining the dog.

"It would be easy for a person to go 'off his rocker' here," Dick wrote. "It is miles from nowhere and the mosquitoes are driving us crazy."

It began to rain and without the tent, Dick could only curl up in his sleeping bag and wait for morning. By 3:00 a.m. too cold and wet to sleep, he got up and went looking for the moose. When he returned, again unsuccessful, Pup was lying in camp asleep.

Meanwhile, it began to snow in the mountains and Dick could see the weather was headed in their direction. It was time to move again, but Pup refused. Exasperated, Dick took the pack and left the dog behind.

As it began to snow, poor visibility made hunting impossible. He set up camp at a tributary of the Shaviovik River. By the next morning Pup had arrived and so had three inches of fresh snow. Even with the snow there were no signs of game, not a single track.

"We can't move out of here until we get something to eat," Dick wrote. For the first time he felt overwhelmed and unsure where this all might end.

"I'm hundreds of miles from anyplace, overextended, and way beyond my abilities. I'm in big trouble. I would bag this trip in a heartbeat if I could. I don't belong here," he wrote.

Then he made a choice reminiscent of his youth in Wyoming, when his father had forced him to put down his own horse and dog.

Dick shot Pup.

He skinned the dog, built a fire, and spent the day making dogmeat jerky.

"The dogs needed the meat as badly as I did," he remarked. Then he fed himself and the dogs their first meal in many miles.

While Pup had been less than useful as a pack dog, he was now providing life-sustaining nourishment until they could find game. Dick now carried

Making jerky out of dog meat.

the gear from Blackie's and Whitie's packs so that neither dog had to carry much—at least until he could get more food into their bellies.

In the search for food, Dick was zigzagging across the landscape rather than moving southwest toward Anaktuvuk Pass. He hoped his luck in finding game would change once he reached the Ivishak River.

As tough as the trail was and as hungry as he and the dogs were, Dick still managed to find rewards along the way. "It's always a thrill to drop into another major drainage," Dick wrote. "It's the rivers crossed that seem to count, not the miles traveled."

Finally through his rifle scope, he spotted five caribou bulls lying on a wide swath of ice. After a four-mile stalk, Dick managed to put down one of the bulls. It began to rain and Dick found a stand of willows to build a fire. He stayed up most of the night making caribou jerky. He also boiled pots of meat and fat for the dogs.

Dick always spent an hour each evening in camp reading. He used the pages that he read to build the next day's fire. On this trip he brought along the books *The True Believer* by Eric Hoffer and *Mainsprings of Civilizations* by Ellsworth Huntington—a 660-page tome.

He also had time to think and write. "As yet I'm not lonesome ... I have discovered that you must be alone with yourself and like the company you keep in the empty moments."

Crossing Ivishak River.

He also thought about his family back home. "I don't consider this trip without a lot of self doubts," he wrote. "Kimmer is four and Barney is two and both are too young to have a father wandering the Arctic not knowing from day to day where the next meal will come from. Often I feel a gnawing sense of irresponsibility about being away."

Even though the dogs now had plenty to eat, Blackie was in bad shape. He was old and had to be lifted to his feet in the morning before they left camp. After walking some distance, Dick sat down, built a fire and drank several cups of tea while the dogs rested. Although he knew several large river crossings still lay ahead, Dick decided to abandon his boat. Carrying fifteen pounds of jerky was now more important than carrying the weight of the boat. Still, he wondered with all the rain, how he'd manage to get across those rivers. Back on the trail, Blackie followed until they crossed a pass between drainages. When Dick looked around, the dog was missing.

"I walked back over the hill and found him lying there, dead. I brushed the mosquitoes off his nose for the last time and walked away," he wrote.

Throughout the day, Dick kept looking over his shoulder watching for Blackie, having to remind himself that the dog was gone. It had been just four days since Pup had perished. Now Blackie had succumbed. This trek was proving just too much for the dogs. Whitie followed along, hollow-eyed. Dick gave him half of the remaining jerky.

The rain persisted and the rivers continued to rise. Devoid of vegetation, the mountains looked deep blue and forbidding. Fast flowing torrents now replaced what had once been creeks with stepping stones to cross. In one place, a sheet of ice four miles across flowed wide with water. Whitie refused to cross the expanse. Dick went ahead knowing the dog would have to make his own way. When Dick reached the other side, he built a fire, made camp, and waited for the dog to arrive.

The dog never showed. Dick hoped that Whitie had decided to return to an earlier moose carcass, where he could eat and rest. But deep down, Dick realized that in the dog's weakened state, Whitie had probably drowned.

"The dogs could have worked as pack dogs if I had only stopped for three or four days at a kill to let them thoroughly rest," he wrote. "I've always been in such a hurry. There's so much country out there that I have to have it all—NOW."

Later, months after his trek, Dick saw a photo in *Life* magazine of a white dog on the tundra close to Lake Peters (near the Naval Arctic research camp where his friend Hungry had stayed behind). Dick recognized the dog as Whitie. It turned out he had not drowned after all—he had simply abandoned the expedition. Whitie had presumably survived on the carcasses of the caribou and moose Dick had shot along the way. Dick contacted the photographer, who sent him a negative of the photo.

Now Dick traveled completely alone and he too was wearing down. His clothes were rags, his shoes were in tatters, and he had grown gaunt. He had trouble getting up in the morning and it took a long time to get started each day. But the lure of the next hill, the next bend in the landscape, daily sparked his energy and by 2:00 p.m. most days he was a self-professed "walking fool." Deeper in the mountains, the terrain was growing steeper. His biggest challenge was river crossings. The water was cold and often deep. Without the boat, he worried about losing his gear in the current, or being swept away himself.

On July 16, as he reached the top of a knoll, he was startled to see a helicopter overhead. It landed nearby and two geologists and the pilot from the chopper had a hard time believing what they saw. Wild haired, bearded, and far too lean, the man standing before them looked, for the life of them, like he needed to be rescued.

The men insisted Dick return with them to their nearby camp and Dick accepted the ride. Richfield Oil Corporation had sent this team to look for oil on the coastal plain. At camp, Dick enjoyed a meal while the men tried to convince him to return on the next flight back to civilization. By then he had walked more than 336 miles and had roughly one hundred miles more to go before he reached his destination of Anaktuvuk Pass. He wasn't about to quit.

Dick spent the night and accepted every morsel of food they offered– he was more than willing to eat something besides jerky and the tea he had been living on. The next day, it took all day to walk to the Itkillik River where he set up camp in a driving wind. It began to snow and Dick spent the night—in a tent nearly flattened by wind—sleepless and wondering how he would manage to cross the river.

The next morning he packed up his tent and considered his options. He wished he had the boat he'd left far behind on the tundra. Finally he decided to forge across as best he could. He walked into frigid water that was at first waist deep and then chest deep. When the ground gave way under his feet Dick was forced to swim. He was so thin that his trousers slid off his body and disappeared into the current. Dick turned back toward shore and crawled out—wet, shivering, and nearly naked. After putting on a set of long-johns, he decided to hike back to the geologists' camp. Maybe one of the guys would have a pair of pants to spare. He remembered how he had built rafts of driftwood and shoelaces on the Barranca del Cobre; maybe there would be a few empty gas cans at camp that he could tie together to float across. If he could just build a boat …

The raft idea seemed insane to the geologists and they were fearful for Dick's life. This time the men insisted. If Dick refused to return to the safety of civilization, then he most certainly could accept a short helicopter ride to cross over the swollen river. Dick relented and took the ride, leaving behind the idea of a raft made of empty gas cans.

At last the going grew easier. Many of the mountain passes now lined up so that instead of crossing one ridge after the next, he was able to walk parallel with the mountains, which allowed him to cover as much as thirty miles in a day. The ice sheets and tussocks were gone, the wind and rain had eased. The water level dropped in the rivers making crossing them relatively easy, but the mosquitoes were still fearsome and Dick's feet were beginning to deteriorate. He had infected blisters that he knew would not heal until he stopped walking.

Finally, after thirty-eight days on the trail, in the heart of the Brooks Range, Dick looked up to see two small dots on the vast expanse. He looked through his rifle's spotting scope and saw two families on the roofs of their sod huts peering back at him with binoculars. These were the homes of Simon Paneak and his father-in-law, Elijah Kakinya.

Dick knew Simon Paneak. He was a well-known Native and while he was being treated for tuberculosis in Anchorage, Dick had gone to visit him in the hospital. Dick had spoken with Simon about his plans for this trek, but Simon had shaken his head. He doubted it was possible, especially for a white man without an Eskimo companion.

When Dick arrived at the sod huts, he learned that Simon was away hunting caribou. Simon's wife, Suzy, and the rest of the family were all home however—including Simon's father-in-law, Elijah. These were Nunamiut people, inland Eskimos who over the centuries had subsisted along the valleys and rivers of the Brooks Range. The twentieth century was bringing about profound changes for indigenous cultures in Alaska. As it turned out, Simon and Elijah's families were the last of their people to practice the traditional nomadic way of life.

Traditional sod hut.

Elijah's wife, May, took one look at Dick and made him a skillet full of fried caribou and offered coffee with sugar. Elijah took great interest in Dick's travels and in broken English, asked how Dick had managed his nearly five-hundred-mile trek. A few hours later, Elijah decided that Dick was still hungry, so May prepared another plate of caribou and offered more coffee with sugar.

Dick enjoyed learning from Elijah, the translations of the names of the rivers he had crossed. Ivishak River meant "the place where you find iron." Sagavanirktok meant "fast river." The Itkillik was "the place where Eskimos had a big battle with Indians." And finally, Anaktuvuk was the combination of two Eskimo words Anak—"shit" and tuvuk—"caribou."

Dick stayed the night accepting Elijah's hospitality. As he closed his eyes, Dick lay his bone-weary body onto the soft bed of a caribou hide. The next day would be the last one of his first Arctic trek.

Elijah Kakinya.

Five-thousand-foot peaks reached on either side of the pass as Dick traveled the final sixteen miles into the village of Anaktuvuk Pass. Except for an infection festering in his feet, he said the final miles were easy.

Anaktuvuk Pass later became a modern village.

FLYING OUT OF THE VILLAGE THE NEXT DAY, Dick once again looked at the Brooks Range from the sky. He was no less inspired by the view than when he'd flown over it nearly two months earlier. The wide expanse of peaks and valleys seemed as formidable and fascinating as ever.

Dick had learned a great deal about Arctic travel on this trip. And he'd learned a thing or two about himself. The challenge of the trek, he said, was twenty-five percent physical and seventy-five percent mental. He'd stretched himself on both accounts.

Now, below him lay a wilderness too vast for words, a place remote and daunting and utterly indifferent to the footfall of a man traveling across its stoic face. The Arctic consumed him and yet he'd only just touched the hem of it. He had just tasted the bittersweet hold it would come to have on him. Of one thing Dick was certain, as he watched the mountains pass beneath him. Someday he would be back for more.

Chapter 9

The Raven Years

Beaten men follow beaten paths.
—Unknown.

IN A SECRET CREASE OF LANDSCAPE between the town of Girdwood and Eagle River valley sits a small cabin, tucked away off the trail of even the nearest backcountry path. Deep in the Chugach Mountains, the Raven Cabin was a sanctuary that drew Dick back again and again for the sustenance of wild untamed places.

In autumn of 1959, after his walk through the Brooks Range to Anaktuvuk Pass, Dick decided to return to school for a degree in Civil Engineering from Marquette University. He and Isabelle and the kids moved to Milwaukee, Wisconsin, and lived with Isabelle's mother until they bought a house. It was not the happiest time, being with a mother-in-law who had always considered Dick a ne'er-do-well.

"She was right about that," Dick likes to say.

As it turns out, Dick's mother was not particularly fond of Isabelle either. "My mother thought she was a Bohemian because she didn't wear a bra."

As is often the case, neither Dick's nor Isabelle's personas quite fit a more complicated reality. They both certainly proved their in-laws wrong. In the end, Dick would have a successful thirty-year career in government service, retiring from the Federal Aviation Administration after building airports all over rural Alaska. Isabelle finished her career at Providence Medical Center as a medical technician. All the while, Isabelle would hold a secret that even Dick would not discover for nearly fifty years—one that may explain, in part, why after their move to Alaska, Isabelle no longer accompanied Dick on his adventures.

The family returned to Anchorage in 1964 shortly after the Good Friday Earthquake that devastated Southcentral Alaska. The earthquake measured a magnitude of 9.2 on the Richter scale—the most violent earthquake ever recorded in North America and the second largest in the world. Roads and rail lines, ports and towns along Alaska's coastline were decimated. The earthquake scrambled much of Alaska's infrastructure so there was plenty of work available in rebuilding the state when Dick went to work for the FAA.

He became a self-described "weekend warrior," exploring the mountains near his home. With a half-million acres of wilderness, Chugach State Park is the third largest state park in America. This became Dick's playground in the years that he raised his family. Perhaps no one came to know the folds of earth, the zigzag of streams, or the crinkled collection of glaciers in the area as well as Dick. When map makers went to create a map of Chugach State Park, they sought out Dick to help them.

One of Dick's favorite destinations over the years became Raven Cabin. Originally an old trapper's cabin, the cabin was rebuilt in 1973 by Larry and Kathy Tedrick. The couple had a young son, Larry Jr. Along with rebuilding the cabin, the couple helped construct a new trail to a visitor center alongside Eagle River. Dick befriended the little boy who enjoyed the rare guests to their remote home. Dick brought apples and oranges and children's books by Richard Scarry. One time, father and son accompanied Dick out to the end of the valley—a good ten mile walk—which impressed Dick immensely. The boy, who was only five at the time, never once complained.

One day when Dick stopped by, the cabin lay empty. Although the cabin had endured, the couple's marriage had not. They had returned to civilization, leaving behind many of their belongings and a single family photo. To his consternation, Dick later learned the couple had given the little boy up for adoption. Dick took the family photo and made copies. He returned one photo to the cabin. He kept one copy for himself and another he hoped to one day give to the little boy. (Dick discovered only years later that the boy—now grown—had lived in Hawaii and then the Midwest. He was not interested in Dick's photo remembrance of the past.)

From the time that the Tedricks left, Dick became the unofficial and self-appointed care-taker of Raven Cabin.

He also became a renegade. The cabin was officially in the care of Chugach State Park. Over the years rangers often stayed there with Dick and his friends. But later on, park authorities did not always approve of Dick's unauthorized work on the cabin or nearby trails. At one point, park officials helicoptered into the site and removed all of Dick's tools including a chainsaw. It would be years before he recovered his chainsaw and by then, he said, it was ruined.

The cabin log book became a voluminous testament to the comings and goings of people, bears, and wolves. Dick wrote the rules of Raven Cabin, which were posted in the log book:

Cabin Rules
- Cabin use not to exceed four nights.
- Don't fill gas lantern with chainsaw gas (only white gas). It's okay to introduce friends to cabin but not friends who are smart enough to find their way back.
- Black bears are a problem. They are always trying to gain entry either through the roof, door or windows. Be sure to inspect premises. Put the bear proof window shutters back like you found them.
- Use tools in cabin but don't take them. This cabin is used for working on the trail on the other side of the river. We keep this side of the river and the "general public" can have the other side. "Beaten men follow beaten paths."
- Do not ever cut any alders, trees or branches on the trail leading to this cabin. This cabin must remain hidden or it will be quickly destroyed.
- It's not mandatory to leave anything in this log book but it is a good chronicle of what is happening in this area.

Many entries from the log book were banters back and forth between hikers who knew each other; and many thanked Dick for his upkeep and work on the cabin. One passerby commented, "Who is Dick Griffith? Is he faster than a speeding bullet? Does he leap over high buildings?"

Another entry said, "When Dick chews the tree gum it gives him hyper speed, Dick's super drug."

Dick often wrote only "Passing through" in the diary. He began to sign the register "Me again." He made as many as nine trips a year, up and over Crow Pass, along Eagle River to the visitor center and back again. Some days he traveled alone. Other times he took friends. He often took his daughter's dogs, Sam and Quillpie. The dogs slept in front of the cabin door and had the job of keeping bears away. Bears were a continuous nuisance over the years and broke into the cabin on many occasions.

It was early dusk one morning in late May when Dick heard a yelp outside the cabin.

"I ran out into the early morning darkness and called for Quillpie and Sam," he wrote. "There was no response so I ran over to the general area where I heard the distress. A large grey wolf was dragging Quillpie away. The wolf dropped the dog when I blew on a whistle. Quillpie was very much dead when I reached him. I searched another hour before I found Sam, dead also."

Dick placed the dogs' collars on a nail inside the cabin. By the next morning all that remained of his companions was the stain of blood on the forest floor. What the wolves left behind, the bears had taken away. It was a grim reminder of the realities of life and death in the wilderness.

That evening his journal entry read, "I wanted to work on the trail up to Thunder Gorge but I am tired, discouraged, and lonesome." The next day he wrote, "I am leaving this morning—don't know if I will come back."

But he did come back—many times after that. The log book entries offered their condolences about the dogs. It also included entries by Kimmer and Barney, Dick's now adult daughter and son. He continued making treks into his eighties, keeping the cabin in good repair, cutting and splitting firewood, and working on trails and bridges along the way.

DICK ENJOYED WATCHING THE CROW PASS wilderness race, an annual event that passed through Eagle River valley. The race course treks more than twenty-five miles and includes a mountain pass, a glacial river crossing, roots, rocks, and snow. Obstacles include encounters with startled bears and recalcitrant moose. Dick didn't compete—but he did walk the course in Griffith fashion, one long stride at a time. When he reached the river crossing at Eagle River, rather than ford to the other side, he inflated a packraft and leapfrogged ahead of the other runners by eight miles. Then he packed up his raft before hiking to the finish line.

While other competitors collapsed at the finish, Dick would shrug and say, "Well, I gotta go get my car," and set off to hike the trail back to Girdwood—a round trip distance of nearly fifty miles.

"I just did it to make fun of them," Dick said. He was amused at the hoopla of the whole thing—the great effort expended on the one-way course that he easily traversed in under six hours several times a year.

THE ALASKA MOUNTAIN WILDERNESS CLASSIC was another outlet for Dick's compulsion for walkabouts. The Classic has become known as one of the world's toughest wilderness races—a punishing 150-250-mile trek across untracked wilderness. There is no set route—just get from point A to point B under your own power. Every three years, the race location is changed so that trekkers don't get too familiar with the terrain.

Rules of the race offer ample warnings of the rigors ahead: "*No help will be available. No rescue can be anticipated ... We are warning you. Any decision you make is your own and you are responsible for it. Your injuries or death are not our responsibility.*"

This was Dick's kind of race.

A test of wilderness skills, the event requires competitors to carry with them all the provisions they would need for the trek. The race is so grueling that in the nearly thirty years since its inception, only about half of the competitors have finished. The event has no sponsors or prize money. The liability alone keeps sponsors away; besides, media coverage of the race would involve watching a dozen or so people disappear into the wild with hopes that they would, at some point, all show up at the finish line. Dick ran the

Alaska Wilderness Classic, Nabesna to McCarthy.

inaugural Classic in 1982, traversing the wilderness from Hope to Homer across Alaska's Kenai Peninsula. The race application asked what the competitor was doing to prepare for the event.

Dick wrote, "Sitting on the couch watching TV and eating peanuts."

Roman Dial, a fellow competitor who himself won the race multiple times, remembers Dick as the old man of the race. At age fifty-five, Dick already sported a shock of white hair.

"Dick clearly had some experience, but he wore it so very modestly, with an 'aw, shucks' demeanor. He was the kind of guy even a twenty-something punk like me wanted to be: Clint Eastwood in a backpack and tennis shoes," Dial wrote in his book, *Packrafting!*

One of the obstacles on that first race was the potentially lethal Skilak River. The icy torrent churned gray with silt from the melting glacier that fed it. The water was deep and fast and mean. Several of the competitors camped at the river's edge hoping that by morning the water might subside. Dial described the scene in his book:

> *"Whadda you guys doin' here? I'd expect you to be half way to Homer by now! I can't believe you let an old man catch you."*
>
> *We mumbled something about waiting for the water to go down before swimming the river.*
>
> *"Swim?" Dick asked incredulously. "You can't swim these rivers. They're too cold and fast. How you gonna swim with all that stuff on your back?"*
>
> *He'd voiced precisely what we were wondering. Then he pulled out a fuzzy red hat with blue horns and pulled it on over his white hair. It was some sort of crazy Viking hat.*
>
> *"You may be fast," he said glancing at Dave and me, "but you guys eat too much and don't know nothin'."*
>
> *... Dick started pulling gear out of his pack.*
>
> *"What's that Dick?" someone asked, indicating a gray pile. "Your secret weapon?"*
>
> *"Yep, my secret weapon," he repeated proudly.*
>
> *His secret weapon was a gray vinyl, inflatable "two-man" raft. Dick was going to row the Skilak crossing in a "rubber ducky." ...*
>
> *"You guys might be fast, but old age and treachery conquer youth and skill any day!" Dick crowed.*
>
> *Seemed like he had a point.*

After his crossing, Dick stayed at the far shore to make sure the others made it safely across the turbid, thirty-three-degree river. One competitor, Dave Manzer, got swept downstream as he tried to cross. The rope that was tied around his waist got tangled in the ripping current and wrapped around his legs. As Manzer tumbled downstream, weighed down by his backpack, Dick ran along the bank to grab him. He and another competitor pulled Manzer to shore.

Dick's son, Barney Griffith (left), often accompanied Dick in the Alaska Wilderness Classic race.

Later, while other competitors thrashed and bush-wacked through fifteen hours of alder thickets, Dick floated the distance in just three hours, most of it with just one oar because the second one had broken somewhere along the way.

It was Dick's use of the Air Force survival raft on his trek down the Barranca del Cobre and his "rubber ducky" in the Alaska Mountain Wilderness Classic that earned Dick the distinction of being the grandfather of packrafting. On that first race, it seemed as if he was folding his six-foot frame into a pool toy. The strategy worked however, and from that race forward, savvy competitors included it as part of their wilderness gear.

Dick was one of only four finishers in that first race, along with Roman Dial, Dave Manzer, and George Ripley, the founder and director of the race.

IN SUBSEQUENT YEARS, HEADLINES FROM the *Anchorage Daily News* called competitors "Crazed Souls." Gordy Vernon competed in the Classic as a rookie in 1991, and ran alongside Dick and Dick's son, Barney. Vernon claims he found religion as a result of the race, in particular along the Goat Trail that traverses a steep slope above the swirling Chitistone River between Nabesna and McCarthy.

"Every step counts. The path heads straight up and then disappears into a trail across a crumbling sandstone cliff, etched only by the mad scrambling of the person before," Vernon wrote in a 1991 article for *We Alaskans*. "You watch the rocks you knock loose bounce 1,000 feet down, picking up speed until they shoot out and are swallowed by the river gorge."

He said he prayed like a zealot.

Dick and Barney dubbed Vernon the "Leprechaun," because he had a habit of disappearing along the trail behind them and then mysteriously showing up ahead of them. With the help of the Griffiths, Vernon placed third in the race that year. (Vernon's standing in the race was momentarily challenged however because, instead of ringing the bell in front of the McCarthy Lodge, he headed straight inside to the bar.)

Dick did not compete to win, so much as to traverse the back country and to be amused by other wilderness travelers. When asked once about who he thought might win in the lineup of competitors, he nodded toward a wisp of a man from Fairbanks—a guy who installed burglar alarms for a living. Vernon recalled that when asked why he thought that fellow might take the title, Dick said, "He has to be back to work on Wednesday."

Competitors from outside Alaska rarely finished the race, and Dick chuckled when a Utah team of Outward Bound instructors got lost.

"We don't need to worry about them," he said. "They teach survival skills."

JERRY DIXON, A FELLOW WILDERNESS TRAVELER, wrote about his experience competing in the Classic alongside his friend, Dick.

> *Even following Dick, we end up taking six hours to go three miles.*
> *After about five hours I am ready to call a helicopter. I just want out.*
> *We end up cliffed out and start to descend a waterfall as it is the*

only place the brush and deadfall will allow passage. We are down climbing in a stream when Dick falls six feet and lands on his head. My first thought was, "Medivac." Dick leaped to his feet and with a few choice words continued to lead the next 120 miles to Homer. A fall like that would have left me in a heap in the streambed. I was astonished and asked Barney, his son, "Did you see that?"

"Yes I did. Hey Dad, this is getting too steep. Let's head right and see if we can't get out of these cliffs."

... We continue edging right until we find a passage. Barney and I scout ahead and literally slide to the gravel plain of the Skilak River. Later Dick offers a laconic, "Good work."

At the end of each day of the race, while other competitors forged ahead through the twilight of Alaska's summer night, Dick would stop, build a campfire and sleep.

"I like sleep," he said. "I never miss my sleep."

Over the years, of the half or so competitors who managed to get across the finish line, many came in using their packraft paddles as crutches for blistered feet and strained joints. Some were hallucinating from lack of sleep.

Dick usually finished his races with a strong stride. "I don't push myself. In the end I still have good feet and can turn around and go back."

Between 1982 and 2008, Dick finished the race seventeen times—more than any other competitor in the history of the race until his friend John Lapkass broke Dick's record in 2011. Dick ran his last race at the age of 81.

In the history of the race, as of 2012, he also holds the following distinctions:

First to use a packraft: In 1982, at age 55, Hope to Homer
Oldest finisher: In 2004, at age 78, Eureka to Talkeetna
First place finisher Master's Division: In 2008, at age 81, Chicken to Central
Oldest finisher in Master's Division: In 2008, at age 81, Chicken to Central

THROUGH THE CANYONS of the Green and Colorado rivers and the Barranca del Cobre, Isabelle's voice played a prominent part in the telling of Dick's story. But after arriving in Alaska, and after the birth of a daughter and son, she stopped accompanying Dick. Their daughter, Kimmer, says Isabelle was an avid berry picker and always enjoyed the outdoors. But she never again made the long arduous treks into the backcountry.

One reason may have been that floating together on a rubber boat, she could keep up with her husband. But trying to keep up with him on foot—when Dick had the stamina of a Tarahumara Indian—was another story. Kimmer acknowledged that trekking with her father was a challenge for her and her brother. They didn't stop to ponder scenery or smell the wildflowers. It was all about going the distance and Dick did so at a brutal pace.

Barney Griffith and John Lapkass on the Talkeetna River, Alaska Wilderness Classic.

Barney knew his parents as fundamentally very different people.

"Dad had a lot of ambition, a spirit for adventure," Barney said. "There was a part of him that wanted to adventure full time, but he had family responsibilities."

Although Isabelle's interests had turned toward more domestic endeavors, she didn't worry when Dick went trekking for long stretches at a time.

"No one lost sleep over it," Barney said. "There was nothing you could do about it anyway. Not knowing where he was or when he'd get back was, in a way, its own safety net."

Isabelle did, however, hold a $200,000 life insurance policy on her husband. She also held a closely guarded secret which was not discovered until late into their forty-seven years of marriage.

She had told Dick when they met that she was only three years older than his twenty-two years. She maintained that difference in their age throughout their lives together and even doctored her birth certificate to reflect it. But when, at age sixty-two, Dick went to apply for Social Security for both of them, he learned that Isabelle had a large sum waiting for her—one that took him by complete surprise. His wife was, in fact, nearly a decade older than him.

Dick found the whole thing amusing. Isabelle, however, did not.

"She was vain," Dick said, chuckling.

Their daughter, Kimmer, said her mother was able to pull off the secret because her beauty was not diminished by age. Isabelle was an attractive woman her entire life. She passed away in 1996 at the age of seventy-eight of heart disease and breast cancer.

Dick was sixty-nine when Isabelle died. By then he was more than halfway through a stunning odyssey across the Arctic. One that he very nearly didn't survive.

Chapter 10

Landscape of Anguish

I'm discovering there are degrees of desolation.
—Dick Griffith

IT'S THE LITTLE MISTAKES that kill you.

Shivering, with frozen fingertips, Dick could not thread the zipper of his sleeping bag back onto its track. Stunned, he wondered for a moment if this was it. If this would be the one small detail that tipped the balance.

He quickly wrapped himself the best he could in his sleeping bag and crawled into the two-foot-deep snow trench he had dug for himself. This would be his shelter for the night. At minus thirty degrees, with winds howling up to forty miles an hour, the windchill factor was more than one hundred degrees below zero. He had staked his sled and backpack into the snow using his ski poles to keep them from blowing away.

Snow drifted in over the trench, covering him with an insulating layer of snow. He began to feel warmer. As his body warmed, so did the frostbitten parts of his anatomy. The wind that had pressed at his back all day—which had been strong enough to push his sled out in front of him– had frozen the flesh of his backside and legs.

He was terribly thirsty.

Less than two days earlier, on March 10, 1980, Dick had been lying in the loft of his friends Roosevelt and Beth Paneak's home in Anaktuvuk Pass. It was the night before his trek and the plan was to ski from Anaktuvuk Pass to Bettles and then over the mountains to the village of Tanana and on to the Yukon River. It was to be a three-hundred-mile trek through rugged country with snow deep enough to swallow snowmachines (the Alaskan term for snowmobile).

With snow conditions as they were, Dick decided to lighten his load. He left his tent behind, opting instead for a large, heavy-duty sleeping bag that would shelter him from the cold. A layer of spruce boughs would be his bed. If necessary, he could build snow caves for shelter. He also decided to leave his stove and fuel at home. He liked a wood fire best, and as he had on previous trips, he would gather wood as he traveled. He also left his Gore-Tex bibs behind. His plan was to keep moving at a good clip and take as little as necessary to stay agile and quick.

The 1959 trip from Kaktovik to Anaktuvuk Pass had taught him a great deal about wilderness travel in the North. Later in 1977, Dick walked 150 miles and floated 450 miles from Anaktuvuk Pass to Kotzebue with his friend Bruce Stafford. Between mosquitoes, rain, and rivers swollen with floodwaters—he learned that travel was best done before "breakup"—the time of year when Alaska's daylight grows longer but before the warmer weather of spring melts the ice on rivers. Two years later in 1979, he traveled solo on foot and by ski from Nuiqsut to Anaktuvuk Pass, a distance of two hundred miles.

People asked him why he took these trips, and sometimes he wondered himself. On his 1979 solo journey he reflected, "There are moments I don't know why I'm here. It's cold and the landscape is monotonous. Progress is slow and the distance ahead seems to be unreachable. You need the capacity to see beauty even when it's not pretty every day."

He learned he could travel much lighter. On the solo trip, he'd dropped a lot of gear—a thermos, food, a wet down jacket, even his sled. "This is a situation where possessions can forfeit freedom," he wrote. On that trek he also noted, "Comfort is best when interspersed with moments of great discomfort."

Bruce Stafford on the Noatak River.

He would soon discover the slender thread between discomfort and disaster.

This trip in 1980 already had an ominous beginning. On his airplane flight en route to the Brooks Range, a defective engine on the plane had thumped to a sickening stop. In his career as a civil engineer for the FAA, Dick had worked on airports all over the state. The irony of dying in a plane crash on his way to traveling overland on skis was not lost on him. The pilot managed to turn the crippled aircraft around and with one engine return to Bettles.

Then, as Dick boarded a different airplane to reach his starting point, a snowmachine roared up to the Piper Navaho. One of the men on the sled cradled his hand, which was wrapped in a blood-soaked rag. The pilot agreed to take the injured man to Fairbanks. But the door to the plane refused to close. It was minus twenty degrees and Dick and the pilot took turns removing their mittens to fix the door.

"By that time I was ready to go back to Fairbanks and call it quits," Dick wrote. "Nothing was going right."

When Dick finally arrived in Anaktuvuk Pass, it was late in the evening.

The stove glowed as the wind buffeted Paneak's small house. Dick thought about finding Elijah before heading out of the village the next morning. It was rumored Elijah was a shaman, wise as he was old. At one time the Nunamiut man had hunted moose and caribou with a bow and spear. Dick felt privileged to know a man who knew the old ways of subsistence, who lived before the introduction of television and snowmachines. Elijah had offered the bed of caribou hide on the last night of Dick's journey through the Brooks Range in 1959.

Dick gazed outside the window and saw hundreds of caribou grazing nearby. It had been a tough winter so far in Anaktuvuk, with temperatures regularly dipping to minus fifty and winds gusting to fifty miles per hour.

Anaktuvuk Pass.

"The snow was worn out from the wind blowing back and forth through the pass," Dick wrote in his journal that night. The loft was cozy though—even a little too warm—and Dick unzipped his bag, not noticing that the zipper had come off its track.

The next morning he found Elijah. It had been almost twenty years since Elijah had translated the Native meanings of the rivers Dick had traveled between Barter Island and Anaktuvuk. He had at one time been a sled dog driver for the famous explorer Vilhjalmur Stefansson. Now, nearing the age of ninety, Elijah's memory was hazy.

"Elijah was the type of person you could set down any place in the world, bare naked, and he would soon surface with clothes, much caribou meat, and a wad of greenbacks," Dick said. It was the kind of resourcefulness and self-sufficiency that Dick held in highest regard.

When Dick said goodbye to his old friend and left the village with his loaded sled it was 11:00 a.m. A stiff wind was still blowing but ski conditions on the hard-blown snow were excellent.

"The 30 mile-per-hour wind was at my back and I was actually being blown down the John River. There was no drag on the sled because the wind pushed it," he wrote.

Minus thirty didn't seem that cold. The trick was to keep moving. As he traveled, he came across hundreds of caribou standing with their backs to the wind. The animals hardly noticed Dick's presence in their midst. They were stoic, braced against the wind. He could have touched them with his ski pole.

His plan was to reach the tree line by nightfall where he would find spruce trees that offered firewood and shelter from the wind. At 2:00 p.m., when he reached for his water bottles to get a drink, he discovered that even with the insulation of being wrapped in his sleeping bag, the containers held only solid chunks of ice. He would have to do without water until he could build a fire. By 4:00 p.m., temperatures began to drop even further from minus thirty to minus forty. The wind increased to forty miles per hour. Dick had to stop now and then to beat his hands together to regain circulation. He felt a tingling sensation on the back of his legs and backside. He was regretting leaving the Gore-Tex bibs behind.

The tree line was nowhere in sight and although he skied faster, the wind created a ground blizzard that made visibility nearly zero. There was no shelter, not even a meager stand of willows. He was skiing through a white funnel of snow.

As evening descended, Dick knew he'd have to stop and make some sort of camp. He dug a two-foot-deep trench in the snow and crawled in. Thirsty and shivering, he didn't think things could get a whole lot worse. Then he discovered that he could not zip his sleeping bag.

THROUGHOUT THE NIGHT, HE USED his mittens to punch holes in the snow for air. He slept fitfully, hoping that by morning the weather would let up. It didn't. Late in the morning the sun rose over the mountains offering only a thin hint of warmth. He thrust his frozen boots in the bag to thaw them. His mouth felt woolen. He needed water badly. By 11:00 a.m. he was able, painfully, to get back on the trail. He needed a fire in order to thaw something to drink. And the only way to build a fire was to get to the tree line.

He finally reached the tree line at 3:00 p.m. but the still-raging wind made building a fire impossible. He managed to spark a feeble flame, but it was quickly swallowed by blowing snow and wind. So much for thawing ice or snow to drink. Once again he dug a trench to sleep in. This time, with fingertips now blackened by frostbite, he somehow managed to get the zipper back on the track of his sleeping bag. He put the frozen water bottles inside the bag with him, pressing them against his shivering body. Maybe his body heat would thaw the ice a little—even a few teaspoons to drink would be better than nothing.

"The intense cold has become the overriding sensation; it hovers in my dreams and wraps around my body. The cold is so intense that the moisture in my eyes freezes to form tiny icicles between the upper and lower lashes. I live deep inside the tunnel formed by the hood of my parka," he wrote.

The human body chooses to stay alive first and to function second. The next morning, Dick had a hard time getting out of his sleeping bag. As the cold seeped deeper into his body, his brain sensed the danger. By slowing blood flow to the extremities, his body circulated more blood to the vital organs. Dick's limbs moved woodenly now, almost as if they belonged to someone else. Putting on his boots was a major undertaking.

At this point he was twenty miles from Anaktuvuk, where he'd started, and another sixty miles from Crevice Creek. Even though the distance back to Anaktuvuk was less than half the distance to Crevice Creek, the terrain back to the village was mostly uphill. With winds continuing to howl fiercely from that direction, a return trip would have been difficult if not impossible. Dick knew Bill and Lil Fickus had a homestead at Crevice Creek and made the decision to set out for their cabin. But he didn't really know where the cabin was. Or even Crevice Creek for that matter.

What he did know was that he needed water. And that by following the John River he would eventually get to Crevice Creek.

Below Hunts Fork on the John River, he came to a large overflow area where water seeped over the top of the ice. An open spot in the river appeared and at last he was able to drink. He sipped greedily at the icy water. With one cold swallow after the next, he finally slaked his thirst.

The pain in Dick's legs and rear were intense. Exposure to the cold and lack of oxygen causes cells to die. Dehydration furthers their destruction. As blood flow returns to the extremities, it leaks out from damaged blood vessels, creating inflammation and further tissue damage. As Dick warmed himself in his sleeping bag at night, and then traveled in the cold wind each day, the frostbite only worsened. He could hardly bend over; the pain in his backside was so severe. As he skied, he could feel sticky fluid from his injuries seeping down the back of his legs.

By midafternoon on the third day, he stopped and set up camp. This time he set his sleeping bag on an insulating layer of spruce boughs. His ski boots were frozen at the toes from skiing through the river's overflow. He hammered the ice off with his saw and in the brittle cold, the saw broke. He put the boots in his sleeping bag to thaw.

On the fourth night, as he stomped a platform to lay his bag on, he broke through the river ice with one foot, sinking thigh-deep in the frigid water. Climbing out to firmer ground, his leg was immediately encased in ice. He used his ski pole to shave off the ice before climbing into the sleeping bag with the frozen boot still on. By now his underwear was glued onto his skin and he began to note the fetid smell of decay.

Dick was now near a state of total exhaustion. Each morning it grew harder to get out of his sleeping bag. Traveling became a slow, painful slog. His focus narrowed to the path directly in front of his skis. Keep moving, he told himself. Just keep moving. His map showed two cabins. If he could find one of them, he could stop for a few days.

"I'd like to just stay in my sleeping bag and not get up anymore," he wrote. "I have to discipline myself to move on—no matter what environment you are subjected to, it is willpower that makes you survive."

That night, with a weariness more pressing even than the cold, Dick considered the choices he'd made.

"We have choices between living life to its fullest and trying to live life to its longest," he wrote. "When I started this trip I would have opted to live life to its fullest. But now I want to live life to its longest. It is the reality of life; Mother Nature wants us dead."

The next morning he got up again and headed slowly, painfully, down river. At this point he was no longer thinking clearly, just sliding one ski ahead of the other, one hour after the next. He had done this before, gone long distances without stopping. He was no stranger to the cold. As a boy in Wyoming, he tried to sell Christmas trees door-to-door from the back of his father's truck. At one point, he and his brother were shivering so intensely that they could barely speak. A kindly old woman took them in, set them next to a warm stove, and fed them hot cocoa. His father, also shivering, waited outside. They sold not one tree. Not even after discounting them from fifty cents to a dime each. It was the Great Depression and no one had money to spare.

The cabins on his map were not materializing and he was growing weaker. A hard oozing crust had formed on his legs and rear end.

THE ARCTIC IS A LANDSCAPE INFUSED with tragedy. It strains the fragile filament between life and death; between the cold indifference of the elements and the stamina of a beating heart. It can test every wilderness skill, every ounce of resolve.

"Boatloads of people perished in the Arctic," Dick said. "Mostly out of stupidity."

The most famous and tragic expedition was led by Sir John Franklin. In 1845, Franklin led two ships and 127 men through the ice-covered waterways north of the Canadian mainland, in search of the Northwest Passage. Their boat was frozen in the ice for two years. Those who did not die of starvation or scurvy resorted to eating their dead. In the end, not one man survived. More crews perished as they searched the Arctic to learn what had become of the Franklin expedition.

There were other stories. Dozens of them. Some were stories where one big mistake or a series of small mistakes tipped the balance. Others were the stories of just plain chance, where circumstances beyond anyone's control shifted. Where luck drifted from the center line into a collision course with disaster.

And sometimes, against all odds—call it a stroke of luck, or divine intervention—Providence offered, at precisely the right moment, another chance.

Six days after leaving Anaktuvuk Pass, Dick happened upon a snow-machine trail. It was a trapline trail crossing the John River.

A lifeline.

He followed the track into a timbered area nearby. Following the snow-machine trail was easier than following the rough snow of the river. Besides, it presumably would lead to a cabin.

It was nearing dark when he saw a shadowed figure ahead. It was a lynx, alive and caught in a leg hold trap. Dick paused. The lynx lay next to the trail in a V-shaped hollow of terrain. Making a wide berth around the lynx would require a climb over and around the draw. He would not even attempt it.

He and the lynx eyed each other silently as Dick passed by, just feet away from where it lay. He felt sorry for the creature.

"Both of us were in bad shape," Dick wrote. "The lynx was at the end of a chain and so was I."

He pushed ahead. Several times he nearly lost the trail where it crossed frozen lakes. But somehow the track always reappeared, faint but welcome

Bill and Lil Fickus in 2003.

on the other side. Then at 9:30 p.m., he looked up to see a thin line of smoke threading from the chimney of Bill and Lil Fickus' homestead. The temperature was minus twenty-nine degrees.

IT'S NOT OFTEN IN A WILDERNESS CABIN—where there are no roads or neighbors for dozens of miles—that someone comes knocking in the deep cold of the night. At their door stood a gaunt man, encrusted by cold, his nose blackened by frostbite. His eyes alone held the warmth of a man still living. "They were very surprised when I knocked on their door," Dick said.

He entered a modern home with lights and heat and inside plumbing. Bill poured a tub of warm water and peeled off Dick's bloody underwear.

Lil, who was trained as a nurse, knew by looking at the black hardened skin and blisters that Dick was in trouble. Bill went outside and hooked up the engine heaters to his airplane and the next morning he and Lil flew Dick to Bettles. From there Dick caught commercial flights to Fairbanks and then on to Anchorage. Other passengers sat as far away as possible from the stench of his decaying flesh.

Dick was admitted to Providence Hospital's thermal unit with a fever, elevated blood pressure, dehydration, malnutrition, severe frostbite, and gangrene. He was in the hospital for nearly a month during which time he wrote most of his journal entries recounting his experience. On the trail he had only a small thermometer to read temperature and wind speeds he later learned by checking the weather reports for the day. They were able to save Dick's fingers, but he needed surgery to remove the frostbite from his rear end and his legs followed by the long painful process of skin grafts. When Dick returned to work at the FAA on crutches, he had to stand because he could not sit.

"They amputated my butt," Dick likes to say.

It is the reason he has earned the nickname "Black Ass." Dick credits Bill and Lil Fickus for saving his life. "I could never have made the remaining 40 miles to Bettles. I doubt if there were even four miles left in me," Dick wrote. That night, in the salvation of the warm cabin and before attempting to sleep, Dick drank two quarts of home brew.

(Left) First day in the hospital. The aftermath of frostbite. (Right) Three weeks later; injuries required skin grafts. (Photos by Dr. William Mills.).

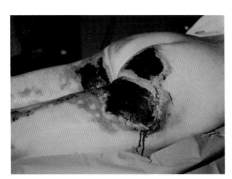
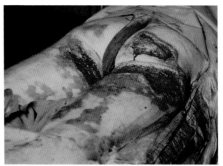

Arctic explorer Vilhjalmur Stefansson, who experienced ill-fated expeditions of his own in the early 1900s, is quoted as saying, "Adventure is a sign of incompetence." Throughout Dick's life, he always maintained that he'd rather be lucky than skilled. And on this trek between Anaktuvuk Pass and Crevice Creek he had drawn on ample measures of both.

Later on, Dick would write that the Arctic was a landscape of anguish. But it would repeatedly draw him back. As he recovered from his injuries, he was already thinking about his next trip. And he was formulating an idea to traverse the entire Brooks Range and beyond.

Chapter 11

Rabies

Hundreds and hundreds of men have perished in the arctic (entire shiploads)
and each and every one died with hope on his lips.
—Dick Griffith

IT WAS EASTER SUNDAY, 1989, and Dick was in church. Not that he'd planned it that way exactly. But he was grateful for a place out of the wind and blowing snow. This was the only structure that had not been completely drifted over in the abandoned Alaska fishing village of Sheshalik. He moved the crude benches and stack of Bibles to the side before shoveling snow off the floor. With wind rattling the small plywood building, and after finding a can of sixteen-penny nails, he nailed his tent to the wooden floor.

At age sixty-one, just days after retiring from government service, Dick took off on his longest trek yet. The plan was to travel from Unalakleet, Alaska on the coast of Norton Sound, across the Seward Peninsula and on to Barrow, a distance of nine hundred miles. By now he had traversed the entire Brooks Range from East to West, more than eleven hundred miles total, the first person ever to do so. He had learned a great deal and had his share of mishaps.

"I consider myself to be a seasoned Arctic traveler now because I have been severely frozen, destroyed a tent by fire, lost expensive equipment in the wind and skied over a thousand miles across the interior of Alaska to reach Unalakleet," he wrote.

He said he was at the point in life that he was not willing to repeat past mistakes but quite willing to make new ones. And always there was the persistent question, why did he make these arduous expeditions?

"I have no idea why I want to attempt such a long, cold trip. I should perhaps be going to Florida or the Caribbean to sit on the beach and watch girls," he wrote. "A successful person graduates from college, gets a job, marries, has kids, retires, and dies. I have done all that except die; I want more out of life, a lot more."

This was his second attempt out of Unalakleet. The previous year in 1988, he had upgraded his gear with a new tent and a high-end down sleeping bag. He had left in the light of a full moon with his loaded sled and traveled several miles looking for a good place to camp. Winds were gusting forty to fifty miles per hour when Dick decided to call it a night. He looked for a snow drift to anchor down his tent. As he set up the tent, the open end of it tilted toward the wind, and filled with air, instantly becoming a sail. Twisting out of Dick's grasp, the tent soared thirty feet up like a big balloon. Dick watched it drop back onto the sea ice and bounce out of sight. He quickly followed the trail of the tent, hoping it would stop against one of the thirty-foot-high pressure ridges along the coast. Pressure ridges are jumbles of large ice slabs piled on top of each other. In areas where ocean waters are shallow, the movements of the tide break the ice apart, bulldozing building-sized chunks of ice onto the shore. Some of the ridges reached twenty to thirty feet high.

But he found nothing. He went another mile out onto the ocean where open leads of water shimmered in the moonlight. Still he found nothing.

Leaning against the wind as he made his way back to his sled, he at one point had to crawl on his hands and knees to cross the slick, wind-scoured ice. When he reached his sled, he discovered that in his absence, the wind had also stolen his new sleeping bag and air mattress.

And that was that. He returned to the village, spent the next day searching for his gear to no avail, and returned to Anchorage.

"To say the least, I was very disappointed with my incompetence," Dick wrote. "I had to remind myself that the purpose of life is to grow and learn. No life is without regrets!"

Later, in the spring of 1988, he made his first of two attempts on Mount McKinley (Denali). At 20,230 feet, the mountain is the tallest in North America. In both of his tries he suffered from pulmonary edema—a dangerous condition caused by the effects of altitude—and had to turn back after reaching elevations just shy of the summit.

Now HE WAS BACK IN THE ARCTIC, determined to make the nine-hundred-mile trek along Alaska's northwestern coast. He started about the time the Iditarod sled dog race was getting underway, and when the dog teams caught up with him past the village of Shaktoolik, he commented, "I won't get up when they come. I need to take care of my own two dogs, the right and left foot."

Dick was never a big fan of the race. He found the notoriety that had grown up around the event—the money involved in corporate sponsorship and the media hype—all a bit much. To him, Arctic travel was about traveling in solitude. The occasional interlude with local villagers was all he cared for or needed. He was always heartened by the locals' generosity and their interest in his travels. They gave advice that he often took, especially when it came to route-finding through wild country. He normally set his course by looking at rudimentary aeronautical charts, using a compass, and sometimes by following snowmachine tracks. But the people who lived on the land knew the landscape best. And they often knew shortcuts that in some instances saved him dozens of miles.

Dick had been on the trail for two weeks when he reached the abandoned fishing village of Sheshalik, where, on Easter Sunday, he found himself in church. It was also Isabelle's birthday. Snow drifted to the eaves of every other building in the village. But the church was open and his only concern was that he keep the doorway clear of snow, since it opened outward. Most doors in the Arctic opened inward, to keep from getting trapped inside.

Throughout the night, strong winds rattled and shook the flimsy plywood building. But it was a dry, warm camp. The next morning the wind continued, so Dick stayed an extra day sleeping.

Rest and food were key to staying strong on the trail. Dick determined he needed five thousand calories each day to maintain, but he rarely managed to eat that much and lost weight as he traveled. A typical day's meals were:

Breakfast
¾ cup Cream of Wheat or cracked wheat cereal
1 oz. butter
½ cup raisins
1 tbsp. brown sugar
½ qt. milk
All this cooked in at least a quart of water.

Lunch
1 granola bar

Supper
Macaroni and cheese, rice, or Top Ramen
4 oz. corn beef
2 oz. cheese
½ qt. milk
1 qt. water
2 oz. butter
1 tbsp. brown sugar
1 jigger 151 rum

He didn't ration food, just ate until he ran out, resupplying his sled as he passed villages along the way. He also read books in the evenings. On this particular trip he was reading *Mary Queen of Scots* by Antonia Fraser.

He passed several cemeteries as he left Sheshalik. Earlier on this trip, before reaching the town of Kotzebue, he had passed a large wooden cross which read, "Alice____ died 1952 age 22."

The Arctic was a lonely place to die.

The second day out of Sheshalik, Dick had the opportunity to ponder that fact firsthand. All along the way, villagers had been warning him about rabid fox and polar bears. No one could believe he traveled unarmed. Dick always maintained that he'd rather carry eight extra pounds of food than an eight-pound rifle. Besides, the moisture and cold inside a tent would freeze the action of a rifle—rendering the weapon useless.

Morning sunlight angled behind Dick on the horizon as he slid one ski in front of the next. From the corner of his eye, he suddenly noticed a long shadow next to his. In the instant that he realized he was no longer alone, a fox lunged toward him and anchored itself firmly into his calf.

"I reacted immediately and tried to reach behind me to stab the fox with my ski pole," Did wrote. "I fell down on the slick ice, hopelessly tangled–skis tied to my feet, sled harness around my waist, and ski poles tied to my wrists."

The fall knocked the fox loose from Dick's leg, but it lunged again, this time at his chest. Dick's repeated blows dislodged the snarling animal, but it lunged yet again and grabbed the back of his gloved wrist.

"The fight seemed to go on forever," Dick said. He managed to get in several hard blows to the fox's head before it finally released its hold and ambled off to a nearby rocky hillside.

Dick got to his feet, shaking. For once, he wrote, he was truly scared. The rabid fox had torn holes in his pants, parka, and gloves. He looked at the damage to his throbbing calf and found bruised marks—but no blood or puncture wounds. Even so, at that moment, he said he would have paid $500 for a snowmachine ride back to Kotzebue.

Instead, he took off for Kivalina, following the sea ice next to the shoreline where the terrain was flat. He hoped he could at least find a snowmachine trail that could lead him into the village. Instead, as he rounded a corner, he was met with a daunting expanse of pressure ridges. He decided to go inland but could find no snowmachine trail—nothing but soft snow and hummocks. So Dick turned back toward the ocean, picking his way through the pressure ridges toward smoother sea ice. When he finally reached flat ice, his thoughts were still preoccupied with the unnerving fox attack. He badly wanted to reach Kivalina and as he hurried along he vaguely sensed something wasn't quite right.

"The new ice was rubbery and dimpled with small puddles of slush," he wrote.

With skis strapped to his sled, he walked out about two hundred yards, pulling his sled behind him. Suddenly the ice gave way under his feet. In an instant, Dick plunged into the Arctic Ocean.

The icy water sent a shockwave through his system. Suddenly he was fully and intensely focused. He used his gloved fists to break away the soft, crumbling edges looking for ice strong enough to support his weight. He was still wearing the sled harness. Finally reaching firmer ice, he managed to haul himself, dripping, out of the frigid water. As he lifted himself into the cold Arctic air his wet clothing immediately froze and he became stiffly encrusted in ice.

Now he needed to make camp and make it quickly. With no time to pick his way back to shore and land, he built his camp on the ice in the dubious

Tracks leading into the opening where Dick fell through the ice.

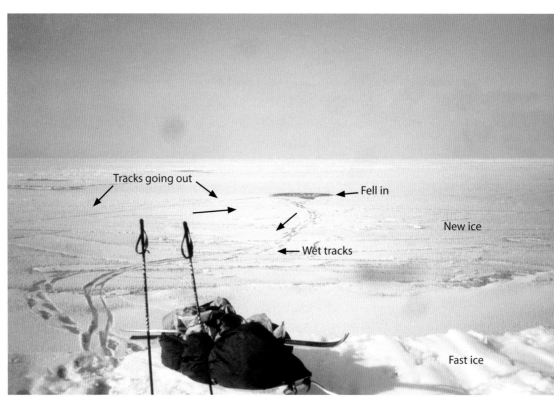

shelter of the pressure ridges. As he left the scene of his accident, he dug out his camera and snapped a photo.

Later he wrote, "I'm going to blow up the picture of the place I fell in and frame it so I won't forget that stupid mistakes are made … the mistake I made was not concentrating on what was directly in front of me… One should never allow the mind to race ahead."

He hung his wet clothes in the tent to dry. He carried no spare clothing, so he wrapped himself in his sleeping bag as he started up his stove. He hoped to get the clothes partially dry before the next day's travels.

As he tried to sleep that night, the sea ice popped and groaned, sounding as if it would detach from the shore. It was a long night, knowing that the force that had created the giant pressure ridges was a force that could easily crush his small camp. The movement of tides could also open the ice beneath him, swallowing him up into an indifferent ocean that had claimed its share of northern travelers.

The next morning when he crawled out of his sleeping bag, the tent walls were solid with ice from the sublimated moisture of his wet clothes. His sleeping bag was frozen now too. He packed up his sled and took off wearing clothes still damp from his dunking. By following the coast, he eventually arrived at Red Dog Mine, a new zinc-lead mine that had begun its operations that year, in 1989.

As he approached the sprawling complex of red buildings, a woman driving a service truck stopped to investigate the solitary man on skis. She invited Dick to the mining camp for dinner; it was steak night and Dick gladly accepted. He also welcomed the opportunity to dry out his gear and get a hot shower.

Now he was able to examine his wounds from the fox attack more closely. He had a three-inch scratch across his groin but otherwise was just bruised. He spoke with the camp EMT who confirmed the threat of rabies. Someone at camp had been bitten, too, but like Dick, had enough clothes on to keep the fox from causing serious injury.

That night, it was too warm inside the buildings and too dark outside to pitch his tent. So Dick slept under the stars. As he lay in his sleeping bag, a spectacle of northern lights shimmered across the Arctic sky.

"According to Eskimo legend, the northern lights are spirits carrying torches to guide nomadic travelers to the afterlife," Dick wrote. Lying under that star-filled sky, he thought about the miles he had left to travel with feet and skis still firmly planted on the rounded curve of the earth.

By now he was eighty-two miles north of Kotzebue, fifty-five miles from the Chukchi Sea, and 106 miles above the Arctic Circle. It took him half a day to reach Kivalina where he bought groceries and repacked his gear in the yard of an Eskimo elder, Tom Adams. A man of few words, Tom could hardly fathom the distance that Dick was still proposing to travel.

"As far as Tom was concerned, Barrow was the end of the world," Dick wrote.

Tom advised Dick to stay off the sea ice and to cut across the Lisburne Hills on the other side of Point Hope. He noticed Dick's torn glove and listened to Dick's story about the fox attack.

Tom warned Dick, "Man travel country on foot is dead man and man go without gun is dead before he starts." Tom pointed out there were rabid fox all the way to Point Hope and that polar bears regularly patrolled the shoreline.

"That was a bit much for me to absorb," Dick wrote, "If I stayed, he might convince me to catch the next airplane back to Anchorage. The old man had a keen mind and I sensed that he held both the past and the future in an equal balance."

Dick quickly headed back out of town.

Along with writing daily in his journals, Dick wrote letters home to friends and family, mailing them at villages along the way. He wrote about the fox encounter to his longtime friend Jill Johnson. Concerned, she relayed the news to a doctor friend who strongly recommended Dick return home to Anchorage for a series of rabies shots.

But Dick was on the trail, oblivious to the series of events that his retelling of the fox attack had set into motion. He had begun to build snow shelters along the coast as he made camp, cutting blocks of snow and ice to create a wall that protected his tent from ferocious winds. Fox continued to plague him. They sometimes circled his camp and peed on the snow walls surrounding his tent. And now he had another creature to contend with. He was now crossing trails with the tracks of polar bears.

He skied along the rocky cliffs of Cape Thompson on his way to Point Hope. Crossing under sea arches made of stone, Dick marveled at the Arctic's stark beauty. Some days she glimmered like a brilliant jewel that he held in a singular cup of solitude. Other times, he grew frustrated by her monotonous indifference and the unrelenting challenge. She could be fickle. In one moment the day would sparkle and in the next, the sky grew black and menacing. And just then, a storm was blowing in.

Sea arches at Cape Thompson.

Sea arches at Cape Thompson.

(Top) During a storm. (Bottom) After the storm at the same location.

"The black horizon was mesmerizing and the black clouds rolled right over me and appeared to fold into the ground," Dick wrote. "Visibility was almost zero. I had to find Point Hope but didn't have the slightest idea where it was."

It was getting dark and he needed shelter from winds that had increased to fifty miles per hour. He skied hard and fast until his ski tip struck a wooden grave marker. He was in the middle of a graveyard. He knew that Point Hope couldn't be too far away.

"When I found the village, a high wall of snow surrounded it. It looked like a fortress," he wrote. "I had to ski around the impenetrable barrier until I found a break. The snow removed from the streets had been piled there by front-end loaders. The wall provided a windbreak for the town."

He camped inside the snow walls of the village, but even so, by morning the wind had nearly buried his tent with snow. He went to the washeteria to shower. Few village homes had indoor plumbing and the washeteria was the place where the community came to collect fresh running water. It was a laundromat, a shower facility—and by default, a community center—all rolled into one. At home, most families used a five-gallon bucket covered with a toilet seat—known as "honey buckets." Dick met one of the villagers as he did his laundry, and within an hour, thanks to CB radios throughout the community, all of Point Hope knew that Dick was in town and that his plans were to travel to Barrow.

The mayor of Point Hope, David Stone, met with Dick and expressed his concern for Dick's safety. Dick ate boiled walrus for lunch at the senior center. The elder Eskimos were skeptical of Dick's plan to travel along the storm-battered coast to Point Lay. They advised him, "Take the airplane to Point Lay and we will tell no one. That's how we do it."

Dick thanked them, waited out the storm, and then struck out again in a heavy fog. As he traveled, he considered his options. He could go inland and cross the Lisburne Hills where the wind blew all the time, the snow was deep, and polar bears were denning. Or he could go around Cape Lisburne on the sea ice where the wind blew continuously, and where the ice was rubbery and had a propensity for pulling away from shore. There were polar bears there as well.

"I understand, now that I'm sitting here facing a decision, that the choice is mine alone," he wrote. "I look at the pressure ridges and they're piled 30 to 40 feet high against the shore—what a tremendous force it took to push the huge slabs of ice on top of the other."

He remembered from his reading that explorer Ejnar Mikkelsen and his companions had nearly lost their lives traveling around this cape on the sea ice.

"Now that I'm here, I almost wish that I did have rabies so I could back out of the mess gracefully," he wrote.

The wind had packed the recent snow along the inland route making it easier to ski, so he chose to cross the Lisburne Hills, just as the elder Tom Adams in Kivalina had recommended.

For three days he traveled in the fog, not sure exactly of his position. As he skied into the gauze of gray, he hoped the fog would lift. He needed to find the pass that would lead him through these mountains. The fog did not subside. Instead, in a stroke of good fortune, he crossed paths with deep ruts made by migrating caribou. He followed their tracks, which led him through the pass and on to the other side of the range.

"I was sorry that I crossed these mountains without seeing them; they are probably beautiful ... I must have had divine guidance—I just crossed a range of mountains and I was lost the entire way," he wrote in his journal. He had set up camp in the wind just as another storm came rolling in from the south.

By now Dick had been on the trail for more than five weeks. He was seeing more polar bear sign, including a den that he very nearly skied over. He cut out the mosquito net vent on his tent so he could drop a flare outside the tent if a bear came around. He also tied a tin can to his ski pole in the hopes that the sound of it clanking in the wind would keep them away.

The isolation was getting to him. The south wind brought rain and made his travels a wet slog. The wind was unremitting. Nights were spent trying to keep the tent from blowing away. One night the wind dismantled the snow wall he'd built, flinging hard chunks of ice against his nylon tent.

"I desperately hung on to the snapping and flapping of nylon in the wind which overshadowed the pounding of a heart audibly loud as you wonder if the tent will survive and you with it," he wrote.

Polar bear tracks. Cape Lisburne has the highest concentration of polar bears in Alaska.

He also wrote, "Now I know why Vilhjalmur Stefansson left the Arctic at the youthful age of 56. He couldn't stand it anymore. I can't either."

The weather refused to cooperate. "Every hour of the day I hope for a break in the weather, I hope for dry clothes, I hope for more food and fuel … Hope is a frequent word in the journals of early explorers. The word spills out on maps; ironically I just left the village of Point Hope."

Finally, the storm abated and the sky briefly grew clear. Dick had laid out his gear to dry in the sun when he noticed the whop-whop of a helicopter. It flew in from one direction, turned around, and then flew back along the coast as if searching for something. Or someone.

The helicopter had launched from Barrow and was indeed looking for Dick. But even with his clothes and tent strewn out on the snow, searchers did not see him. The next day a Cessna 185 on wheel skis followed his tracks up the beach, flying just two hundred feet above the ground. After spotting

Dick, the plane circled several times and left. Later it reappeared with a larger Beaver aircraft that also circled.

Friends and family back home were concerned that Dick might be suffering from rabies. Meanwhile people from Point Hope and Point Lay were worried he'd disappeared on drifting sea ice. The whole world seemed to be looking for him. Dick later learned that the North Slope Borough Search and Rescue had launched a search for him. Once they found him they were unable to land the aircraft near Dick's camp. However, upon a closer aerial look, they were sufficiently satisfied that Dick was okay and called off the rescue.

"I don't know exactly where I am, but I'm not lost," he grumbled. "It cost big bucks to bring that helicopter all the way from Barrow. Next time I see that Jill Johnson, I'll wring her neck."

Dick always traveled with two white-haired trolls. Made of hand-carved ivory, the small talismans were tucked alongside his gear in the

Gale force winds destroyed Dick's camp and tent.

Camped next to a thirty-foot pressure ridge.

sled. Between the constant, battering storms, the poor traveling conditions, and the lost ski he had to backtrack to find, he decided to tell his trolls that they were falling down on the job. "They're supposed to give me unlimited protection and should prevent Little People from causing these mischievous mishaps."

In Native lore, "Little People" are mythical, childlike characters who delight in creating trouble. Dick was low on gasoline, food, and patience. The weather had turned bad again with low visibility. He'd been wandering for what felt like days, looking for the village.

"Point Lay has to be around here someplace," he wrote.

Seventeen days after leaving Point Hope, he woke up to clear skies and a vision he'd been waiting to see. There in the distant horizon, but *behind* him, was the village of Point Lay. Not able to see in the previous day's blowing snow, he'd bypassed it altogether.

He turned back and entered the village cold, tired, hungry, and discouraged. There, he picked up his mail—a letter from Isabelle, two from Jill, and one from Dr. Dave whose help Jill had enlisted. Dick's rabies case had caused a raging controversy in the office of the State Epidemiologist. The letters from Jill and the doctor implored Dick to return to Anchorage for a series of rabies shots.

Reluctantly, he booked a flight back to Anchorage, but bad weather rolled in again, delaying the flight. Meanwhile, Dick called the State Epidemiology Lab. The doctor there told him that it was unlikely he had the disease and explained that the fox usually dies before the rabies virus reaches the saliva ducts. But to be on the safe side, the doctor recommended Dick return to Anchorage to get the series of shots.

"I haven't been on the safe side since I started this trip!" Dick scoffed. After eating, getting warm, and resting, Dick was in better spirits than he'd been in weeks. He was glad the weather had kept the plane from landing. Rabies or not, he would continue his trek to Barrow.

He spent two days in Point Lay, a friendly Eskimo village of 150 people. It had a health clinic, fire station, and washeteria. He took a day to pine tar his skis; he had skied so far that the grooves had worn off. By now he had traveled seven hundred miles in forty-nine days with another two hundred miles left to go.

For weeks now, he'd been seeing polar bear tracks, but had seen only one bear so far, startling it while traveling in poor visibility. It had quickly run off. He knew he had probably passed dozens of bears without seeing them. "I've come to the conclusion that polar bears are rather retiring and unaggressive, especially in comparison to grizzly bears."

Dick had many bear encounters over the years.

"I have come into physical contact with three black bear and inches have separated me from a grizzly bear," he wrote. "When I was nine years old, I stuck my foot into a caged black bear and it bit the toe of my tennis shoe off. Another black bear tried to enter our tent while Isabelle and I were sleeping. I kicked it in the belly to get rid of it. On the Hope to Homer 160 mile Alaska Wilderness Classic race I was sleeping under an open fly with two women. I always sleep on top of the food and a bear reached beneath me to get the food. I used a small flare pistol to drive the bear away."

Kathy Sarns, who was one of those women, remembered the incident in a 1988 interview with the *Anchorage Daily News*. "We're all under the same tarp (trying to find protection from the rain). And the tarp comes down on our faces. This bear had stepped on the line," she said. "Dick goes 'Hang on, girls. I'll take care of it.' He jumps up and fires off this flare gun. Everything lights up. And Dick says, 'There I think I showed him.'"

Dick didn't believe in hanging food in a tree to keep it away from bears. "No damn way."

Other than the polar bear encounter of the previous year, the most frightening bear incident may have been the one with the grizzly bear in Chugach State Park. Dick's son, Barney remembered the event in vivid detail.

Barney was about fifteen years old when he and his father hiked from Ship Creek to Indian Valley in the Chugach Mountains. They were above the timberline and Barney was in front with Dick bringing up the rear. They had a dog along. When they came up over a rise, Barney saw a grizzly sow with two cubs just three hundred feet in front of them. Barney simultaneously knew two things: Their dog would go after the bear if given the chance; and, mother bears will defend their cubs with fierce finality.

"I said, 'Dad, grab the dog. Grab the dog!'" Barney said. "Dad wasn't paying attention to the dog—he just wanted to know why I was saying that. By that time the dog saw the bear."

The dog started barking and took chase. When the bear charged, the dog turned tail and came running back, bringing the bear in hot pursuit. Whatever Dick and Barney had been taught or thought about responding to a charging bear, they reacted instead on instinct. They ran. Barney remembers well those fractions of seconds as the angry bear bore down on him and his father. He was running, ahead of Dick now, adrenaline surging in great strides, when from the corner of his eye, he saw the bear running up the other side of the hill with the cubs scrambling behind her.

"Dad had dropped his pack," Barney explained. So instead of coming after Dick and Barney, the bear had mauled the pack. Once the threat was "neutralized" the bear cleared out with her cubs as quickly as she could. When they went back to pick up the pack, Barney said the Kelty aluminum frame was punctured by tooth holes. "That would have been us if he hadn't dropped the pack."

THE FOX ON THIS TREK WERE FAR MORE WORRISOME to Dick than polar bears. They were bold and unafraid. Some nights they barked outside his tent, making the odd sound that Dick described as "something like donkeys with a muted braying."

Two days out of Point Lay, the warm spring sunshine enticed Dick into taking a long lunch break. "There are glorious moments on a warm sunny day ... you become detached from everything and seep into the landscape," he reflected. "It has been rather stressful traveling through all these tight places and dealing with one storm after another. In many places I had to drag the sled up a slick incline that dropped into the ocean. If a tow strap were to break, all my equipment would slide into the ocean. I am constantly harried by the enigmas of this huge landscape."

He thought about the black wolf he'd encountered, feeding on a caribou, and the hundreds of seals sunning themselves on the ice. He suspected the polar bears left him alone in part because of their abundance of food.

He gazed at the snowy horizon where it met the blue sky and noticed a white fox coming toward him at a steady trot. Dick was out of his harness and poles, standing near his sled. He yelled at the fox, but it was not dissuaded.

"I fired one round from my 25-mm flare gun," Dick wrote. The flare passed just over the top of the fox, but it just kept coming. This time Dick was taking no chances. As it boldly approached his sled, he took both skis and bashed it over the head. "I stunned the fox and knocked him off his feet. Then I ran around the sled and stabbed it to death with my ski poles," he wrote.

AS DICK APPROACHED WAINRIGHT and then Barrow, he encountered men, women, and children traveling back and forth on snowmachines, setting up whaling camps to launch their spring hunts. It was May in the Arctic and the sun would not set again until late in August. Because the warmer weather made the snow soft and sticky, Dick had taken to traveling at night when cooler temperatures hardened the snow to ice. He started his day at 3:00 a.m. and then stopped traveling by midafternoon. As he approached Barrow, he was glad that he'd continued on his trek. With all the worry about rabies, he'd almost gone home at Point Lay.

By the time he reached Barrow at 9:30 a.m. on May 8, 1989, he had traveled sixty-three days across nine hundred miles.

"I'm glad it's all over," he wrote. "Right now, I don't know if I'll ever return to the Arctic. I'm burned out physically and mentally. However, once I'm on a jet flying south, I know I'll change my mind ... There are thousands of miles along the Arctic coast that I can travel that will put me deep into Canada. I know how to do it; I just don't know why I do it. A wise man once said, 'the ultimate quest has no end.'"

Chapter 12

Outlaw

His life is the wilderness and he embraces it all the time.
This Grand Canyon trip of his in March—three weeks—does not feel right to me.
But who can lock the wind in a closet? I never try.
—Isabelle Galo Griffith in a letter to her friend, Henrietta Marcott

IT WAS A WILD RIDE IN THE DARK. Some areas of the river were bathed in moonlight while other places were shadowed beneath the canyon's vertical walls. Alone on the river, Dick was trying to make a getaway—and retrieve the gear he had stashed downstream. As he quickly paddled his five-pound packraft downstream, Dick noted two lovers standing on the suspension bridge spanning the Colorado River near Bright Angel Creek. As he floated under them on the river below he remembered the influence of canyon magic—and hoped the couple had eyes only for each other. He needed a bit of magic to pass by undetected—the last thing he needed now was someone to report him to the authorities.

THE YEAR WAS 1991, AND DICK WAS NEARLY sixty-four years old. Sporting a shock of white hair, he was strong as a tree. He still had more stamina than most men half his age and he was ready to run the Grand Canyon again—this time in a packraft. The "rubber ducky" had been used in Alaska for eleven years—ever since Dick had introduced a small inflatable Air Force survival boat during the first Alaska Mountain Wilderness Classic in 1982.

Forty years earlier, in 1951, Dick had been the first person to descend the famous Lava Falls in an inflatable boat—a feat no one thought possible. With Isabelle and Johnny looking on, Dick had maneuvered his boat through the falls' wild waters in a sensational ride that left everyone breathless and triumphant. That event would herald the way the rapids would be run in the future. Derivations of the inflatable boat would soon become the customary means of traveling through the Grand Canyon. Thirty thousand tourists float the Colorado River each year in oar rigs and large motorized inflatable crafts weighing up to five tons. But in 1991, no one to date—as far as Dick knew—had tried it with a five-pound pack-raft, alone and unsupported. It seemed entirely fitting that Dick should be the first.

Dick's son, Barney, had inherited his father's physical prowess and Dick wanted him to come along on the trip. At eighteen, Barney had been the first to kayak through the nearly impossible Devil's Canyon Rapids in Alaska. Now at thirty-four, he was also an avid mountain runner, one of a handful of elite athletes that gobbled up Alaska's extreme terrain.

"I needed him to keep the old man out of trouble," Dick wrote.

Dick wrote a letter to the National Park Service asking for a permit for the 226-mile journey. The NPS denied his request. In their letter they wrote:

> *A backpacking trip of this magnitude has been attempted in the past and normally takes 30-45 days to accomplish ... Your proposed trip is of much shorter duration than those accomplished in the past, and you have chosen a route that does not allow passage by foot ... Your proposed use of inflatable boats to pass "difficult" areas via the Colorado River is not an acceptable method of travel for backcountry permit holders ... In your letter and itinerary you indicate that by using these boats you will be able to traverse great distances rapidly on available water sources. We feel this does not comply with the spirit of backcountry travel but is in essence a downstream trip on the Colorado River.*

"The last sentence of the letter correctly summed up the purpose of the trip: We fully intended to make a downstream trip on the Colorado River," Dick wrote.

The letter did not deter Dick in the least. Barney, whose strength also lay in caution and good judgment, decided not to go without the permission of the National Park Service. The park service was more than willing and ready to enforce the rules. Dick's friend, Andy Embick, had recently been apprehended at Diamond Creek for illegally running the Grand Canyon in a kayak.

"The rangers stepped out of the brush as he got out of his kayak, pointed a pistol at him, hauled him off to jail in Flagstaff, confiscated all his equipment, fined him $300 and made him appear in court at the South Rim," Dick recalled.

Dick knew if he got caught, the price would be steep. But he'd made up his mind—"afflicted," he said, with that dogged mindset that often drove him to doing what others said couldn't (or shouldn't) be done.

"I was committed to go because I'm too old to wait years for a permit that I would probably never obtain," he wrote. He surmised it would take a minimum of seven years to get the permit and he was sixty-four. Dick also knew his trip would not meet NPS rules for carrying required gear. The steel fire pan alone would weigh more than his five-pound raft.

He arrived at Page, Arizona at midnight, on March 5. He'd decided to make the run in early spring because the river would be relatively quiet—tourist season wouldn't start for a month or two. From his hotel room the next morning, he could see Lake Powell. How the place had changed.

"It is hard for me to imagine the Glen Canyon gone forever," he wrote, reminiscing about the days when he'd worked for Harry Aleson and floated the Colorado with Isabelle. "We always walked up the side (Forbidding) canyon from the Colorado River just to see Rainbow Bridge. Just below Rainbow Bridge I remember a hanging garden in each alcove. Now there is a boat dock with floating rest rooms under the bridge ... Gone are the grottos of gentle seeps and lush greenery, Music Temple, Cathedral in the Desert, Hidden Passage. Gone are the clean sandbars that we camped on, the huge cottonwoods, thousands of Anasazi Indian sites. Only the memories remain."

It was forty miles from Page to Lee's Ferry, where Dick planned to launch his trip. A young woman who worked at the hotel where he stayed the first night agreed to drive him there for $50. On their drive she asked Dick about his plans. He claimed he was a fisherman. She looked him up and down.

"I've hauled many fishermen from Page to Lee's Ferry and they all look like fisherman," she said. "You aren't going fishing on the Colorado River."

Dick paused and then confessed. His plan was to first run Marble Canyon and then the Grand Canyon in a small raft that he had concealed in his backpack. His paddles were also in the pack. He carried a seven-foot metal walking staff which attached to the paddles.

"She dropped me off and by this time she was apprehensive about my plans," Dick wrote. "So was I."

He hid in the bushes out of sight of the ranger station and inflated his raft. The sky was gray, the air cool. This would be no summer lark—nighttime temperatures were dipping into the forties. By 4:00 p.m. Dick was impatient to get started. He launched into the Colorado River, floating past the ranger station in plain view of anyone who might notice. No one did.

The river had changed dramatically since Dick's early days as a boatman. "The water flow is not a natural process but a gift from the engineers who control the Glen Canyon Dam," he wrote. There were now 160 rapids in the 226 miles between Lees Ferry and Diamond Creek. "The wide variance of flow is determined by the power requirements of the large cities in Arizona … low water produces many more rapids, exposing large boulders."

Dick's packraft was five feet long and three feet wide. In calm waters, the craft was as maneuverable as a kayak, moving easily at the whim of Dick's weight and paddle. But through the many rapids, Dick stashed the paddle and just rode the waves hanging onto the boat. With all of its lightweight advantages, it was not a comfortable ride. Waves sloshed over the sides so that he was kneeling in cold water most of the time. For the most part, he was alone in the canyon. The first night he camped on a sandbar beneath red limestone walls, "a poor camp exposed to the very cold wind."

By morning the wind had abated leaving a calm, clear-blue day.

It wasn't long before he encountered a group of backpackers whom he assumed would report him when they returned to the rim of the canyon. He ran most of the rapids, even though he had little control of the boat in white-water. A portage meant Dick had to carry the boat and paddle in one arm and his pack in the other. He would then have to crawl over boulders and beat his way through heavy brush. He much preferred to stay on the water. He traveled nine hours before calling it a day.

As Marble Canyon merged into the Grand Canyon, Dick looked at the sheer red walls rising up on either side of the river. Marble Canyon would start at a depth of five hundred feet and by the time he reached the Grand Canyon, the walls would rise up five thousand feet from the river. Once again Dick marveled at the raw beauty of the canyon. Words simply fell short to explain the power of the landscape

To truly understand, he wrote, "You have to live down here many weeks, feel the tremendous force of the rapids, explore the many side canyons." Most visitors to the Grand Canyon glanced over the edge of the rim for a half hour and went on their way. It was something else altogether to live in the grip of the canyon's more hard-earned wonders.

He would have liked to stop at some of the landmarks that he enjoyed when he ran the river as a younger man—the Indian ruins, North Canyon, Stanton's Cave, Bert Loper's boat. But the packraft was too small to carry the amount of food he needed for an extended trip. Besides, "I must constantly be on the move down river to lessen the prospect of being discovered."

Temperatures dipped at night and direct sunlight was rare deep in the canyon. He wished he'd brought his winter rather than summer sleeping bag. He heated water, poured it in his water bottle, and held it close trying to stay warm at night.

On his second night he camped near the gravesite of one of the two men lost in the 1889 Brown-Stanton expedition and the grave of the fifteen-year-old who drowned in 1951, the summer he, Isabelle, and Johnny had run the river. Coyotes howled through the night.

"Today I almost drowned my two white-haired trolls that I always carry for luck," Dick wrote that evening. "One of my waterproof bags leaks ... My trolls are more valuable to me than my food so I packed them in another waterproof bag with my sleeping bag. I need all the help I can get."

The next day, Dick portaged around Nankoweap Rapids, not because it wasn't navigable, but because he needed to warm up. He felt chilled with the ache of an oncoming virus. This was not a good time to get sick. As he climbed around the rapids, he heard the steady chop of a helicopter approaching. Quickly, he ducked under his boat, which, overturned, looked like a boulder. Once again, luck was with him. Had he been on the water at the time the helicopter passed overhead, he surely would have been discovered.

Continuing his portage around the rapids, he stumbled upon a cache of food and equipment marked with the bold black letters FWS—Fish and Wildlife Service. Dick looked around but saw no one. So he rummaged until he found a stash of Jack Daniels whiskey and took a long swig. Cold medicine.

Making a hasty retreat, he launched his boat and ran the lower half of the rapids. Near the end of the falls, he passed three people camping on the shore. They ran for their cameras and field glasses. The campers were volunteers for the Bureau of Reclamation Glen Canyon Environmental Studies office. Unbeknownst to Dick, he was also being observed by eagle researchers from a viewing platform one thousand feet high up in the cliffs.

"I gave them a good show for I ran several more rapids below," he wrote. "I made up my mind not to worry about NPS rangers any more until I get to Bright Angel at milepost 88. There is a ranger station there."

At the confluence of the Colorado and Little Colorado rivers, Dick saw four large motorized boats tied to the bank. It was starting to get crowded in the canyon. He back-paddled, thinking he would sneak around them by climbing over the cliffs. As he paddled backward into a side eddy, he nearly bumped into a large motorized boat with radio antennas protruding at every angle. Two men sat in the boat, likely as startled to see a white haired man in his little "rubber ducky," as Dick was to see them. Dick was sure he'd been caught.

One of the men said, "You can have a beer if you tell us a story,"

Dick paused. There was no outrunning these two in their big boat. If they were rangers, his trip was over anyway.

"I'll take the beer but no story," Dick said. There was no need to incriminate himself any more than necessary.

As Dick paddled closer, the larger man said "We know what you're up to and we aren't park rangers."

It turned out the man, Brian Dieker, was a boatman. He had been contracted to assist a group of scientists in a multi-million-dollar study of the Grand Canyon. Brian had made over two hundred Grand Canyon trips in motorized boats. He kept offering beer to Dick, shaking his head and saying, "You have brass balls." He and his colleague, renowned fish biologist Randy Van Haverbe were tasked to put radio transmitters in humpback chubs, a fish native to the Colorado River. Their work was part of the research in studying the downstream effects of the Glen Canyon Dam. Dick's new friends had to return to work, but promised to bring him a bag of gorp from their stash.

Dick continued downstream, taking on three minor rapids that on most days would hardly be worth a mention.

"The last rapid dumped me," Dick wrote. "A large whirlpool grabbed my boat, pulled it straight down backwards."

The boat flipped as it surged through the churning water and Dick tumbled into the water, hanging tightly onto the paddle tied to the bow of the boat. Dick somehow managed to climb on top of the overturned boat and paddle it to shore.

"To be dumped in a rapid without a name was devastating to me," Dick wrote. Between being drenched by the cold water and the wind, Dick grew hypothermic. He shivered as he lit a small fire.

He realized that if he could be overturned in the minor rapids, it could happen anywhere along the river. He had no change of clothing, no coat, no spare gear of any sort. A fire was the only way to get warm and dry, but he was near the sacred Hopi salt seeps where ancient Indians had once collected salt for trading with other tribes. It was an illegal place to camp.

On their way back upstream, Brian and Randy saw Dick huddled around his meager fire and convinced him to spend the evening at their camp. Dick left the raft and his gear behind and joined his new friends around a warm fire. They spent much of the night swapping stories. Things had changed considerably since Dick had been a boatman working for Harry Aleson.

In those days, he explained, they threw tin cans and waste in the river. "Now they're smashed flat and hauled out of the canyon. We peed—girls upstream, boys down—anyplace. Now you are required to pee in the river. Human waste was left any convenient place. Now it is hauled out in cans. We cooked on wood fires leaving charred rocks and partially burnt wood. Now they cook on propane stoves. Wood fires are now allowed during the winter months but must be contained in a metal fire pan. We carried canned goods, potatoes, onions, flour, slab bacon, powdered milk and eggs, tea and coffee, now they bring freezer chests of perishables that can keep on ice for several weeks. Drinking water was obtained from side streams or the river without filtering."

Brian and Randy listened raptly as Dick described his early days of boating. There is a culture among boatmen, a grudging respect for pioneers and a fierce competition to be the first to achieve a new feat on the river.

"Without exception, all the river runners in the late 40s and early 50s had tremendous egos," Dick explained. "We believed that we were the only ones capable of running the rapids and we alone possessed the canyons. We were few in number and had exclusive rights to the river and were accountable to no one."

Among Dick's contemporaries were Norm Nevills, a competitor of Dick's boss Harry Aleson, who "firmly believed that inflatables would never negotiate the canyon rapids ... we proved him wrong when we passed through in 1951."

Nevills was a showman and would drag driftwood to the top of a rock wall and set it on fire in the dark. Then he would throw the burning embers over the cliff to create a fiery display for his clients. "It made an unsightly mess at the bottom but in those days no one seemed to care," Dick remembered.

Other famous boatmen's names came up in conversation—Bert Loper, Otis Marston, Amos Burg. Their talk eventually turned back to Dick's outlaw trip.

"If NPS finds out there's an old, white-haired, crazy man running Colorado River rapids in a small inflatable, they'll hunt you down in a helicopter and you'll pay for it," Brian said. "You stick out like a sore thumb."

It was true. Dick was conspicuous wearing his red polypro long-johns underneath yellow shorts, a brown jacket, yellow life vest and a red baseball cap. The bottom of his boat may have camouflaged him as he hid among rocks and boulders, but the sight of the six-foot man in a five-foot boat made an impression whether someone was looking for him or not.

The two men made a plan to meet Dick at Diamond Creek, where Dick planned to finish his trek. They would stow him and his gear in one of the scientist's metal boxes to help him evade authorities. By then law enforcement of the entire canyon would be eager to apprehend him.

"The rangers will have a net stretched across the river at Bright Angel to catch me," he worried.

The next morning the boatmen delivered Dick back to the sacred Hopi salt seeps where he discovered that his campsite had been vandalized.

"My camp was completely devastated by ravens and ring-tailed cats, for in my haste I left my dry bags open," he wrote. "Ravens tore holes in the Zip-Loc bags and ate all my gorp, freeze-dried beans, and Lipton dinners. And the cats drug off the little stuff like my trolls, which I recovered."

All he had left to eat were two oranges and two cans of tuna—not much for the few days it would still take to get to Bright Angel. There he planned to climb out of the canyon and resupply his food.

Downstream he began to run into more scientists and backpackers; many glared and others took photos as if collecting evidence.

"I am paranoid with good reason. I really can't expect to win any popularity contests down here," he wrote. At Tanner Rapids, he had to cross a swirling current in order to get to the side of the river that allowed for a portage. He had just a few feet to spare before being swept into the Tanner Rapids, a gutsy maneuver he pulled off in front of two camera-toting scientists.

"You'll never make it," one of them growled. Later, at Hance Rapids, backpackers took photos and gave him surly looks. He just hoped their print film could not be developed before he reached his destination—these were the days before widespread use of the internet or digital photography.

Aside from the threat of being caught, Dick also had the river to contend with. He formulated a new style of running the rapids in his tiny rubber boat.

Entering Inner Granite Gorge.

"It's not the waves that I plunge through that give me problems, but the tail end of the rapids where the whirlpools, boils, and undercurrents form," he wrote. "These areas are flat and look benign. I increase my buoyancy by flailing my kayak paddle. As I'm about to be sucked under, I'd paddle rapidly and drag myself out of the whirlpool."

On March 10, he woke up in the full grip of the virus that had been chilling him throughout the trip. "I have a cold, sore throat, slight fever, am hungry, but most of all I'm scared," he wrote.

He was facing two big rapids that day, Sockdolager (rated V-VII) and Grapevine (VI-VII). He knew the waves would be higher than his boat was long and that the undercurrents and whirlpools could be stronger than the pack raft's ability to float. The night before, as he entered the dark canyon of Inner Granite Gorge, he'd reflected, "I feel as if I am jumping off the cliff into the abyss! I wish I had a decent boat."

The first rapid at Hance Creek sucked the boat straight down, leaving Dick swimming and clinging to the paddle, which was tied to the boat. Dick thought he would be pulled to the bottom of the river. The boat was completely submerged, but managed to surface again.

The next rapids were Sockdolager. The steep narrow canyon walls would not allow for portage, so Dick was forced to run it. Again the boat filled with water in the first hole. "The continuous waves, one after the other, washed over me which left me gasping for air at the bottom of the rapid."

Grapevine also had vertical walls that forced Dick's hand. "I had to dump over a five-foot ledge rather than get out in the big waves," he wrote.

Looking upriver into Inner Granite Gorge.

"I should have flipped when I dropped over the ledge but didn't. This kind of luck can't continue forever."

Finally, around the corner in plain view was the suspension bridge that hearkened his arrival at Bright Angel. He knew his chances of getting apprehended at this point were very real. It was the most popular place to view the Grand Canyon—with a small village on the rim and a multitude of tourists clamoring up and down the trail. But circumstances were once again in Dick's favor. Rain in the canyon and snow on the rim reduced the likelihood of less-than-friendly encounters.

"I ate my last sandwich, deflated the raft, and buried everything in a pile of rocks," he wrote. "I am sick and all my food is gone."

The day of exertion and excitement had taken its toll. He was feeling poorly but still had to climb five thousand feet to get to the rim. He struck out at 4:30 p.m. and reached the rim four hours later, using a flashlight to follow the last two miles of the trail.

As he checked into a hotel, sick, bedraggled and unshaven, he made up an alias and gave a phony address. Too many people had seen him on the Colorado River and after eluding the authorities this far, it hardly made sense to let them know his whereabouts through a hotel register. Just as he paid cash, he heard a familiar voice.

"Hi Griffith, what are you doing here?" It was Richard Gunther, his neighbor from Anchorage, Alaska, traveling with his family to see the Grand Canyon in a more conventional way.

"So much for secrecy," Dick said, drolly. Then he cleaned up and ate an enjoyable meal with friends.

The next morning Dick was too sick to get out of bed.

"I lie on my back, staring at the ceiling, a white void. My mind races backwards then forwards, wondering what to do next. I have to buy more supplies, climb back down the canyon, dig up my priceless boat and trolls and go another 138 river miles," he wrote. "Today is one of those days that I wish that I could say 'This is enough. I don't have to prove anything to anybody.' But somewhere deep down, I know I cannot stop."

Earlier, eleven years to the day, Dick had been on the trek where he had nearly frozen to death. As he liked to say, "I froze my butt off." Since then he had traveled another two thousand miles across Alaska and the Arctic, one step at a time. The dangers inherent in the task seemed formidable but never impossible. In spite of the bone-tiring exertion, there was always some inexplicable call to return to great expanses of landscape. To endless days of solitude.

This canyon trip, however, was getting crowded. And he was sick. The following day, still feverish, he flew back to Alaska.

In the end, it proved to be possibly the only reason he evaded capture. Ten days after returning home, Dick called Brian Dieker, the boatman who was by then in Flagstaff, to explain why he had not arrived at their rendezvous at Diamond Creek. Dick asked if there had been any rumors as to his whereabouts.

"You are now known as the Mystery Man," Brian replied.

ON MARCH 28, DICK FLEW BACK to finish what he'd begun. The park rangers had stopped looking for him. He arrived in late afternoon with eight inches of snow covering the ground. He took a taxi to the rim and started down Bright Angel Trail carrying a heavy pack with enough food for nine days. This time he also brought a spare raft and paddles. He left the rim at 6:30 p.m. The trail had just reopened after an accident in which four mules had slipped over the edge of the trail, three of which had to be put down as a result of their injuries. As he jogged down the snow-laden trail, he ran into a woman ranger sporting a pistol. She stopped him and chastised him for jogging in such slippery conditions.

"I secretly wanted to tell her that's how we do it in Alaska," Dick wrote.

"Where's your backcountry permit?" she asked.

Dick had never held a backcountry permit in his life.

"I don't have one, I'm day hiking," he replied.

She looked at his pack. "How come you're traveling at night and carrying a heavy backpack if you're day hiking?"

Dick hesitated. "I'm carrying groceries to a party camped down on the Colorado River," he lied. "They're walking the Tonto trail."

She wasn't buying it. "You have to walk all the way to the bottom of the canyon, then turn around and walk back out. You cannot stop to sleep or camp (without a permit). You're too old for all that."

Dick told her that he looked a lot older than he really was.

"Okay," she said. "How old are you and where is your identification?"

By now Dick was getting impatient, standing in eight inches of slush with nothing on his feet but running shoes.

"I'm almost sixty-four years old," he said, "and my driver's license is in the car."

She looked down in the canyon and repeated again. "You are much too old to walk five thousand feet down and five thousand feet up without camping."

Dick didn't know what to say or do next. He was desperate. So he pulled up his pant leg and showed her his calf muscle. "Look at this," he said, his skin exposed.

For the first time, she grinned, stifling a laugh.

"Okay," she said. "Go."

He reached the river three hours later in the light of the full moon. He dropped his pack and headed upriver to retrieve his raft, life preserver, dry suit, and two white-haired trolls.

"Everything was as I left it, wet but okay," Dick wrote. "I was particularly concerned about my trolls. I am superstitious and can't travel without them."

Then he inflated the raft and began his wild ride in the dark. It was here that Dick noted two lovers standing on the suspension bridge. How well he remembered the influence of canyon magic. And how he hoped like hell they would not notice him. Still, he knew he was in plain view and that they might report him.

"Tomorrow morning the rangers and everyone in the campground will be aware that someone is sneaking down the river without a permit," he wrote.

He stopped briefly to pick up the pack he'd left along the shore and discovered that ringtail cats had climbed into his waterproof bag and stolen all his oatmeal raisin cookies. His favorite.

He traveled until almost midnight, made camp, and was up before dawn eager to be on his way.

"I ate a candy bar for breakfast but barfed it up because I was so tense," he recalled. "Rangers behind and big rapids in front don't make for many relaxed moments."

It took him six days to complete his run to Diamond Creek. He rafted and other times portaged some of the most challenging rapids of the trip including Horn Creek, Crystal Rapids, and most notably Lava Falls. Again he met surly backpackers, but befriended others who marveled at the exploits of this white-haired fellow in his little raft. He reminisced as he passed the places that he and Isabelle and Johnny had traveled.

There was Bedrock Rapids, where Johnny Schlump had almost drowned in 1951. There was Tapeats Creek and Deer Creek Falls where he and Isabelle and Johnny had fished and gathered prickly pear fruit before continuing on to Boulder Dam. So much was familiar. And so much had changed. When he

Five-pound packraft next to a five-ton inflatable boat.

passed the area where he and Isabelle had spent their first anniversary, he saw that the long overhanging shelf had collapsed.

Grudgingly, Dick acknowledged that the National Park Service had done an excellent job of keeping the canyon a pristine place—there was not a cigarette butt or candy wrapper to be found. He learned from other boaters on the river that park rangers were closing in on him, so for the last sixteen miles to Diamond Creek, he packed his raft and paddles to join a girl and her boyfriend on their bigger raft. When they dropped him off, he noticed "three men who had just come down river in motorized rigs sitting in the shade, drinking beer."

"Boatmen drink lots of beer," he noted. "Rangers don't. They were contract boatmen working for NPS."

Dick asked for a lift on the back of the flatbed truck that was coming to pick up their gear.

"No," one of them said, "you're too hot. You are known all the way up and down the Colorado River."

Dick was flabbergasted. "They had me pegged the minute I stepped off my friend's boat … They even admitted that they had been looking for me for two days. All this time I thought I was very clever!!"

Although they didn't give Dick a lift, "they did feed me NPS food and beer, a good thing because I was hungry and thirsty." One of the men turned out to be Ted Hatch, son of the famous boatman Bus Hatch, from Vernal, Utah. Dick had stored his raft in Bus's garage during his early years of boating.

Ted warned Dick that he should leave since they were expecting NPS rangers to arrive soon. He took the advice and hitched a ride with three young men and a woman—not realizing that "the rest of that night would be the most hazardous journey since leaving Lee's Ferry, 226 miles upriver."

He rode in the back of a pickup where beer cans and bottles had accumulated from an evening's bout of drinking. The pickup stopped periodically for the party to get out and pee and at one point two of the men got into a fight over the girl. The owner of the truck seemed to win the scuffle, and he along with the girl disappeared into the bushes. Meanwhile the other two men took the truck and drove off with Dick still lying in the truck bed.

The truck weaved all over the road so Dick pounded on the cab and offered to drive. They agreed.

"I was now driving a stolen truck and my new friends had just passed out," Dick said.

He pulled into a hotel parking lot in Flagstaff, placed the $50 he'd promised them on the dash of the truck and walked away.

IN REFLECTING ON HIS OUTLAW TRIP, Dick wrote, "I have ... acquired the habit of making up my mind without asking the opinion of others. I am neither a follower nor a leader, which makes it easy to be a loner. [Henrik] Isben once said 'The strongest man in the world is he who stands most alone.'"

Chapter 13

Meandering a Great Emptiness

Some days I feel that I am on a treadmill that goes nowhere.
I get depressed when the great emptiness envelops me.
I struggle for nothing, in nothing, about nothing!
—Dick Griffith

DICK WAS PULLING HIS SLED through rough ice along the coast of the Beaufort Sea when he looked up to see a polar bear seventy-five yards away. He paused. They looked at each other with calm regard. The polar bear was an adult male, powerfully built and regal in its white mantle of fur. Its black eyes absorbed the sight of the man on skis, its nose breathed in the scent of him. Dick was thrilled to be in such close proximity to the animal. Here stood the monarch of the Arctic, perfectly adapted to the cold with its thick, hollow hair and massive paws. The largest land carnivore in the world, it fed primarily on seals and could weigh as much as fifteen hundred pounds.

An enigma of the Arctic, these bears often travel alone across hundreds of miles of frozen tundra and ice. With no natural enemies, it walked the Arctic with impervious authority.

"This part of the world has belonged to him always," Dick wrote.

In their sojourns, it seemed the white-haired man and the polar bear were not so unlike one another, traveling as they did, mile after mile across ice and snow.

THE YEAR WAS 1992. DICK WAS SIXTY-FIVE and on a trek from Barrow to Barter Island and the village of Kaktovik. Many things had changed since Dick first began his Arctic journeys in 1959. His children were grown, he'd retired from a career in civil service, and he now had the experience of thousands of miles of traveling Alaska's backcountry behind him. A map of his travels to date looked a little like the spokes on a wheel with Anaktuvuk Pass at the center. This trek completed the wheel, bringing him back to where he had started thirty-three years earlier. To date he had already traveled nearly three thousand miles in Alaska's Arctic and sub-Arctic.

Barrow had changed dramatically since he had worked as a professional engineer on the Barrow runway in 1967.

"Then nearly all the inhabitants of Barrow were Natives driving dog sleds, dining on seal oil, living hardworking lives ... Now they have flushable toilets, screaming snowmachines and imported food from all over the world," Dick wrote in his journal. In just his lifetime, he had witnessed the dramatic influence of Western culture on Alaska's Native lifestyles.

Dick's attitudes and ideas about life and death had changed too. On his first Arctic expedition from Barter Island to Anaktuvuk Pass, he had toted a rifle and killed caribou and moose at will, taking only what he and his ill-fated dogs might need for the coming few days. The rest of the animal he had left to the wolves and bears. This Hemingway-esque approach came largely from his readings of explorer Vilhjalmur Stefansson, who proclaimed in his 1921 book, *The Friendly Arctic,* that the tundra was a place where the land could provide—endlessly.

These days Dick knew better. Nature was not a thing of conquest or exploitation, but rather a place of careful balance—one that was both cruel in its indifference to life, but also at times generous in its abundance. It was a place that mesmerized him with its paradoxes. Always, life in the Arctic seemed to be on the march—caribou and whale migrated to and from spring calving grounds; foxes, bears, and wolves were in perpetual motion looking for their next meal. Even inanimate objects moved—the sea ice broke up with the tides, always shifting and sometimes thrusting slabs of ocean ice onto the shore. And here he was too, on the move. Always moving forward.

Dick had also begun to think in earnest about the steady march of time. Isabelle was beginning to have health issues. And while Dick was still stronger and had more stamina than men a fraction of his age, his powerhouse strength was not what it used to be. He was beginning to take pleasure in small comforts along the trail. He carried a radio Walkman, a gift from his friend Jill Johnson. Now he could listen to music on cassette tapes. He also carried two stoves, one that used gas for fuel and the other that used wood. He enjoyed long evenings feeding the fire with wood that he found along the trail.

"It won't be old age or loss of physical strength that keeps me from making these trips," he wrote. "One day I'll just become too lazy."

Woodburning camp stove.

DICK REGARDED THE POLAR BEAR before him with wary respect. Over the years, he had developed a kinship with bears and questioned the fear that many local residents had of them. Villagers often traveled between communities on snowmachines, heavily armed with rifles. Yes, there had been bear attacks and even cases of humans being hunted by polar bears. But Dick pointed out that more people were killed by lightening, bee stings, and dog bites every year than by bear attacks.

It was time to move on so Dick shouted and waved his arms. The bear looked over his shoulder at Dick as he ambled away.

The polar bear sighting was a treat, some eighteen days into this trek, but these had not been Dick's best days of travel. He'd made a number of mistakes along the way. For one, he had traveled too far north on the sea ice. He'd run into rough ice—pressure ridges and rippled, windblown dunes of snow called *sastrugi*. He kept thinking he'd break out of the rough patch any moment but the uneven terrain blocked his view and he had no way of knowing how much farther he needed to go before finding better trail conditions. He wound up traveling eight miles too far and it took ten hours to pick his way back out of the tangled maze of ice.

The next day, the jagged teeth of the snow saw rubbed a hole in the one-gallon can of gas in the sled he was pulling. Most of his fuel for the stove spilled out. He could still use the wood stove, but he'd already traveled more miles and taken more time than he intended—he was also down to the very last of his food.

"I realize that some small, potentially fatal accident could occur to me and I could die without help," Dick wrote. "But without the possibility of death, life would be meaningless."

When Dick's daughter, Kimmer, reflected on the years and miles that her father traveled alone, she said that family and friends would not hear from him for weeks at a time.

"We grew up never knowing where our Dad was and never knowing if he would come back," she said. "There was an unspoken understanding that if he didn't return, there would be no search party, no bringing him back. We were to leave him out there."

With a Depression-era sensibility, Dick blanched to think what it might cost to try and find his body—a small speck in a great white emptiness.

SHORTLY AFTER STARTING THIS TREK, the local radio station in Barrow, KBRW had warned of an incoming storm. Dick watched as the winds picked up and earth and sky became indistinguishable from each other.

"The landscape of blowing snow is dull, undefined, a world without proportion, unbroken, and above all a monotonous white ... Here it all merges into one. There is no horizon, no hills, no outline; nothing that one can focus on, just hundreds of smoky plumes of snow running along the surface before the wind," he wrote.

Dick made camp on the sea ice, not the best place, but he needed to hunker down. The radio said twenty-nine below with winds gusting to forty miles per hour. The windchill was one hundred degrees below zero—as cold as the time he nearly froze to death on his trek from Anaktuvuk Pass to Nenana. This time, however, he had a tent for shelter, a stove, and water to drink.

"There's no room for mistakes or carelessness out here," he wrote, "I made one of each last night. I was careless and burned a hole in my sleeping bag. Then, by mistake I poured hot water into my pee bottle instead of my water bottle."

Dick discovered his mistake when he took a swig the next morning.

The wind continued to blow with visibility remaining at zero. Dick spent the day in the tent and took stock of his food and wood supply. Although the tundra was void of trees, he was able to gather driftwood from beaches along the frozen coastline. The driftwood had been transported there from inland rivers flowing into the Arctic Ocean. Along with faraway trees brought in on the tide, Dick burned remnants of others Arctic misfortunes—planks of broken whaling vessels and washed up fishing boats. Salt water and cold preserved these fragments of the past. One piece of tropical hardwood gave him pause; perhaps he was even warming himself with the remains of vessels belonging to early explorers.

When the weather cleared, Dick was back on the trail. He now had a parka with a wolverine and wolf ruff, a vast improvement over the balaclava facemasks he'd used in earlier years. His progress this trip seemed slow. Weather had him holed up in his tent more than he liked. And he knew he wasn't traveling in a straight line.

Driftwood can be found all along the treeless Arctic coast.

"Snow and wind buries the Arctic and levels it off with such uniformity that you have to shovel snow away to find out if you're on land or sea," he said. "There are three clues to watch for: grass means I'm on tundra; sticks of wood indicate beach; and if there's no wood or grass, I'm on sea ice."

He had his compass to judge the direction he needed to go. And he basically followed the prevailing snowdrifts east.

"I'm not lost, I just don't seem to know where I am," he wrote on several occasions.

Later he explained, "Even if you're lost, it's no big deal. You've got your compass and you just follow it north. Eventually you'll come to something. Go north and you'll reach the Arctic Ocean. Go south and you'll hit the Brooks Range. As long as you keep going in a straight line you'll get somewhere."

Still, on this trip he was exasperated with himself. At the rate he was meandering, he would take twice as long and travel twice the distance that he intended. One day he saw a benchmark with a mast and flag surrounded by fifty-five-gallon barrels. He decided to check it out and detached himself from his sled to ski towards it. After skiing three hundred yards, he discovered it lay another three hundred yards away. He continued to follow it and skied three miles before he realized the benchmark was a mirage—a phenomenon of the north that had led many Arctic travelers astray. When he looked back over his shoulder, the sled was nowhere in sight—he'd gone too far to see it. He followed his own tracks back.

"When I returned to my sled, the benchmark was still three hundred yards away. I lost six miles, two hours of travel time and didn't get any wood," he grumbled.

He sometimes followed the occasional snowmachine tracks eastward, which made traveling a bit easier than trying to ski across rough *sastrugi* or pressure ridges. But the snowmachine tracks could be misleading—one day he got turned around completely. When he thought he was traveling east, he was instead following his own trail back to Barrow. He didn't discover his mistake until the next morning when the sun came up on the wrong side of the tent.

He eventually reached Rolligon tracks between Barrow and Prudhoe Bay. He had entered oil country and Rolligons were dinosaur-like vehicles that carried supplies from villages to and between oil production camps. The wind chill was minus fifty when a convoy drove by. The drivers stopped their rigs, incredulous to see a lone man on skis pulling a sled. A driver asked if Dick needed any help. Dick gladly accepted a four-by-four piece of lumber to burn in his wood stove. But he turned down the offer of food.

"The driver wanted to give me all his apples and canned goods, but I was too proud to take anything more than an apple," Dick said. Already on the Colville Delta, he knew he would soon be arriving at the homestead of Jim Helmericks. He didn't believe the driver who told him it was still another seventy miles to reach the family compound. "Tomorrow I'll either be at a drill rig or at Helmericks; either location I can get more food."

The next day he discovered he was not on the Colville Delta after all. And another storm was rolling in. "I still have a little 151 rum left," he wrote. "The next several days without food should be interesting. I do have lots of tea bags."

The wind rattled and shook Dick's tent for two days. He cut blocks of snow and stacked them around his tent, but the blocks eroded away with the wind. Inside the tent, Dick cut and chopped wood and at one point the fire grew toasty enough to blow a seam on his air mattress and put a blister on his plastic pee bottle.

"Sometimes I don't know what I'm doing here," he wrote. "Perhaps I am here because there is no other place to go."

The same four Rolligons that had passed him two days earlier stopped again as they traveled through the other direction. The same driver stopped and yelled, "What do you need?"

Dick stuck his head out the tent door and sheepishly replied, "Something to eat and firewood."

The driver handed Dick a sack of canned goods. Dick was grateful and wanted to get the man's name—but the howling wind made conversation impossible.

Dick wondered how these Rolligon drivers navigated the tundra, especially in storms where there were no landmarks and visibility was zero. He later learned they were using the new technology of the Global Positioning System, equipment he recognized could give him the ability to travel as the raven flies. His current meandering course was costing him untold miles and time.

The wind continued for a third straight day and when Dick woke up in the morning, he was trapped inside his tent by a hard-packed snowdrift. The wall he'd built created a wind break that allowed snow to drift on top of the tent. He had to tunnel upward through the snow to make his way out. The only place to put the snow was inside his tent, where it promptly melted, soaking all his gear.

He'd once read how, in 1956, a group of Inuit travelers had tied their dogs at the foot of a cliff to protect them from a strong south wind. Their own tent was on top of the cliff. The vacuum of the sheltered space below the cliff had drawn in snow so deep that it had suffocated the dogs.

He loaded his wet gear into his sled and found the ice haul road. He was hungry and knew he needed to find the Helmericks' or a drill rig oil camp soon. Once again a convoy of equipment and crew-cab trucks drove

The tent after a three-day storm.

by and this time when they stopped, Dick did not ask for food or wood. He asked for directions. One of the drivers knew the way to the Helmericks so Dick put his sled in the bucket of the front-end loader and crawled into the warm cab of the truck. The men offered him their lunches and then drove him four miles to a place where a thin snowmachine track diverged from their Rolligon trail.

"See that faint track? Just follow it four miles and you'll come to Helmericks," the driver said.

"I would have never found the place without their help," Dick wrote.

The Helmericks' three-generation home site lay sixty miles west of Prudhoe Bay on Anachlik Island on the outer edge of the Colville River Delta. It was first settled in the early 1950s by Bud and Martha Helmericks and began as nothing but a wall tent on the tundra. By the mid-1980s, there were two-story modern homes, a hangar for airplanes, storage buildings, greenhouses, ice cellars, and guest quarters. The couple had written several books about Alaska, all of which Dick had read. The homesite, which they called Colville Village, had become a well-known waypoint for dog mushers in winter, and birders and fishermen in the summer. Jim Helmericks and his two sons met Dick at the door. They had seen a lot of people come through, but they had never seen a man on skis traveling alone.

Dick and Jim talked late into the night about the Arctic, about other travelers who had come through, and the nuisance of rabid fox on the tundra. One winter Jim had killed fourteen rabid fox in their yard. Only one rabid fox had come through this winter, chasing Jim into the woodshed, where he managed to slam the door on its neck, killing it. It was easy to tell a rabid fox from a healthy one; the rabid fox had matted fur and walked with a drunken wobble.

The next day Dick bought groceries and white gas and continued on his way. The weather was good and he easily traveled the sixteen miles to his next stop at the Oliktok Saltwater Treatment Plant. Dick seemed to have friends all across the Arctic—and here he contacted his good friend Cathe Grosshandler, who offered a bed, laundry, shower, and "some of the best food in the world." She also insisted he take along a roll of duct tape for his trip; it might come in handy.

It was here, less than a year later, one mile from the saltwater treatment plant, at the Oliktok Air Force early warning site, that a worker was severely mauled by a polar bear that entered through a second-story window. The camp cook shot the bear as it attacked his coworker. The story garnered national attention and resulted in a lawsuit against the Air Force for requiring that all firearms be locked up—a regulation that the cook, thankfully, had ignored. And it was one more strike in favor of the bear's reputation as a vicious predator.

When Dick arrived at the Endicott oil production camp three miles offshore in the Beaufort Sea, he was four weeks into his trip and once again needed to resupply his food. He'd begun this trek with a sled loaded with ninety pounds of gear and food. To keep the sled weight manageable, he took only enough food to get him down the trail to where he hoped he could resupply. Expeditions of this sort had the reputation of costing tens of thousands of dollars in gear and equipment, but Dick was always quick to point out that his only sponsor on these lonely treks was the Salvation Army, a place he could "get clothes cheap." Aside from the food he carried, the list of his gear included only bare essentials:

Tent
Sleeping bag
Vapor barrier liner for the inside of his sleeping bag
Inflatable mattress
Hatchet
Wooden skis
Ski poles
Extra tent poles
Gas stove
Wood stove, plus 3-inch stove pipe
Water bottle
Pee bottle
Walkman radio/cassette player
Flares (railroad fuses)
Snow saw and small shovel
Fuel can with white gas
Chemical heat packs to keep fingers warm
Books (to read and start the next day's fire)
Music tapes
Duct tape

Except for tent poles, Dick brought no spares of anything, including clothing. He wore:

Capilene longjohns   Wool socks
Polyester trousers   Leather ski boots
Fleece pile jacket   Gaiters
Gore-Tex bibs   Gloves
Unlined parka

Dick knew there would be no grocery store at the Endicott camp; he just hoped the camp cook might spare some provisions from the pantry. He also hoped to enter a side door without causing any fuss.

"I circled the building, and the only unlocked door I could find led to the front desk with a security guard," Dick wrote. The guard, Charlie, looked at the grizzled, white-haired sixty-five-year-old with astonishment. "He couldn't understand how I was able to walk all the way from Barrow and continue to Kaktovik. The Arctic was the end of the world to him," Dick wrote.

Dick handed Charlie a grocery list, which he promptly passed on to the cook. Meanwhile, Dick spoke with a U.S. Fish and Wildlife biologist doing research on polar bears from the camp. He warned Dick that seismograph crews had been recently run off by bears at Flaxman Island.

"I'm going to be a little more careful," he wrote. "I have a 25 mm-flare pistol with three charges, two m-88 firecrackers, and two fuses."

Dick only stayed a few hours, then packed up his food, and continued on the trail promising Charlie that he'd be careful.

The bears were not the problem. Fox were a nuisance however, braying and yipping all night, sometimes circling his tent for hours. Was it the smell of cooking hotdogs that attracted them? And Dick's gear was beginning to wear out. His leather ski boots had thousands of miles on them. His wool socks had holes in the heels. The carbide tip on one of his ski poles was broken, so he couldn't use it on ice. Then while crossing some rough *sastrugi*, one of his wooden skis broke.

"I taped it with duct tape that Cathe made me bring," he said. The tape kept his skis from gliding smoothly, but using skis helped to bridge the cracks in the sea ice. These cracks ranged from a few inches to several feet wide and were caused by the movement of ice from fluctuating tides. With skis he was able to straddle over the top of the cracks and keep moving. Without skis, he had to scramble in and out of the cracks, exerting energy and time.

In the hours and miles of traveling across the great white emptiness, Dick occupied his mind with daydreams. "Some days I dream of a large plastic bubble equipped with a warm soft bed, stereo music, video movies, exotic food and a few other amenities," he wrote. "This bubble follows behind me, and when I get ready to camp I just crawl inside it. To endure, I let my mind wander sideways, uncontrolled."

For several days the weather grew sunny and Dick could see the Brooks Range eighty miles away. It had been thirty-three years since he had last seen this part of the mountains.

"There are three magic places in this world," Dick wrote. "The Brooks Range, the Grand Canyon, and the Himalayan Mountains." Along with his treks across the Arctic, Dick had also made treks to Nepal and Ladakh in northern India with Barney and Kimmer.

The Arctic landscape was beginning to shrug the dark mantle of winter. It was the time of year, in April, when the sun would rise and not set again until August. Dick was crossing, for the second time in his life, the Arctic

One good day in the Arctic made up for many difficult ones. (Canadian Arctic.)

National Wildlife Refuge (ANWR)—a place larger than the states of Connecticut and Massachusetts combined.

On April 29, the fourth week of the trek, a strong wind out of the west blew yet another storm into the area. Visibility was so bad Dick lost the Rolligon tracks and found himself once again trying to navigate through rough pockets of *sastrugi*. He took his skis off and tucked them in his sled, hoping to make better progress without them. But the tide cracks were numerous and without skis, he repeatedly fell, with the sled overturning behind him. At one point, without his realizing, his one good ski fell out. With only the one broken ski remaining, he would now be forced to make the rest of this trek on foot.

As the weather worsened, he decided to set up camp. He constructed a wide snow-block wall as a shelter from the howling wind. He knew he would need to shovel snow during the night, but he couldn't be without some sort of windbreak. Without it, his tent would be flattened in no time. He used his saw to cut blocks fourteen inches wide and stacked a wall nearly as high as his tent. Bracing against the wind's fury, he gathered wood along the gravel delta. After setting up camp, building a snow wall, and collecting wood, he crawled into the tent and built a fire. But snow collected on the warm stove pipe. As it melted, the slush slid down into the stove's fire chamber, extinguishing the flames. The fire sizzled out and water ran out the bottom of the stove. Discouraged and exhausted, Dick gave up and crawled into a wet sleeping bag and slept. He woke up cold and went outside to shovel the snow that was collecting around the tent. Then he wrapped a bungee over the stovepipe chimney to keep snow from collecting. From then on he was able to burn wood, get warm, and cook.

He listened to the Barrow radio station as he waited out the storm. He enjoyed "The Birthday Party" radio program where one-by-one, villagers from all over the north called the radio station to wish each other a happy birthday. He learned that the villagers of Kivalina had killed their first bowhead whale of the season. And he heard that riots in Los Angeles had broken out following the acquittal of four police officers accused in the beating of black motorist Rodney King. Such different worlds.

During the night, winds raged to fifty-five miles per hour, blowing a snow block off of the protective wall he'd built. The block struck the tent with such force that it snapped a tent pole. He had a few extra sections of pole for just such occasions, but the repair would have to wait until the wind subsided.

"One thing I've learned—the Arctic is no place for dreamers!"

The snow came down and the wind blew so fiercely that had he remained in his tent much longer only the stovepipe would have been visible from the drifting snow. "I should have shoveled out the tent every six hours to be on the safe side," Dick wrote.

He awoke to pain in his leg and surmised that he'd sprained something in one of his falls into the tide cracks the day before. Movement was painful as he made his way, ski-less now, across the white landscape. Towards evening, hobbling in the drifting fog, Dick saw the eerie forms of bare trees, protruding upside down from a long narrow peninsula half a mile away. The trees were the ghosts of an old Eskimo summer camp. Trees were scarce on the tundra, and collecting those delivered by the tide, Natives would bury dead trees upside down into the ground, leaving the tangle of roots exposed five feet high. These became racks used to preserve fish and meat, and a place to store dogsleds. Since sleds were lashed together with rawhide they were often the targets of hungry sled dogs.

At the sight of these odd formations, Dick realized it was the same spit that Hungry and he had walked to reach the mainland in 1959. Now he knew he was very close to his destination of Kaktovik. He was in considerable pain and decided to camp early on what he realized would likely be the last day of his trek.

The next morning he followed the series of satellite dishes along the coastline. These Distant Early Warning (DEW) sites were remnants of the Cold War, designed to detect incoming Soviet bombers and provide early warning of a land-based invasion.

On May 1, one month after setting out from Barrow, Dick arrived in Kaktovik windburned, his nose slightly frozen, with a scraggly beard and mess of white hair. "I am a wild man," he wrote. Since April 2, he had traveled 450 miles—give or take several dozen miles for the days he was lost.

As always, in his travels, he was barely on the airplane back to Anchorage before he was thinking about his next trip.

Trees buried upside down indicate an abandoned village. Trees were used as storage racks.

"I can only move eastward now into Canada," he wrote.

He reflected on the hundreds of people who had perished in the Arctic seeking the Northwest Passage. The exploits of John Barrow and especially the John Franklin Expedition fascinated him. Approximately seventy British corpses had been uncovered to date.

"In decades to come, explorers would pick wonderingly through the bundles of cloth, whitened bones, personal articles, stacks of supplies and scraps of wood that comprised the remains of the best supplied Arctic Fleet to have left England's shores," Dick wrote. "Because of the Franklin Expedition, the Northwest Passage gained a macabre allure. I have an uncontrollable desire to reach this disaster. There is at least 2200 miles more to go. I may not be able to cover the entire distance because of my age, but then I'm reminded that the ultimate quest has no end."

And on his next trip, he would leave his meandering course for a more direct route across a great white expanse.

Chapter 14

As Far as Thought Can Reach

Arctic writers have filled books with flowery, evocative, romantic descriptions of the Arctic. Writers use similar wording when describing a harsh, barren desert. The real Arctic I have found is less about romance and more, much more about adversity, struggle, and hope.
—Dick Griffith

SUPERIMPOSED OVER A MAP of the continental United States, the western tip of Alaska sits in Sacramento, California, its northern tip in Duluth, Minnesota, and its eastern tip in Savannah, Georgia. At 570,374 square miles, Alaska is larger than all but eighteen countries in the world and has more coastline than the rest of the United States combined.

To grasp the distances that Dick traveled in his treks across Alaska and the Canadian Arctic, imagine walking or skiing from Seattle, Washington, to New York City. Upon arriving in the Big Apple, you would have to turn around and walk back to Seattle. Still not finished, you would then have to trek south to San Diego to come even close to the more than six thousand miles Dick traveled in the Arctic and sub-Arctic over the years.

Dick calculated that in an eight hour day, each foot picks itself up 19,200 times. In the 445 days he spent walking the Arctic and sub-Arctic, he took an estimated 8.5 million steps. He traveled those distances with no fanfare; no sponsors, reporters, or reality TV shows. He traveled largely alone, one step at a time across the wilderness.

The remoteness of the landscape he traversed is also hard to comprehend. Alaska's population density is 1.09 people per square mile—with an even lower density across the Canadian Arctic. If Manhattan had the same population density as Alaska, there would only be twenty-five people living there instead of more than 1.5 million.

In nearly every trek's journal, Dick asked himself why he did it—why did he brave wind chills to minus one hundred degrees, difficult terrain, polar bear encounters, rabid foxes, and days of unrelenting solitude? "Hour after hour I trudge along pulling my sled," he wrote. "I try to come up with reasons for my obsession with the Arctic. The first few years I made lengthy Arctic trips to satisfy my ego. The next few trips were made because I knew that I could do better. Now I make Arctic trips because it's that time of year."

He returned to Kaktovik in 1993, at age sixty-six, to continue his eastward sojourn along the Northwest Passage, a route defined by twenty-six hundred miles of sea ice along the Arctic Ocean from Barrow, Alaska, to Repulse Bay, located at the north end of Hudson Bay. On this trek from Kaktovik, Alaska, to Tuktoyaktuk, in Canada, he would travel four hundred miles without resupply. His sled weighed 134 pounds.

For the first time, he was using a GPS. "I feel like I'm cheating, but I need to go as straight as possible," he wrote. "I can't afford to waste energy wandering as I have in previous years using a compass course."

In later years, he would lament that the GPS caused him to lose his earlier navigation skills—he would come to depend on technology rather than his own ability to read the prevailing snowdrifts to determine the direction he was traveling.

In Kaktovik, snowdrifts reached up to the eaves of the houses. The windy sides of taller, two-story buildings were caked with a hard crust of snow. It was a landscape encased in cold; the frigid fingers of the Arctic seemed to claw at life itself. Dick often found himself despairing at the beginning of these treks. There would be discomfort and danger and the possibility that he might not return. But the familiar dread always disappeared once he got on the trail.

"After several days of travel, I am in my element," he wrote.

In his journals, he often commented about the changes in Native life since his earlier encounters with rural villagers.

"In 1959 when I visited this village the Eskimos were living on the bluff facing the ocean. Every family had a dog team staked nearby. No water or sewerage existed. The smell was indescribable ... Hunters left every day with dog teams to hunt inland for caribou and out on the sea ice for seal ... The villagers now live in modern stick built houses with sewer and water," he remembered.

As he packed up his gear in Kaktovik, he realized he'd forgotten his copy of Ayn Rand's *Fountainhead*—and he needed books for his travels. So he stole two "bodice rippers" from the Waldo Arms store—a commercial contractor's camp in Kaktovik. "One of the covers had the hero's embrace squishing the swooner's breasts out of the top of her dress," he wrote. The books might not provide much in the way of intellectual stimulation but surely they would be entertaining.

Dick used the term "stolen" loosely in his journals. To his chagrin, people he met in the villages rarely took his money. They all regarded him with a measure of incredulousness that superseded the need for normal commerce. If he was willing to walk thousands of miles across a frozen landscape, a gallon of fuel or a bag of rice was usually on the house.

At the store, he also caught up on local gossip. He listened to talk of the nine polar bears feeding on a beached whale nearby and how many of the fox in the area were rabid. The weather was also getting warmer, meaning the water could pour out over the top of the Mackenzie River before he arrived. "My diminishing youthful enthusiasm was about to completely evaporate, so I left the village," he wrote.

He soon discovered that his GPS did not work in temperatures colder than minus ten degrees. He would have to use it at night, get a compass bearing for the next day, and then set out. He would check it again in the evening after he stopped to camp and could warm it up again. In his tent at night, the GPS told him how far he'd traveled and where he was; no more guessing on that account. Now he could better move in raven miles rather than wandering as he'd done on previous trips.

Dick's schedule was to wake up at 6:00 a.m. and light his stove with the "fire bomb" he'd prepared the night before—pages from his book, camp trash, and select wood shavings. He'd then go back to sleep for an hour. By

Polar bear feeding on whale carcass.

(Photo by Robyn Becker, 2004)

7:00 a.m. the water he'd put on the stove would be hot and he could drink a cup of coffee while he prepared breakfast. By 9:00 a.m. he broke camp, loaded up his sled and was on his way.

When necessary, he could set up and break camp in minutes. He pitched the tent first, pulled the sled inside, unloaded the stove and fired it up. To break camp he would pull the sled in and load it up, leaving the tent for last.

But on more leisurely days, he would stop at 5:00 p.m., put up his tent and then set out looking for wood. After gathering enough to burn for six hours, he took what he'd gathered and sawed or chopped it into pieces small enough to fit into his stove.

"Gathering wood is a spiritual task that I perform daily. I enjoy poking through the driftwood piles for the perfect pieces of wood that will burn hot and fill the tent with a nice aroma," Dick wrote. "Some of the washed-up trees are sixty feet long, straight as arrows, and several feet in diameter. I always get carried away and cut more wood than I need and end up dragging it to my next campsite."

In a later journal he again commented about the task he so enjoyed: "I have collected little pieces of wood like some women collect tea cups: small board of Douglas fir from a shipwreck, a short piece of white spruce from the Mackenzie River and a willow from perhaps the Horton River. Today I use them for firewood."

After preparing the wood and lighting the stove, he would put water on to boil for his nightly hot buttered rum. The other pot simmered lentils, rice, macaroni and cheese, cracked wheat, oat germ, or dried boiled spuds.

He limited his sleep to ten hours a night. His dreams were filled with colorful images and people. Sometimes they were humorous. Other times they were extensions of his conscious thought—a problem solved on the trail somewhere. Always his dreams were populated by people and animals—as if to keep him company on these long lonely treks. He looked forward to each night's encounter. He often dreamed about his granddaughter, Yarrow.

On this trip, he was once again paralleling the Brooks Range, a mountain range that was as familiar as it was enigmatic. These mountains gave way to the steel blue Richardson Mountains which lay to his right. Herschel Island lay to his left.

He had finished traveling for the day, set up his tent for the evening, and embarked on his evening ritual of gathering wood along the icy shoreline. He was a quarter of a mile from camp when he looked over his shoulder and there, foraging through his sled, was a polar bear. Dick dropped his arm load of wood except for one piece which he wielded like a club. Then he ran yelling towards the bear—it could destroy his gear in seconds, leaving him with no food, shelter, or provisions. The bear took one look at the white-haired man screaming toward him—and high tailed it over the sea ice. When Dick reached his sled, he grabbed his flare gun and fired a round—but the bear was long gone. He also shot off a "seal bomb," which he described as a large firecracker or mini-stick of dynamite. Dick then followed the bear tracks to see where it had come from. He quickly discovered that the animal had been following him for miles. Because the afternoon had been foggy—and polar bears were difficult to see on ice and snow—Dick had been unaware of his pursuer.

He went back and took stock of what the bear had pilfered from his sled. The only thing missing were eight Power Bars. Dick decided not to move camp. But he did gather enough wood to keep the stove burning all night. He also dug out his Swiss army knife in case he needed to cut his way out of the tent. The tent zippers were always frozen and had to be thawed with bare hands in order to exit each morning.

That night in his tent, Dick reflected on his encounter.

"If you have to die, what a way to go. To be killed by a polar bear has class and I can live with that," he wrote. "To die of natural causes in a hospital must be boring and degrading ... It matters not to me to have an unmarked grave or to have my remains scattered randomly across the Arctic in little brown piles. The earth turns and the sun inexorably sets and one day, for each of us, the sun will go down for the last, last time. It is a day that I do not fear."

Even so, Dick did not sleep well that night. "I kept waking up to see if the polar bear had come back." Apparently Dick had left a formidable impression and the bear stayed away. "I think the polar bear hated those Power Bars as much as I did."

The spring weather was growing warm and Dick complained about the heat. With his Arctic clothing and the exertion of pulling his 110-pound

Following the occasional snowmachine track near a circa 1900 abandoned igloo.

sled, any temperature over twenty degrees became uncomfortable for traveling. With cold temperatures and sunshine, it was like moving through a crystal ball.

"In the morning the sparkles from the snow are spectacular. They surround me for a radius of at least 200 yards," he wrote. "Some random ones glitter half a mile away—they look like flashing mirrors."

He was following a snowmachine track along a rolling landscape when he heard the drone of approaching snowmachines. Suddenly a flurry of machines burst over the hill and the drivers circled back and surrounded him. There were seventeen snowmachines with at least twenty-five people on board. The group was traveling back to Kaktovik after visiting friends and relatives in Aklavik in Canada. One of the snowmachines pulled a sled with what appeared to be a large blue doll house on top. The house was complete with a door and windows. Inside sat two elder women in their little home-built camper. Dick had to wonder how often the top-heavy structure toppled over along the way. One woman in the group recognized Dick as Barney's dad. Barney, a telecommunication specialist, installed GPSs on their whaling boats every year.

"There were young people, old people, little kids, big and little people. Everyone was joyful. It was a carnival atmosphere," Dick remembered. Everyone asked questions.

"How old are you?"

"Where are you going?"

"How long have you been walking?"

"Aren't you afraid to sleep out here alone?"

Someone offered him hot coffee with sugar.

Dick pulled out his maps. "I was the one that needed to ask questions."

Dick wondered about the best way to cross the upcoming Mackenzie River Delta. The delta is one of the largest in the world and the largest river system in Canada. The wide expanse where the Mackenzie River flowed into the Arctic Ocean was a maze of braided steams and islands. Warm springtime temperatures would likely create hazardous overflow and with few landmarks, it would be difficult to navigate. One of the young men in the group told him the person that could give him advice lived in the nearby village of Shingle Point.

The lively group then bid Dick farewell and continued on their way to Kaktovik.

"When they took off towards Barter Island, they looked like the Oklahoma land stampede. What a happy, carefree group," Dick wrote. "I was very much amused by this brief, joyful encounter with the Eskimos."

When Dick arrived at Shingle Point two days later; it was a community of twenty mostly vacant cabins scattered over three miles. The cabins were built of driftwood logs collected from the beach. Next to each cabin stood a teepee made of logs which was used to store firewood. At one time a permanent village, Shingle Point was now used mainly as a summer fish camp. In springtime, it became a base camp for Native hunters looking for polar bears.

The weather continued sunny and warm and Dick sported a badly sunburned lip. It didn't seem to matter what he did, the crack in his lip got deeper, breaking open and bleeding every time he moved his mouth.

Shingle Point.

"I'm carrying Gore-Tex bibs, a parka with an extra wide wolverine ruff, mittens with extra outer fur covering, insulated over boots, expedition-weight Patagonia jacket, a sleeping bag good for-30 degrees F, and chemical hand warmers that will hold heat for seven hours," he wrote. "I don't need any of this stuff. Today it is 15 degrees."

He decided to stay and rest. The hunters had left. "It is once again very quiet," Dick wrote. "There's no one left here but the ravens and I."

The wind had picked up and wispy coils of snow rolled across the tundra like lonesome Arctic tumbleweed. That evening Dick received an unusual visitor.

"A very old, white-haired Eskimo rode up to my tent on an old, beat-up snowmachine. His machine pulled an equally beat-up narrow toboggan, typical of those used in this country ... It's not often that you see an Eskimo with snowy white hair like mine. I asked him, 'Where are you going?' He said, 'No place.' He wore ragged clothes and looked very poor, but he walked with a regal bearing, and when he spoke it was with a deep, slow voice. This man appeared to be ageless. I'm guessing he must have been in his 70s. I invited him in for tea," Dick wrote.

Dick liked the old man immediately. He had a mystic presence about him. The elder wanted to know more about Dick's travels. In halting English, he relayed his heartache for a vanishing way of life.

Dick offered him more tea and sugar in hopes of learning more. When Dick asked again where the old man was headed, he replied, "I am going back to my youth."

Then without a word, the white-haired man got up and left Dick's tent, climbed onto his snowmachine and disappeared into a heavy fog.

Dick was stunned. Where had the old man come from? Where was he going? It seemed as if he'd just seen a phantom or a ghost.

Dick thought about Maniilaq, a powerful figure of Inupiat legend. Maniilaq was born in the Kobuk region of Northwest Alaska and lived in the 1800s just as the Russians and Europeans were making first contact with the aboriginal cultures. Maniilaq was a hunter and a healer with prophetic visions about the arrival of white men. He had predicted their boats and flying machines long before they arrived. Airplanes had not yet been invented. He also traveled the North extensively—he was an oracle during a transitional time in Alaska Native cultural history.

Dick did not consider himself a religious man, but he was superstitious—carrying his ivory trolls with him as talismans during his travels. Dick couldn't help but wonder if the man with whom he'd just shared tea was in fact the prophet, Maniilaq.

The next night, after beginning his trek across the Mackenzie River Delta, Dick had yet another visitor. Sitting inside his tent, he heard the sound of scratching from inside his food bag. Dick poked at the bag and a weasel popped out to look at him.

"I chased it out the way it had come in, through the hole in the floor of my tent," Dick wrote. This opening gave Dick access to snow to melt for water. "I laid some heavy objects over the fabric and went back to bed."

Twenty minutes later the weasel was tunneling back into Dick's tent. Rather than chase him off, this time Dick gave him a strip of dried salmon. Greedily the weasel grabbed it and left and did not come back until the next morning.

"The weasel returned looking for another handout," Dick wrote. This time the weasel tried to climb his pant leg. "A vicious looking critter... but he got no more salmon."

The delta was as difficult to navigate as Dick had anticipated. There were few landmarks, just a wide flat expanse of ice and treeless islands. He was traveling a labyrinth of frozen channels. Sometimes after a long day of travel, after warming the GPS in his tent, Dick would discover he had traveled off course.

"I made camp at the usual time and checked my GPS; it shows that I'm in the wrong channel. I'm headed south; somehow I turned off at Caribou Channel and went into another channel," he wrote. "Tomorrow I'll have to retrace my steps ... this error cost me eight miles. The enormity of everything sometimes gets to me."

He decided to start packing the GPS against his water bottle filled with hot water. That gave him a five hour window to use the device before it once again was too cold to function. Even so, the GPS didn't account for terrain or extensive *sastrugi* that sometimes forced him to alter his course.

So far, this trek had been the least hazardous in terms of stormy weather, but even the sunshine had its hazards. Dick's cracked bleeding lip had now grown infected. Puss oozed from the deep painful split. He knew that even small accidents could create serious problems.

"I'm careful not to get injured in any way," he wrote. "I cut shavings with a knife, chop wood with a hatchet, and cut wood with a saw. Any one of these operations is a potential small accident that, out here, could be big trouble."

A week after leaving Shingle Point, without seeing even one other human, Dick met up with an ice road indicating that he had finally completed his crossing of the delta. This road would lead him to his destination, Tuktoyaktuk.

The ice road was peppered with gravel so Dick put his skis in the sled and walked. The horizon was punctuated by pingos—earth-covered mounds of ice found in the Arctic and sub-Arctic. The term pingo was derived from the Native word for small hill; these geologic formations reaching heights up to 230 feet were prominent features on an otherwise flat landscape. Tuktoyaktuk had more than 1,350 pingos, one of the largest concentrations in the world. The area also had large herds of caribou moving through and Dick saw dozens of gut piles along the way, evidence of the hunting endeavors of the locals.

People stopped on the ice road to talk to the solitary traveler. One dropped off a bag of groceries. A polar bear hunter wanted to buy Dick's camp stove. After persistent requests, Dick finally agreed to sell it after he reached Tuktoyaktuk.

Spring was quickly arriving, and according to one of the Natives, the road would officially close in the next couple of days. Already Dick had to navigate around flooding on the ice road. At night, Dick slept restlessly to the rifle-crack sounds of moving ice.

"The volume of water in the Mackenzie is rapidly increasing; temperatures in the interior are much warmer," Dick wrote. "When the larger volume of water reaches the Arctic Coast it has to go someplace and pushes up the ice, forming cracks, and eventually spilling out onto the surface. Breakup is dramatic in the Arctic."

Roman Dial, a longtime friend and fellow competitor in the Alaska Mountain Wilderness Classic race once remarked that while most competitors came dragging exhausted and bedraggled to the finish line of that race, Dick usually looked better and moved with more vigor than when he'd started. Aside from an infected lip, Dick approached Tuktoyaktuk feeling strong and capable of traveling hundreds of miles farther along the Northwest Passage.

After three days on the ice road and on the last night of this trek, an elder stopped his truck and came over to Dick's tent. Dick invited him in for tea. The elder wondered about his travels and commented that no one had ever done what Dick had done—traveled under his own power across thousands of miles across the frozen Arctic. Dick pointed out that Native people had always pulled sleds for long distances along the coast.

"Never in my lifetime," the elder replied.

Water running on the ice road at Mackenzie River. Complete breakup followed two days later.

Historically speaking, the man was right. In terms of European explorers in the 1800s and early 1900s, hundreds had died trying to navigate the Northwest Passage. Many became famous in their attempts. But no one could remember anyone—Native or otherwise—who had ever gone that distance traveling solo under his or her own power.

Dick was quietly carving his name among the legends of the North.

Chapter 15

Walking Among Legends

Mountain ranges eventually end, rivers terminate in the sea,
deserts are limited in extent but the Arctic stretches
into infinity as far as thought can reach.
That is the power of the Artic, it is endless.
—Dick Griffith

DICK LAMENTED AT TIMES ABOUT having been born too late to have joined early explorers as they discovered the Arctic. The maps of the world were already drawn and he considered himself a mere adventurer in places already charted by the great legends of the North.

Dick had read all about the exploits and travels of Roald Amundsen, Sir John Franklin, Vilhjalmur Stefansson, Hudson Stuck and others. He has an encyclopedic knowledge of the Arctic's early explorers and his journals are punctuated with stories from his reading and research. From the time he was a boy, these explorers had been his heroes.

They were, as Dick described, "Men who were courageous, adventuresome, and sometimes foolhardy. They were also those who were bullheaded, eccentric, quarrelsome, cruel, pompous, and self-seeking."

In search of a northern ocean passage that would connect the centers of European commerce with those of the Orient and India, most early explorers came on expensive, well-equipped expeditions.

Mistakes and plain bad luck often proved deadly for early explorers of the Arctic. No tragedy was more famous than that of the doomed expedition of Sir John Franklin that departed England in 1845. Franklin had served on three previous successful Arctic expeditions. This fourth voyage was meant to traverse the last as yet unnavigated section of the Northwest Passage. But the ships *Eribus* and *Terror* became icebound in Victoria Strait near King William Island. In the end, the entire expedition, including Franklin and 127 men, perished.

"It is curious that the world is often more impressed by spectacular failure than success," Dick wrote.

Pressed by Franklin's wife to find them, a reward was offered to learn the fate of the missing men and a search was launched in 1848. The first relics of the expedition were found on Beechey Island, including the graves of three crewmen. The first crewmembers most likely succumbed to pneumonia or tuberculosis. Others died of scurvy, hypothermia, and starvation. Research later revealed that lead poisoning also contributed to the expedition's woes; the ship's food supplies were made up of badly soldered cans of food.

Explorer John Rae learned more about the fate of the Franklin party from the Native Inuit near King William Island. The Inuit had discovered relics and remains of some of the party. Cut marks on human bones found on King William Island suggested the likelihood of cannibalism as the crew struggled to survive. A hero in his own right, Rae became a pariah for revealing the horrors of men who had since been elevated by the public as national heroes. Rae went on to travel the Northwest Passage on foot and with the use of dog teams.

In Dick's 1979 journal on his trek from Nuiqsut to Anaktuvuk Pass he wrote, "I don't know where I fit into this picture. Lasting fame is a fragile thing—it sometimes has little to do with the magnitude of the achievement but rather with being fortunate to do the right thing at the right time—or to die in sufficiently romantic circumstances to capture the imagination of the public."

Norwegian explorer Roald Amundsen was the first to negotiate the Northwest Passage by sea in 1906. His forty-seven-ton boat, the *Gjoa*, was frozen in the pack ice for three winters before he succeeded in his endeavor. At the end of his trip, Amundsen traveled overland for six weeks in temperatures as low as sixty-below to reach Eagle, Alaska, where he telegraphed his success to the rest of the world. His achievement made him instantly famous around the globe.

At about the same time in 1906, Vilhjalmur Stefansson was doing groundbreaking research as an anthropologist studying Arctic peoples. He made three expeditions to the Canadian Arctic in the early 1900s and his prolific writings carved the public image of a hero. He was a man who prided himself on self-sufficiency even though he accepted ample support from the Native Inuits. That support included the help of Pannigabluk—a seamstress that Stefansson took for his party. A skilled self-promoter, what Stefansson did not make widely known was that he fathered a son in the Arctic.

Dick discovered Stefansson's "forgotten family" when he met a school teacher in Inuvik named Rose. She was the granddaughter of Pannigabluk and Stefansson and was eager to tell Dick their family story.

Dick researched the records and the writings of Stefansson and his contemporaries to learn more about Rose's grandmother. In his search, he ran across a book by Will Hudson with a photograph of Pannigabluk holding her young son, Alex.

"She was a beautiful woman and wearing decorated furs down to her ankles. I fell in love with the image, I wish I could have known her," Dick wrote. In his travels, he learned that many of the early explorers had left behind progeny in the North.

He also learned that explorers made mistakes, some of them costly. Stefansson had a well-equipped and well-financed expedition. But among the tons of supplies, he forgot one absolutely indispensable item: matches. None of the whalers or Mounties at Herschel Island would part with theirs, so Stefansson had to make a one-thousand-mile trip by boat from Herschel Island to Point Barrow to get them. Dick understood the consequence of mistakes—he had made his share during his Arctic travels.

In traversing the Brooks Range of Alaska, Dick often followed the routes of Hudson Stuck. As an Episcopal priest and archdeacon, Hudson traveled thousands of miles by dogsled to minister to a tiny congregation spread over a vast expanse of the north. Hudson believed that Native exposure to western culture would doom them to eventual extinction. He also co-led the expedition of the first ascent of Mount McKinley (Denali), the highest peak in North America.

"I always seemed to be following his tracks," Dick noted. Like Stuck, Dick attempted the ascent of Mount McKinley (Denail). In both his attempts, Dick suffered from pulmonary edema and was unable to summit. (Stuck himself fell unconscious at the summit and had to be carried to a lower elevation to recover.)

As Dick followed the coastline of Alaska and the Canadian Arctic across the Northwest Passage, he traced the footsteps of those who had gone before—yet no explorer before him had ever attempted that distance solo and on foot pulling a sled. The only person who had traveled extensively alone and without dogs was Hubert Darrell in the early 1900s. Stefansson and Amundsen both mentioned him in their writings, yet he disappeared on the trail in 1910 in relative obscurity.

Dick assumed his travels, too, would go largely unnoticed. He wrote, "My legacy is two thin lines left in the snow, which will soon be lost in the drifting snow."

He was sixty-eight years old in 1995 when he traveled from Tuktoyaktuk to Paulatuk, a distance of 350 miles. His trek began in mid-March with temperatures of minus forty degrees. The colder the temperatures, the more resistance the snow placed on the sled. It was like traveling in dry sand. The sled weighed 160 pounds as he started down the trail. The cold temperatures hampered the use of his GPS, which was nothing but added weight until he could warm it up in his tent at night. Several days after leaving Tuktoyaktuk, two Native men stopped by in the dark on their snowmachines. A polar bear hide was draped over one of the sleds. They stopped to see if the lone traveler was all right. They had just come from the Horton River and wondered where Dick was headed.

"You must be a tough old bastard to be out here alone in the cold," one of them said before warning him about polar bears and then continuing down the trail.

A day later another polar bear hunting party stopped to talk to Dick. Three of the men were Inuit and they were guiding a rather large client from Pennsylvania.

"The polar bear hunter was dressed in white. He looked like a polar bear because he was about as wide as he was long," Dick mused. "He stepped to the side of the trail to pee and I think that he was troubled like all of us menfolk in the Arctic: six inches of clothing and two inches of peter."

The guides agreed to meet up and resupply Dick at the Horton River. Travel had been slower than Dick anticipated and a resupply would help him get to Paulatuk without running out of food or gas for his stove. The temperature dipped to minus thirty and as the hunters left, one of them assured him, "Spring is coming."

Wood was growing sparser along the coast and during the nights when he did not light his wood stove, he woke up cold. The wood fire helped dry out his gear, and without it a cold damp seeped deep into his bones. He relished the warm glow from his stove.

"I lay in my sleeping bag and watched my breath form a continuous white lenticular cloud that floated on the cold floor of the tent—then the draft of the stove sucked it into the fire chamber and up the stovepipe," he wrote.

Up until this trip, Dick had used simple leather ski boots on his feet. On this trek, however, he used mukluks, traditional Native footwear made of sealskins and caribou fur. They were warm and light and gave him good traction for pulling the sled. But the severe cold along with the moisture from exertion and snow froze the inside removable liners to the outer shell of the boot itself—encasing his feet in ice. He had to stop for a day just to dry things out.

"Every night I come in discouraged—don't know how I will ever reach Paulatuk with my remaining supplies," he wrote. "Every morning I spring forth with new enthusiasm. Even the sun has a sinking spell at night, but it comes back up every morning."

The cold was relentless and at one point the wind ripped a wide tear in his tent. After three weeks on the trail he wrote, "I am doing so poorly. I would never risk being so far in if those polar bear hunters were not ahead of me ... I look at my map, my goal seems to be unreachable, time and motion—like the sea—is frozen."

On April 1, Dick's spirits were flagging. "My tent rattles and shakes from a wind that is coming from the direction of N40E. It was necessary for me to go out of the tent and build a small snow wall for additional protection ... the world seemed endless and my tent less than a dot upon its face. The extent of my weariness is overpowering, so I returned to the safety of the tent."

The next day Dick had to figure out how to get across the Horton River and past the steep Smoking Hills on the other side. His travels and thoughts were interrupted when three large snowmachines came speeding toward him.

It turned out that one of the motorized travelers was Dick's old friend Roger Siglin, from Fairbanks. Formerly the superintendent of Gates of the Arctic National Park, Siglin had since retired and was making extensive trips in the Arctic by snowmachine.

"I was almost speechless to meet these three people in such a remote place. Like me, they were looking for a place to gain access to the Arctic Ocean. They had powerful wide-track snowmachines (Tundra 2s) each pulling a large toboggan, loaded with gas, food, firewood and camp supplies. They had a large double walled tent, double sleeping bags, camp cots, wood stove and just about everything else," Dick wrote. "My outfit looked very primitive compared to theirs. I looked to be in bad shape for my nose was peeling and I had a two-inch icicle hanging from it."

Photo of Dick taken by passing snowmachiners.

They left Dick with a bag of firewood before heading north. "It was one chance in one million that we should meet in such a remote area."

Meanwhile, the polar bear hunters who had agreed to resupply him at the Horton River did not materialize. Dick tried following snowmachine trails to find them, but this was big country and the tracks were leading him everywhere but forward. The search was costing him time and miles and he decided to continue on—their planned rendezvous never happened.

The weather continued cold and windy and it seemed at times that he had to travel thirty miles to make ten miles of progress. "This can't be the end of the earth but it can't be very far away," Dick wrote. His primary consolation was his wood-burning stove.

"The wood stove gives me so much warmth and pleasure, without it, surviving would be much more difficult," he wrote.

He remembered his mother cooking on a wood stove when he was a youngster in Wyoming and believed heartily in the old adage that food tastes better when cooked on a stove fired by wood.

The terrain had grown jagged with *sastrugi* and pressure ridges. Steep bluffs required him to lower and raise the sled through more difficult passages. The sled overturned multiple times as he pulled it along the serrated landscape. Nearing his fourth week on the trail, he unpacked his sled to set up camp and discovered that his beloved wood stove was missing.

That night he woke up shivering. The next morning he noted, "I miss my stove. It's like having a million dollars, you don't really need it but it is nice to have."

Without the wood stove, he had to use the white gas stove to boil water and cook. Because he had not rendezvoused with the polar bear hunters as planned, he was now down to one liter of fuel. He needed a gallon of water per day for cooking and drinking. To save fuel, he stopped occasionally to build a wood fire on the ground to cook a big meal and fill up his water bottles. He began eating snow during the day to conserve the fuel it took to melt it. He had only a handful of Lipton dinners left—meals that provided only 230 calories each. He also had some fish strips, freeze dried beans, jerky, milk, and three sticks of butter.

Coal seams have been burning for thousands of years in the Smoking Hills. Note beached whale baleen in the foreground.

"My sugar, rum and cereal are long gone," he wrote. "I will make it."

After passing by the Smoking Hills the sea ice grew smooth. Traveling became easier as he pulled a sled that was growing ever lighter as he used up his provisions. The promise of spring was, as the Inuit hunter had foretold, just around the corner.

Winter's deep cold finally broke and the brilliant sun appeared—rising pink on the nearby mountains in the morning and setting gold and blue on the horizon at night. Dick's optimism returned and even the loss of his stove didn't seem so bad.

"If I had my wood stove I would be days behind, camped on the gravel beaches, burning wood and enjoying this beautiful area and spring weather," he reflected.

Now Dick was able to cover fifteen to twenty miles a day. The white hills were turning brown and he remembered how quickly and dramatically spring arrived in the Arctic.

On the twenty-ninth morning after setting out from Tuktoyaktuk, Dick burned his last drop of fuel trying to once again thaw his frozen mukluks. But his timing was good—later that afternoon he arrived at his destination of Paulatuk.

He had traveled some 350 miles, at least seventy-five of which were detours around difficult terrain or meanders in search of the polar bear hunters. He lost one-half pound for every day he was on the trail—a total of fifteen pounds on this trip. As he recovered from his trek, he reflected on how age was factoring into future prospects for adventure.

"I try very hard not to use age as an excuse for not going. I am convinced that all the walking that I have done over the years has provided me with exceptional health into old age," he wrote. "Our two-legged structure is perfectly capable of carrying us to a distant grave—we simply have to be willing to walk there."

And as usual, he was already thinking about the next trek. "I am hooked on this country, hooked on the Eskimo culture and hooked on the rich history of the Arctic. I must continue on to Repulse Bay... I know not why it is so necessary for me to fulfill my destiny on such a long, not-easy section of the earth's terrain."

ROMAN DIAL WAS JUST TWENTY-ONE YEARS OLD when he met Dick at the first Alaska Mountain Wilderness Classic in 1982. While Dick introduced packrafting to outdoor wilderness travel, Dial went on to refine and advance the packraft as a viable mode of wilderness travel.

"Dick was more than just an inspiration," Dial said. "For a bunch of us, he redirected our lives."

Dial himself became a legend for his wilderness exploits and has been featured on the Discovery Channel, PBS, and National Public Radio. Although

Dick lamented living one hundred years too late to be a true explorer, Dial insists that Dick was ahead of his time in many aspects of outdoor wilderness sports.

"It took forty to fifty years for the outdoor community to catch up with him," he said. "He is the conceptual grandfather of long outdoor treks."

Dial also noted the achievements of modern trekkers whose achievements are often touted as "firsts."

"The thing is, Dick's been doing this stuff before most of these guys were even born—before their *parents* were born," he said.

Dial expressed frustration with many modern adventurers' desire for notoriety and recognition. "It becomes all about sponsorship and money," he said. "Dick is not an elitist in any sense. He kept the Alaska Mountain Wilderness Classic pure because he didn't want money to get involved and spoil it."

Dick continues to host a dinner at his home for Wilderness Classic competitors before each race.

Dial said Dick was also ahead of his time in terms of women and adventure. "It wasn't until the '70s and women's lib that women really started showing up in the outdoors," he said. Yet in their early years, Dick and Isabelle traveled together extensively in the canyons and he made many friends in Alaska among women interested in wilderness travel.

Asta Spurgis—who now directs the Eagle River Nature Center in Chugach State Park—credits Dick for fueling her passion for the wilderness. It was Dick who encouraged her discovery of the backcountry, and convinced her to move from Chicago to Alaska.

"He was my summer hiking mentor and the reason I moved to Alaska," Spurgis said. "He had a lot of female companions and enjoyed women's company. He was a really friendly guy and took us under his wing in a fatherly way."

Dick's daughter-in-law, Bobbie Sue Wolk, said that when she sprained her ankle during the Alaska Mountain Wilderness Classic, Dick got up early to help her along the trail before the rest of the group caught up. Without him, she said she couldn't have finished the race.

He has his limits of patience, however. Spurgis tells the story of how she once fired Dick from his volunteer work at the Eagle River Nature Center. She had asked him to take a group of hikers through a backcountry area of Chugach State Park, beginning in Arctic Valley, traveling through Ship Creek, and then on to the Nature Center. It was to be a three-day, twelve person trek overland with no trail—a rigorous hike over unmarked mountains. All hikers were warned of the perils and the importance of being fit enough to undertake this challenging cross-country endeavor.

It soon became clear that one of the women in the group was nowhere near ready for the trip. She was holding up the group. At the pace they were moving, they would need extra days to complete the trek. Finally, Dick had enough of waiting. He sent the hiker back to where they had started while he continued on with the group.

Arriving at their destination at the Nature Center, one of the hikers came in the door and told Spurgis that the group had left a hiker behind two days earlier. Spurgis waited for Dick to come in and explain what was going on. His only words were, "We're back."

"The husband was going to pick up his wife, and we had to explain that she'd not completed the trek," Spurgis said. No harm came to the woman, who made her way back, alone and without incident. "I told him, 'That's it Dick, you're never leading another hike.' If either the woman or her husband had been different kind of people, it could have been very bad news."

Dick wasn't "fired" for long, however. He continues to spend countless volunteer hours at the Eagle River Nature Center working on trails, building public use cabins and yurts, and providing firewood for the cabins' wood stoves. One of his favorite volunteer pastimes is helping Boy Scouts earn their Eagle badges. Together he has helped nearly two dozen young men build bridges, boardwalks, hand rails, benches, and other improvements to trails around the Nature Center and along the Crow Pass trail.

Dick also worked with prison crews from the Hiland Mountain Correctional Center. He enjoyed working with the women crews, many of whom had at one time been prostitutes.

"I thought they were real neat," Dick said. "They were so personable."

The only trouble he had was with a woman guard who refused to pee in the woods. Otherwise, he said they were all hardworking and very appreciative of being outdoors.

Dick can be brusque and charming; tough yet full of good humor. Spurgis laughed to tell the story of her wedding day. She and her husband, Ramunas, had asked Dick to officiate their wedding at Griffith's home in Anchorage. He agreed. When Spurgis and her husband-to-be arrived at Dick and Isabelle's home, Dick pointed to a shovel and told Ramunas to dig a hole for the totem pole that Isabelle wanted in the garden. On their wedding day? But why?

"Because it needed to be dug," he said.

After the hole was dug, Dick married the couple in front of an oosik— the baculum (penis bone) of a walrus—that hung on the wall above their wood stove. To date, Dick has joined a dozen couples in matrimony and each year he hosts a "Still-Married" party for his charges. (Only one of twelve marriages has ended over the years.) The photos of these couples hang on Dick's refrigerator.

"My husband and I have often thought of him as a wolf. He's social and part of the pack," Spurgis said, pointing out his weekly dinner parties for family, friends, and people Dick calls "orphans." She also points out his prodigious volunteer work at the Nature Center. "But every so often he just has to set out on his own. He needs time to be solitary."

And he had a need to complete what he had started. The lure of the Arctic did not wane with the passing years. If anything, Dick's desire to complete the Northwest Passage grew more pressing.

Chapter 16

One Thousand Miles

One by one my toenails are turning black. Perhaps I walk too much.
—*Dick Griffith*

AS DICK LEFT THE VILLAGE OF CAMBRIDGE BAY, he took one last look over his shoulder at the speck of civilization he was leaving behind. It would be almost two months before he would arrive at his destination of Repulse Bay, a distance of 550 miles. He was surprised to see a dark figure between him and the village. Someone appeared to be following him. He detached himself from his sled and skied back to investigate. It turned out to be a woman, an elderly Inuit woman wearing a long caribou fur parka and mukluks. She carried a satchel along with a bedroll made of caribou skin. Her English was poor but she relayed in her Native tongue that she intended to accompany Dick on his trek.

He tried to explain that he couldn't take her along. There was not enough room in his tent, nor did he have enough food for both of them. She did not accept his answer and kept trudging behind him without snowshoes or skis in spite of Dick's rigorous objections.

"She had crows feet around her eyes and her skinny cheekbones were like wings of a raven extending from her nose. Several times I skied back and tried to explain the situation to her. Like myself she was slightly demented and kept coming," Dick wrote. "She probably has no possessions, just memories and dreams ... I thought long and hard as she followed closely behind me for it's a long, lonely, cold journey ahead."

The wind came up and Dick eventually lost his companion in the swirling snow.

He wondered about her during the course of his travels and even wished from time to time for her company. Later in the deep silence after days of solitude he would write, "I should have brought the old woman with me; she looks better with each passing day ... She wanted to go back to the land where life was not easy but a happy one and like myself she must have loved the memories of a simple basic life. I should have checked on her but didn't. Now I wonder if she made it back to the village."

It was 1999 and Dick was seventy-two years old. Isabelle had passed away three years earlier in November 1996, just six months after his trek from Paulatuk to Kugluktuk (Coppermine). She had suffered first from breast cancer and then from heart disease. Her life had ebbed painfully to a close.

"Her family stood by her and watched her die each day but we had no faith in the doctors or the miracle drugs and were all devastated for months before and after she died," Dick wrote. "I would rather break my leg in a tide crack and die here than die the way she did."

The old woman following him out of Cambridge Bay reminded Dick of Isabelle's stubborn resolve to meet him on the Colorado River in 1949 even after he'd tried to send her home. Isabelle, too, had refused to take no for an answer. In the end their marriage had lasted forty-seven years.

"I am very much alone out here; no one comes this far. More alone than ever since Isabelle died," he commented during his trip from Kugluktuk to Cambridge Bay in 1997.

He was getting ever nearer to completing his course across the Northwest Passage. In the thousand miles between Kugluktuk and Repulse Bay he would meet up with his greatest challenges yet. In 1996 he traveled from Paulatuk to Kugluktuk, a distance of 475 miles, in forty-two days. A year later, in 1997, he trekked from Kugluktuk to Cambridge Bay, a distance of 240 miles, in twenty-five days. And in 1999, he would travel from Cambridge Bay to Repulse Bay in fifty-three days and come back in 2000 to complete the 220 miles he'd been forced to bypass because of poor traveling conditions.

By the time he completed his goal to travel the Northwest Passage and reach Repulse Bay, he was seventy-three years old and had travelled more than six thousand miles across the Arctic and sub-Arctic of Alaska and Canada.

BETWEEN PAULATUK AND KUGLUKTUK IN 1996, Dick decided to hire a local, Jonah Nakimayak, to take three bags of food and fuel to a DEW line site, two-hundred miles away. Jonah contracted as an inspector for the unmanned DEW site, traveling there three times a year to check on the facility.

Dick traveled through three major storms to reach the site and had just four days of food to spare when he arrived. He was exhausted. His air mattress had a leak and he'd been sleeping restlessly on the cold ground. It would be a relief to get out of the wind and cold for a time, make his repairs, and wait for Jonah to resupply his food. The radar site had a tower and building with a generator running. On the large steel door hung a sign: "No Trespassing." A ridiculous sign, Dick thought, since no one was around for hundreds of miles—and the door was unlocked.

"I opened the door and entered a small steel room with a 14-foot ceiling. The room was warm but very noisy, I decided to move in and repair my tent and Thermarest (air mattress)," Dick wrote.

Suddenly a telephone rang inside the building. Dick hesitated but then picked up the receiver.

"Who are you and what are you doing there?" the voice on the other end demanded. Surveillance cameras inside and outside of the building had alerted authorities in some faraway city of Dick's arrival.

"My name is Dick Griffith, I am cold, wet, hungry and I need to repair equipment. Jonah is going to meet me here on the 19th with supplies."

"How did you get there?"

"I walked."

There was a pause on the other end.

The voice then informed him that he could stay as long as he notified them by phone when he entered and left the premises. The voice also said if Dick had not picked up the ringing telephone, they would have sent a helicopter to investigate. An hour later, the phone rang again, informing him that Jonah was on his way.

Jonah arrived on a snowmachine the next day with two companions. Because of the remoteness of the site and for safety reasons, Jonah was required to travel with two additional snowmachines. Dick enjoyed the brief company of Jonah and his companions as they shared lunch together. Jonah was amused by the incident, having been called out early to reach the DEW site on Dick's behalf—a trip of four hundred miles round trip. It would be the last people that Dick would see for nearly three weeks.

In the span of seemingly endless miles, there were good days and bad. On bad days in the midst of a ferocious storm Dick wrote, "Twenty-four hours and still pinned down. I hate the Arctic!... I'm getting too old for this sort of stuff ... Most people my age goes south because they don't want to be old and cold at the same time."

On better days Dick would write, "This is an easy life; almost addictive. I lay in my warm tent all afternoon sleeping, reading and eating. In the tent I don't have to deal with the bright sun and wind. Tomorrow morning like every morning I get up before sunrise, drink several cups of coffee, eat cooked cereal with dried fruit and take off ... I'm not sure I ever want to leave the Arctic. I am glad that the people in the southern latitudes consider the Arctic to be cold, dangerous and daunting, an immense place of bleak and barren land bordered by an ice choked sea."

His solitude over the miles eventually became a sanctuary. The longer he traveled alone, the more comfortable he became as he folded himself into the broad landscape and settled into deep silence.

"Very quiet today," he wrote. "I stood five minutes in my ski tracks hoping to hear some sound; nothing but overpowering silence. I stopped another time to listen and I heard the crunching noise of caribou marching single file to the north. They were too far away to see but close enough to hear."

He was interrupted once by men on snowmachines who roared into his camp and stopped to talk. They left him with extra food and warned him yet

Camped on sea ice. Many open leads in this area made for perilous travel.

again about polar bears. As they left, Dick had the disgruntled sense of having been intruded upon.

"It's strange but I feel that these four Natives invaded my space. I am getting very possessive; is this my country?" he wondered.

HE SUFFERED A SERIOUS ACCIDENT at the age of seventy on his 1997 trek between Kugluktuk and Cambridge Bay. He was skiing across a frozen lake, scoured smooth by relentless wind. The wind had deposited snow into drifts that lay in rigid creases across the lake. Dick used his ski poles to push himself across the ice. At one point, the wind pushed his sled into a snow drift, pulling him off balance. He stumbled headfirst onto the ice, striking his head. The blow knocked him unconscious.

Winter in the Arctic conspires to stop movement. The low-growing foliage of the tundra lays buried. Water stops flowing. Blood freezes. The only movements on the landscape are those of living things—caribou, polar bear, fox, or a man—beings whose heart and muscle push back against natural forces that could quickly render life to a small frozen mound on the landscape.

When Dick came to, he lay in a pool of blood, some of it already frozen. The gash on his forehead had stopped bleeding but he was cold. The appeal of lying down and sleeping was nearly overwhelming. It was too cold and windy to set up camp on the lake. He needed to move. So he picked himself up and continued on the trail, not stopping until his own body generated the warmth he needed to stay upright.

He once told Gordy Vernon, a fellow competitor in the Alaska Mountain Wilderness Classic race, "Life is like a bicycle. When you stop moving, you tip over."

That evening in camp, he burned a board made of red oak that he'd found on the frozen beach –the remains of a broken vessel from some distant port. In the glow of his wood-burning stove, he wrote, "I am salvaging someone's disaster." The irony was not lost on him as he considered the thin margin by which he'd missed his own demise that day.

Someone once told him that he was getting so far north and east that he would soon fall off the edge. "She's right. I am on the edge—something I would never admit to my friends or even myself. I still have a nasty gash across my forehead to remind me. Some days I question my sanity and my aloneness. I cannot accept a life—one that holds onto handrails."

ARCTIC WILDLIFE OFFERED DIVERSION, challenges, and at times, comic relief. Depending on the slant of light, herds of migrating caribou sometimes appeared as "brown phantoms floating in the mist." He saw wolf tracks, snowy owls, and for the first time, came across muskox.

Fox continued to plague him. One came into camp and chewed on his ski pole, severing the leather wrist strap. The fox also chewed off a plastic buckle and carried the pole fifty feet away before dropping it in the snow. Another time a fox bit a hole in one of the fuel cans and Dick lost a portion of white gas for his stove. Curious and unafraid, one fox even poked his head inside Dick's tent. He threw a hatchet at it.

"I hate fox," Dick wrote. "I can't leave anything outside my tent. Last night they circled my tent for hours."

Black seals, who lay sunning themselves on the ice, slipped into the water when he passed. One evening two ravens attacked his tent with raucous croaks.

"I don't know what their problem was," Dick wrote.

As he set up his tent in a wind storm one evening, he looked up to see a weasel pass his camp traveling at an unbelievable speed—maybe forty miles an hour. The creature had devised a way of bouncing off the hard-packed snow and letting the wind lift and carry him airborne, one enormous leap after the next. Adaptation. It is one quality common to all life in the Arctic and the little fellow had found an entertaining way to travel.

DURING THESE TREKS DICK BEGAN TO GROW accustomed to the movement of sea ice as winter gave way to spring. The ice popped and groaned as cracks opened in some places and in other places pushed up into icy pressure ridges. In earlier treks, the noise of the ice as it gave way to tides and spring weather had been unnerving. But Dick had begun to shrug off the movement as something as commonplace as the changing seasons.

"I no longer pay any attention to movement under my tent. The sea ice, this time of year, is a large floating mattress," he wrote.

Tide cracks still made travel problematic however. Filled with snow, they were often undetectable until a ski or boot gave way to the softer snow in the gap. Skis help bridge the cracks, but stumbling was still unavoidable and made travel exhausting. In one exasperated journal entry he wrote, "I hope that I stop in Hudson Bay and don't decide to continue the next season towards Baffin Island and Greenland."

As disgruntled and discouraged as he sometimes felt, Dick acknowledged he was in a place as mystical as it was brutal. He described the lure of the Arctic: "The Arctic's magnetism has many elements: It is finding wood when Natives have often told me that there is none... It is the sight of a band of caribou migrating specter like in the blowing snow. It is the thrill of surviving yet another big blow ... It is seeing a raven make artistic patterns in the snow, alternating dipping the left wing then the right wing for several hundred yards. It is the austere beauty—often a landscape that can be described as bleak or beautiful depending on the weather and the mood."

It seemed the closer he neared his destination, the more formidable the challenges. In the 1999 trip from Cambridge Bay, he had several "come and get me" days. He had always scoffed at the notion of radios to call for help in an emergency. Yet he admitted on this trip that if he'd had one he would have used it.

One day, he exited the tent, leaving the door open. The wind lifted the tent and sent it tumbling. Dick tackled it before it got away, but broke a pole and tore the fabric. Later he lost his saw and had to retrace his steps to find it. "If someone were to pay me a million dollars I would not do this. My pockets are filled with drifting snow. Even my compass is encased in ice. My white haired ivory troll is lost on my sled buried under snow. It is a world without a feature, an empty sky, and empty earth, front and back."

That night the wind pummeled his camp from all directions and as he tried to align and then re-align his tent with the wind, another tent pole broke. He had a bad batch of fuel and had trouble keeping the gas stove burning. The stove caught fire twice as he tried to melt snow and cook dinner. Eventually he collapsed the tent over his sleeping bag and went to bed wearing his wet clothes. "It seems I am often on the ragged edge ... Life is fragile, nobody here just me. I have to be focused just to maintain control."

EARLY ONE MORNING HE WOKE TO THE SOUND of crunching snow. The shadow of a polar bear moved across the wall of his tent. He'd often wondered how many polar bear came into his camp at night without his knowing. Sometimes he saw tracks, but often the ice was hard and if bears traveled past, they came and went in silence. But this one was close. Too close.

He let out a yell and charged outside to run the bear off. He grabbed a ski and beat it on his sled to make noise. The bear moved away. When Dick returned to his tent, he discovered a slash in the tent wall. The bear's claws had missed his sleeping bag by four inches. He'd slept right through it.

His hope that the bear would not return was short-lived. After making a quick breakfast, Dick looked outside the tent and saw the bear padding back into camp. This time the bear was not so easily dissuaded. Instead of running away when Dick yelled, it sauntered sideways, still coming, watching Dick from the corner of its eyes. The look the bear gave him raised the hair on the back of his neck.

Dick swiftly broke camp, yelling at the bear as he did. He then took all of the medicine he'd brought—twenty Tylenol and ten Advil tablets—and embedded them into boiled salmon strips. As he left camp he dropped the morsels on the trail.

Zoologist Jordan Schaul, who holds a PhD in conservation and veterinary preventive medicine and serves as a research scientist at the University of Alaska, Fairbanks Institute of Arctic Biology, explained the pills probably did not harm the bear. "Some of the milder side effects of these drugs include dizziness and diarrhea, but neither would likely deter a bear from pursuing a person," he explained. "It was a good move on Dick's part. The medicine might have made the bear feel 'off' enough to decide to take a nap."

That was precisely the gamble Dick was counting on. He didn't have many options. He'd left behind the flare gun and firecrackers he'd taken along during his earlier travels across Alaska. Firearms of any sort were illegal to transport into and out of Canada without special permits and he just hadn't bothered.

The bear followed him at a distance. Dick skied across the snow and ice, looking over his shoulder, gauging the distance between himself and the bear—measuring whether it was moving closer or staying farther behind. Dick knew whatever the distance, in a matter of seconds the bear could be on top of him.

"My Grandmother taught me the Lord's Prayer before I had entered school," Dick wrote. "We said it together every night when I visited her house." He had mostly forgotten the prayer, but today with a polar bear following close on his heels, he needed all the help he could get.

After several hours of following Dick, the bear finally disappeared.

Dick doesn't consider himself a thrill seeker and those who know him well agree with that assessment. Bob Kaufman, who met Dick in 1988 during his rookie run of the Alaska Mountain Wilderness Classic, describes risk as "the interface of danger and one's contingency plan in the face of it." He sees Dick as someone who knew the danger and then prepared for it.

Storms were an exponentially greater threat than polar bears. Dick's decision not to bring along a firearm allowed him to bring more food, which extended his range and allowed him to bunker in for longer periods during storms. In nearly six thousand miles of travel, his encounters with polar bears were—with this exception—rarely cause for alarm.

That night he wrote, "The experience was unnerving. I now understand why Isabelle carried a $200,000 policy for 40 years in the event that I should meet an accidental death or most likely just disappear ... All my life I avoided the 'what ifs' especially those made by friends, family and parents. The 'what ifs' impede moving forward and prevent one from taking risks."

Following the bear encounter, he hoped to camp at the DEW line site near the center of Jenny Lind Island. He looked forward to seeking shelter indoors to dry out and repair his gear. He arrived at the site and shoveled snow from the doors but once he entered, buzzers went off indicating carbon monoxide. The smell of fumes was overwhelming and Dick left disappointed. From there he headed across sea ice toward King William Island. But then he came to a wall of jumbled pack ice that extended as far as he could see. Massive blocks of ice stood on end as high as ten feet.

"I don't know why I should expect easy going when this area is well known for high winds," he wrote. "It is the same sea that crushed Franklin's two ships ... I have to constantly remind myself that the forces of nature are not to be taken lightly."

The back-breaking work of getting through the pressure ridges slowed his rate of travel to a crawl. It took a full day to travel two miles. At this rate his food would not last. He had a bad batch of fuel, which meant it, too, would run out, and he needed to melt water for drinking and cooking.

For the first time, in the middle of an already extended trip, he decided to turn around.

"It was one of those times when one should not confuse ambition with reality," he noted.

On his way back—after seven days of backtracking –he met up with a polar bear hunter who gave him a ride on his snowmachine back to Cambridge Bay.

Jenny Lind Island where poor conditions forced Dick to turn back.

THAT, HOWEVER, WAS NOT THE END OF THE TRIP. Rather than go home, Dick took a flight from Cambridge Bay to the village of Gjoa Haven, located on the south end of King William Island. He took time there to rest and eat. As his strength returned, so did his determination.

"I find my physical strength has not diminished very much in old age. I am concerned if I can always handle the mental part of the Arctic ... Sometimes I am nonchalant about an incident that should require focus. Maybe that's good and maybe not so good. I vacillate from extreme caution to carelessness. If I were cautious I would not be out here but home with my peer group having heart attacks and prostate operations."

As Dick neared civilization, one group of snowmachine travelers after the next stopped to talk and ask questions. How far had he come? How long did it take? How old was he?

He was repeatedly asked one question that always amused him. "My clothes have many holes, my mukluks have holes big enough to expose socks, my white hair is long and scraggly my beard is unkempt and my nose has an ugly scab," he wrote. "And they still want to know my marital status."

His last day on the trail before reaching Repulse Bay was a calm and sunny Sunday. The trail passed between granite knifelike ridges. Small bands of caribou crossed in front of him. A fox brayed from a nearby ridge. Spring had arrived and baby Arctic hares scrambled in front of him.

Granite Hills. Dick was off-course here and Native snowmachiners made a trail for him to follow toward Repulse Bay.

These were the days when the appeal of the Arctic struck a deep chord in Dick. The rewards she parceled out bordered on the mystical. Far removed from the churn of civilization, with a sparse and fierce beauty, it was a place that suffused Dick with wonder and life. There were more difficult days than easy ones by far. Yet as he traveled the final miles of this trek, he knew he would miss the Arctic. Even the days of tempest.

"I have desperately tried to absorb this hostile landscape, but instead I have found that I have been absorbed," he wrote.

Fifty-three days and 550 miles after leaving Cambridge Bay, Dick entered Repulse Bay at the north end of Hudson Bay. Through distant canyons and endless ice, across a lifetime of miles and memories, he had arrived at the farthest eastern point that he would travel in the Arctic.

The entire village turned out for a party with cake and coffee to celebrate his arrival. Everyone signed his sled.

Years earlier as he passed through Fairbanks, he had seen words on a poster from author Lincoln Tritt of Arctic Village that resonated.

I have traveled the land.
I have seen the world.
I have heard it all.
The questions of my childhood,
I have answered.
The things I have dreamed of
I have done.
But when I look into the eyes of an elder
I have not done enough.

Dick would return the following year in 2000 at the age of seventy-three to complete the 220 miles he'd bypassed on this leg of the journey. And even then, it wasn't quite enough.

Chapter 17

The Last One

I am neither explorer nor discoverer; I am just a traveler, just passing through.
—Dick Griffith

DICK'S JOURNAL ENTRIES IN 2000, as he completed the final 220 miles of the Northwest Passage between Cambridge and Gjoa Haven, demonstrated his tenacity in spite of his age and circumstances that nearly made this trip his last one.

It was Easter Sunday when he left Cambridge Bay, and Dick was already frustrated by the delays to get on the trail. His clothing and gear had not yet arrived in the mail and then he'd had trouble rounding up gas for a snow-machine ride to Sturt Point where he would begin his trek. He had already twice crossed this section of the trek—once going out and again when he had to turn back because of bad trail conditions. This, the third time, he was determined to finish crossing the sea ice–first to Jenny Lind Island and then on to Gjoa Haven. Ice conditions were better than the previous year, but the whiteout weather was disorienting.

"No ground surface, no horizon and no sky; only my ski tips," he wrote. "Sometimes when I stopped I became so disoriented that I would tip over because there was no reference point."

He remembered the close calls of his previous trip—the polar bear encounter, the fall on his head, the broken tent in a storm. He did not care to repeat them. "I have a life wish, not a death wish," he said. But he seemed to be brushing ever closer to disaster.

Dick noted that at age seventy-three he was just not as strong as he'd once been. "People want to live longer but they detest getting older," he reflected. Even with the creeping limitations of his advancing years, he still embraced adventure. "I can live with ageism, these are the best years; choose what you want and do it."

Thinking and dreaming as he made his way across sea ice and snow to complete the 220 miles he'd had to bypass the year before, he reflected, "Out here there are no external distractions, only the wind whipping my tent ... Thoughts run deep. Last year I said I would never do this again because I no longer had to prove anything to anyone. I have decided to remove 'never' and 'forever' from my vocabulary."

But it was not to be an easy trip. One morning as he cooked breakfast in his tent, he began to feel off. The feeling progressed to nausea and shortness of breath. He stumbled out of the tent to vomit. His breath came in short jagged breaths. In the enclosed space of his tent, with inadequate ventilation, he was slowly being asphyxiated by carbon monoxide. The fresh air helped. But he wondered how he would manage to go on.

"It is one of those times that I wish I had one of these 'come and get me' radios," he wrote. It turns out the mosquito netting on the tent had frosted over and stopped the flow of fresh air into the tent. "Too many near misses; one of these days it will be a full miss! It's no longer a matter of if but when," he wrote.

It took him several hours on the trail to regain his bearings. His breathing was better but his legs were still weak. Even so, by the time he reached the DEW site on Jenny Lind Island, he decided he was well enough to continue the trek. He passed by the DEW site phone that earlier in the day had been the focus of his travel. Although he said he had nothing to prove, the fact was he still wanted to claim a traverse of the North West passage—*all of it*.

Warm spring weather brought rain, which created a slick glaze of ice over the snow. The ice forced him to put away his skis—there was not enough traction to pull the sled. Without skis to bridge the hidden tide cracks, he often fell. During one fall, he badly wrenched his knee. When he woke up the next morning it was too swollen to bend.

"The sea ice is slick and flat enough that I could make 15-20 miles a day if I could see where I was going and where to place my feet. I have black and blue bruises and my knee does not improve," he wrote. This knee injury would never heal properly and several years later—at the age of eighty-one and after nearly six thousand miles of travel—Dick required surgery for a full knee-replacement.

The fog set in and in exasperation he wrote, "I could do no worse traveling in the dark with a flashlight and compass."

Dick's injured knee slowed his progress toward Gjoa Haven and the lack of a horizon to aim for was disorienting and discouraging. Yet following the monotony of the gray days, his dreams at night were—as usual throughout his Arctic travels—vivid and colorful.

"Last night I was a yellow butterfly in a colorful market place in Asia," he wrote. As usual, he also spent time reading. On this trip he had brought along *The Cider House Rules* by John Irving, *The Poisonwood Bible* by Barbara Kingsolver, and *The Tibetan Book of Living and Dying* by Sogyal Rinpoche.

On May 10, 2000, Dick stepped off of the sea ice onto the gravel beach on the western side of King William Island. This was hallowed ground to him. It was the crossroads of several early, sometimes ill-fated expeditions—an island many explorers considered the loneliest place on earth.

One-hundred-forty-one years ago nearly to the day—and close to where Dick now stood—Lieutenant William Robert Hobson made the discovery of a boat with two skeletons from the Franklin expedition. Inside the boat were two loaded guns and other relics including chocolate and tea. Farther north, the Greely Expedition had also suffered a tragic end. Only six men of twenty-six had survived three years of being marooned in the sea ice—a tragic saga of shipwreck, mutiny, and cannibalism.

That night, Dick had the most vivid dream of his Arctic experience.

"In my dream I was in a white canvas wall tent on a beach similar to the one I crossed yesterday. My black sleeping bag was lying on the coarse gravel inside the tent and I was lying in the bag. I could also see surroundings outside for there was a gentle breeze coming off the blue ocean and there was no ice," he wrote. "A very short emaciated man appeared in the doorway of the tent. His red eyes were deep set, cheekbones protruded, lips blue and puffy and he had a full black beard. He tried to tell me something but nothing was audible. The most remarkable thing about the apparition was his dress. He wore a faded blue coat with a double row of brass buttons, probably a uniform. His black cap had a large visor."

Dick woke with a start and could not sleep the rest of the night. "I have read so much about the Franklin tragedy that the victims/ghosts have gained access to my dreams."

Because of warmer spring weather, Dick had begun traveling early in the morning while the snow and ice were still firm. Packing up camp in the dark at 2:00 a.m., he watched northern lights shimmer across the night sky. Clouds had now given way to clear skies—a welcome change from the gray, featureless fog. The landscape of King William Island lay stark before him. He saw muskox tracks but otherwise the rolling hills seemed nearly devoid of life. No ravens or caribou or Arctic hares. Just foxes—always there were foxes.

As he neared Gjoa Haven, four snowmachines pulling sleds caught up with him and stopped. He had not seen any sign of humans for days, and among the group of travelers was David Amerginik, the man who had ferried Dick by snowmachine to his starting point for this trek.

"I don't think that he thought that I would ever make it," Dick wrote. "They were all overjoyed that I had made it and we celebrated by drinking hot coffee out of their thermos. We compared notes on the crossing— they had to jump three open leads by going very fast on their powerful machines. They can easily cross a lead that is five feet (across). I have to follow the lead, sometimes for miles, until it becomes narrow enough to jump across."

The night before reaching Gjoa Haven, which lay 155 miles north of the Arctic Circle, Dick took inventory of his travels. On this trek he had traveled twenty-three days and made 220 miles.

"It took seven seasons to travel from Barrow to Hudson Bay, which involved 2665 miles and 229 days," he wrote. "If the trip between Unalakleet and Barrow were included it would add another 900 miles and 63 days. There are over several thousand more Arctic miles and days of travel that could be added to the above list. Unlike present day expeditions in the Arctic, I have got by without a satellite telephone, 'come and get me' radio, rifle, companions and sponsors. The only piece of modern technology I have used is the GPS, which saved me an enormous amount of time and miles."

Dick arrived in Gjoa Haven before the village was awake. The shush of his skis was the only sound on a quiet empty street. He had now completed the Northwest Passage. There were no waving flags or cheering fans or clanging bells. No wreaths of roses or trophies or slaps on the back. Just the knowledge that he had done what he had long ago set his mind to doing.

He went to the hotel, checked in, and ordered a hot breakfast.

As always, his mind was moving forward to the next place. He could reach Baffin Island from here. After all, it was just a few hundred miles to the northeast. But that night as he lay down on a real bed rather than the cold hard sea ice, he knew that this was it—the last one. While the spirit might be willing, at the age of seventy-three, his body was telling him that his Arctic travels were over.

Besides, there were still other things left to do.

In 2003, at age seventy-six, Dick hiked with friends from Thistle Cove near Gustavus to Yakutat, Alaska, a distance of 170 miles along Alaska's scenic southeastern coastline. Along the way the group came across LaPerouse Glacier, which spilled into the ocean and blocked their planned route to cross along the beach. The group considered their options. Even at low tide, calving icebergs made it impossible to travel by packraft around the toe of the glacier. Going back would mean a "rescue" pickup by boat or bush plane, since they had been delivered by boat to Thistle Cove to begin their trek. In the end, the group decided to try and carefully pick their way across the glacier. They had no crampons, ice axes, or ropes—not even the most minimal gear to travel safely across a crevasse-ridden glacier. But they went anyway, following each canyon of ice to its narrowest slot and then jumping across.

"We were all aware that if any of us had fallen in a crevasse we would have had to leave them there. We had no rope for retrieving," Dick recalled.

Paul Barnes, Gustavus resident, helps Kathy Lochman and Judy Streveler across a 100-foot deep crevasse. Paul led the coastal trip. (Below) A very careful crossing.

It took them hours to carefully crisscross the glacier's deeply cracked ice. Along the way, Dick found the wreckage of a small airplane. Many airplanes have gone down in Alaska and never been found. Over the years, Dick lost twenty friends to various small airplane accidents. In all adventures lay reminders of the grim consequences of even a small mistake.

Steve Wilson, one of the hiking party, took several pieces of airplane debris and tied them onto his backpack. Maybe these relics could offer authorities clues to a cold case disappearance. Within two years of picking up this debris, Steve and Eric Lochmen— the husband of Kathy Streveler who was along on this hiking trip—would be killed in a small airplane crash in the Brooks Range.

That night around the campfire the group was feeling elated at their successful glacier crossing, but Dick was quick to point out, "We considered ourselves heroes but had we had an accident we would have been labeled inexperienced fools by the public."

Once again, he counted himself lucky.

Two years later, in 2005, Dick and his good friend Jerry Dixon skied from McGrath to Kaltag along a 135-mile section of the Iditarod trail. They helped set up checkpoints for the race at the onset of their trek and then watched as mushers and dogs came through. Dick and Jerry had a history of traveling the backcountry together. They ran several Mountain Wilderness Classic races together and had trekked in seven of Alaska's mountain ranges over the years.

"I have a hard time at my hard-earned 78 years getting up the hills," Dick wrote. "To speed things up Jerry often skis back down the hills and pulls up my sled." Dick eventually took off his skis and hiked the tough terrain. Jerry returned home after two weeks of travel while Dick continued on until he reached Kaltag.

By this time Patricia Jordan had become Dick's partner and new "mate" in life. They had met in 2001 as volunteers at the Eagle River Nature Center. Patricia appreciated Dick's achievements, understood his need for wilderness travel, and looked after him to the extent that Dick would allow. On this Iditarod trek, Dick confessed that age was taking its toll.

Jerry Dixon leads the way on the Iditarod Trail.

"Last summer [when] I had chest pains, Patricia made me go to a doctor. The doctor would not let me out of his office until I agreed to go to the hospital. They put a stent in me," he wrote. "Now I am on six different pills and I am a person who shunned [even] vitamins ... Getting old is a strange and interesting experience."

FROM MAY 1 TO OCTOBER 1 EVERY YEAR, Dick still sleeps in a tent on the hillside of his Anchorage home. Over the years he has occasionally been written about in the *Anchorage Daily News*, *We Alaskans*, and the *Anchorage Press*. His comings and goings have taken place largely unnoticed, which is fine by him.

Whatever legend he would create was noted mostly by those who bore witness to his quiet determination to put one step in front of the other. If his legacy remains "two thin lines" in the blowing snow, it is only because he refused to join the ranks of explorers and adventurers who were as adept at self-aggrandizement as they were at achieving their wilderness exploits.

Dick's real motivation, one that perplexed even him at times, lay more in a desire to live fully awake, to test the possibilities of human endurance; and to spend time with the great love of his life—the wilderness.

Dick noted that author Jack London did not necessarily live up to the ideals he espoused in print, but he fully agreed with London's words:

> *I would rather be ashes than dust, I would rather that my spark should burn out in a brilliant blaze than it should be stifled by dry rot. I would rather be a superb meteor, every atom of me in magnificent glow, than a sleepy and permanent planet. The proper function of a man is to live, not exist. I shall not waste my days trying to prolong them.*

At the writing of this chapter, at age eighty-four, Dick is threading the walls of the Grand Canyon, rafting the white water of the Colorado River. Not many tourists travel the river this time of year because temperatures dip below freezing at night.

Dick likes it that way—just he and a few friends sleeping under the stars.

Epilogue
Return to Raven Cabin

Biographies are but the clothes and buttons of the man.
The biography of the man himself cannot be written.
—Mark Twain

IN THE MONTHS THAT DICK AND I met to write his biography, he never once asked to read the manuscript; he came only to answer my questions and often just to visit. Sometimes he was the interviewer—he wanted to know about my life, what I did for a "day job." One day he brought me a ticket to the Nenana Ice Classic, a guessing pool of when the ice would go out on Alaska's Nenana River every year. After all, he figured I wasn't going to get rich writing books.

The spring before I started writing Dick's story, I'd gone looking for Raven Cabin. I knew it wasn't easy to find. One of the first rules, written in clear language in the diary, was not to tell others its location. It was a secret held by backcountry travelers who knew Dick, knew his friends, or knew friends of friends. Occasionally a bear hunter stumbled upon it.

Knowing I might not find it, I packed my tent along for the trip and headed from the Eagle River Nature Center toward the glaciers at the far end of the valley. I'd hiked Crow Pass several times—it is the main trail through Eagle River Valley to Girdwood—and the namesake of the twenty-five-mile Crow Pass mountain race and Dick's wilderness playground. I passed by sheer rock faces, deep gorges, and waterfalls that tumbled from steep mountain cliffs. It was still spring and the waters of Eagle River ran clear. Within weeks, warm weather would begin melting the glacier and soon the river would churn in a torrent of gray silt. At a quiet bend in the river, I sat on the gravel bank, leaned against my pack, closed my eyes. The summer sun warmed my face. More than an hour later, I woke to a pair of harlequin ducks preening and splashing less than ten yards from where I sat. Even if I didn't find the cabin, the trip was worth it just for this.

After hiking ten miles and taking several bushwhacking forays along various creeks, I was tired. As the cool night air settled in on the valley, I decided to set up my tent and call it a night. I knew the cabin had to be nearby. The next morning, I woke early and took a walk. When I looked across the river I saw a lone white mountain goat carefully making its way down a steep embankment. The animal went down to the water and drank. Then it turned around and clattered back up the rock face. Delighted by what the wilderness unexpectedly offers up, I couldn't help thinking how Dick could count himself among Alaska's more enigmatic inhabitants—the lone polar bear, the white mountain goat, a Dall ram—all white-haired and most at home in the back country. I made coffee and then took one more look around for the cabin. Dick would be happy to know that Raven Cabin was still as well-hidden as ever.

After I told him about my search, he said, "We should take your horses back there and I'll show you where it is."

I hesitated for a number of reasons. For one thing, horses were not allowed in that area of the state park. The other was that my horses had been known to spook, jumping sideways at something scary or unfamiliar on the trail. And I remembered that the last time I got dumped by a horse, it hurt.

"I don't know," I said. "It would sure ruin someone's day to come off a horse on the trail out there."

"Well it might ruin yours," Dick said firmly, "because you'd be the one coming off, not me."

I laughed, seeing as how he'd called me on my attempt at diplomacy. Had I not just implied he was too old and fragile for the trip? Then I remembered his words. "Show me a man afraid to die and I'll show you a man afraid to live."

We finally came up with a plan. I would borrow some mountain-savvy horses from a friend and invite Bill Sullivan to come along. A superb horseman, Bill would be able to help if anything went awry. He would bring his own young horse, Sunny, and make it a training ride through terrain that was new to both of them.

We chose to go late in September when the summer's glacial runoff had subsided to a clear stream. We went during the middle of the week, lessening our chances of meeting hikers on the trail. Asta Sturgis, director of the Eagle River Nature Center, talked to the park superintendent, explaining the circumstances of our ride. Meanwhile I applied for a special-use permit to ride horses in this area of Chugach State Park.

Dick had no use for such formalities, so I didn't mention the permit— he's never had a permit to travel the back country in all his life—he wasn't about to start now. Besides, this trail had once been used by horses and dog teams as a mail route between the seaport town of Seward and the goldfields of Iditarod and then on to Nome. Over the years Dick had even found draft-size horseshoes along the trail. Why people sitting in offices in Anchorage could arbitrarily say "no" to using horses on a trail that historically had used them seemed ludicrous. Just to prove his point, years earlier, Dick had taken a couple of friends and their horses over Crow Pass, across Raven Glacier, and down into Eagle River Valley. Dick's relationship with the park officials was prickly to say the least.

The day of our ride, Dick showed up in a top hat, wearing tennis shoes and sweat pants. Not exactly orthodox riding wear, but comfortable. We loaded the pack horse with feed and some gear. Everything Dick needed was already at the cabin where he'd left it. Sleeping bag, hatchet, coffee pot, dishes.

The day sparkled like a fall gem. Leaves on the birch trees shimmered vibrant yellow. The sky was a deep cloudless dome of blue. The air smelled of fermenting cranberries and crisp sunshine. After weeks of rain, Alaska's moody weather chose a day of benevolence. We rode the trail three miles to Echo Bend and then followed the river off-trail upstream—which meant multiple river crossings for the horses.

Dick rode Rocky, a lanky black quarter horse. I rode a big paint named Sako and ponied the pack horse, Bodacious, leading him by a rope until we

reached the river. Once we got to the river, I let the pack horse go, knowing he would follow the rest of the herd. Bill brought up the rear and gazed with wonder at the scenery. Dick had traveled this valley hundreds of times. I'd gone maybe a dozen times altogether. Seeing it from the middle of the river—Icicle Creek, Heritage Falls, Twin Falls—rather than the wooded trail in the shadow of the mountain, gave the place a vaulted, almost hallowed feel.

Dick explained how the white specks we saw on high mountain meadows and cliffs were mostly sheep on one side of the river and goats on the other. He said there were no bears in the area. Bill and I looked at each other. The riverbank looked like a freeway of bear traffic, one large paw print after the next. Had he just said this to reassure us? Or tease us? Mostly we rode in silence, listening to the clop of hooves and the murmur of water as it tumbled downstream. I couldn't help but wonder what was going through Dick's mind. He had come to an age where he was saying his goodbyes to some things he'd taken for granted most of his life. His knee-replacement two years earlier had allowed him to walk pain-free, but it did not hold up well over rough terrain. What was it like for him not to be able to travel the distances he once had?

"The best thing about getting old is that it doesn't last very long," was all he had to say about that. He never complained.

Neither Bill nor I saw it at first, it blended so well with its surroundings. But less than two hundred yards from the place where I'd camped the summer before, through a thick stand of cottonwood and spruce trees, sat the tiny Raven Cabin. I had been so close! Dick got off his horse and moved stiffly for the first few steps. We had been riding for four hours. Not only did the man have an artificial knee, he had no rear end for sitting on the hard seat of the saddle.

Bill and I took the horses and found places to tie them while Dick opened the cabin. It was a familiar ritual. First he removed the wooden covers from the windows. These were bear shutters, built by Dick, with nails jutting outward to discourage curious paws. Then he opened up the door and went inside.

Meanwhile, Bill and I removed saddles and packs and settled the horses. We were all so busy with our tasks that at one point I looked up and noticed that Dick was nowhere to be found. I looked inside the one-room cabin and then around outside.

"Do you know where Dick went?" I asked.

Bill shook his head. "No."

I walked behind the cabin and found the outhouse. No sign of him. Where could he have gone? Bill stopped what he was doing; should we go look for him? Then through the alders I saw the white shock of Dick's hair moving toward us. He appeared from the woods carrying two metal pails full of water. After four hours in the saddle, he had hiked a quarter mile down to the creek to supply water for the cabin.

Dick delivered the pails inside and then came out and started splitting kindling while Bill and I rationed grain into the horses' feed bags. By

the time we'd fed them and put our gear in order, Dick had a fire crackling in the wood stove.

While I made dinner, Bill broke out the Crown Royal and Dick grabbed a couple of coffee mugs. Bill jokingly asked if I'd brought along some Sprite for his whiskey. "That's okay, it'll be just fine with some water," he teased.

"Why the hell would you water down good whiskey?" Dick said. He reached out his empty mug. "Give it to me straight."

Bill and Dick sat on the bed as a debate ensued. I offered to settle the matter with a taste test. After sipping a little from each cup I declared that drinking it straight tasted better—even if it did burn going down.

After dinner, Dick offered to show us an old bridge that spanned Raven Creek. As we left the cabin, Dick brought out the pot of leftover spaghetti noodles to feed to the horses. We doubted the horses would eat it.

"Why not?" Dick demanded. "My horses would eat anything I gave them."

He told stories about his sheepherding days in Wyoming. Our horses were coddled. All of the horses turned their noses up at the noodles except the pack horse, who happily slurped up a surprise ration of processed grain. "Now there's a good horse," Dick said.

The bridge was half a mile away over uneven ground, but Dick forged the way without hesitation. The bridge was in rough shape; Dick said the bears had eaten the handrails because they liked the taste of creosote. On the hike back, Dick put me in front of the line and told me to find our way back to the cabin.

When I turned into the woods at the right place, he said, "Good."

The evening air was growing cooler and Dick went inside and grabbed his sleeping bag.

"Real horsemen sleep outside on their saddle blankets," he said. Then he proceeded to lay saddle pads on the ground to make his bed. Bill and I protested vigorously. It might be cozy, but there was plenty of room for all of us inside the cabin. There was no need for anyone to sleep outside.

Dick would have none of it.

"The cabin is for the guests," he said. And that was that. Before going outside for the night, Dick threw a few more logs into the stove. Then he nodded at me with amusement. "If it gets too rough in here, you can come outside."

I do believe the joke was on us—the wood stove belted out heat that made the inside of the cabin like a sauna. We propped the door open and lay on top of our sleeping bags. Then we each drifted off to sleep to the scent of wood smoke and the quiet nicker of horses.

In the dark of night, I woke to the sound of a heavy footfall outside the cabin window. Startled, at first I thought a moose was walking through camp. But a moose in close proximity would have stirred the horses up. One of the horses must have gotten loose. Then I thought of Dick lying on the ground outside. I bolted out of bed, grabbing the nearest headlamp within reach. There, wandering around like a white ghost in the night was the pack horse. Dick was up on one elbow looking at the animal which stood just feet away.

"He was nuzzling my head," Dick said. "Guess he was looking for more spaghetti."

I laughed and tied the horse back up again. Bill met me at the cabin door as I went back into the cabin. "Have you seen my headlamp?" he said. Turns out I'd grabbed his headlamp instead of mine. With lights off now, we looked up and saw a velvet sky awash with stars. Dick burrowed deeper into his bag.

Later in the night we were awakened by the howl of coyotes. One of them seemed just yards from the cabin as they talked to each other across the river valley. It was not the normal puppylike yapping, but rather a plaintive yowl unlike anything we'd heard before. This was not only coyote but also wolf country and I thought about Dick's dogs that had been killed by wolves out here all those years ago. Such a savage and beautiful place.

In the morning, we ate a hearty breakfast and talked more about the people who built the cabin in the 1950s and rebuilt it in the 1970s. We talked about Dick's experiences with wolves and bears. He also told us about a pesky weasel that had made its home under the floorboards of the cabin. Mostly Dick and Bill gave each other grief.

"Creamer? In your coffee?" Dick scoffed at the cowboy. Then reaching out with his cup, he said, "Give it to me straight."

Leisurely, we got ready to go. Dick did the dishes while Bill and I saddled up horses. We talked about coming back and staying a couple of days next time. Dick wanted to take us to Heidi's Knob and show us where the old Iditarod road house had once stood. As Dick fastened the bear shutters back on the windows, I couldn't help consider the passage of time. I hoped Dick's cabin would be standing long after all of us were gone.

The horses stepped lively on their way back. We weren't very far down the trail when Dick stopped his horse and nodded his head towards something downstream.

"Bears."

We looked and saw two grizzlies 150 yards away. Then they stood up, shoulder to shoulder, and looked at us. One of the bears was a honey brown, the other the color of cocoa. They dropped down on all fours, seeming to confer with one another. Then the Brothers Ursus stood up and looked at us again. The horses stood at rapt attention. Then the twosome dropped back down and began loping across the river, away from us, looking over their shoulders as they ran.

"Probably two-year-olds," Dick said. "And probably from two different fathers considering their coloring."

We were all elated to see these grizzlies—a wonder of the wilderness that never grows old.

The bear sighting taught me that better photos could be taken if I got off my fidgeting horse. And so I found myself mounting and dismounting to get better shots. At one point, I fumbled and dropped Sako's reins. The horse took full advantage of the situation and left me on the ground while he followed the pack horse, who was trotting at liberty ahead of us. Both horses seemed determined to get home sooner rather than later. I sighed. It might be a long walk back to the trailhead, especially with the number of times we still had left to cross the river. I jogged toward the horses who conveniently trotted just ahead of me and out of reach. Bill sat on his young horse and considered the situation. Rather than try to chase the horses down, he suggested that he and Dick ride back toward the cabin. Most likely the two wayward horses would turn around and come to us. Sure enough, Sako and the pack horse turned around and were quickly back in hand.

Along the last bend in the river before we moved back onto the wooded trail, we came across a pile of driftwood. Tangled near the top lay the bleached antlers of a moose still attached to its white skull. Dick suggested it may have been a wolf kill from the previous winter. Just as the young bears reminded us of the full measure of life in the wilderness, the antlers were a reminder that death could come hard and cruel.

Dick told us about the interlocking antlers he'd once found. Two sparring bull moose had apparently locked horns and the fight had ended with the death of them both. Dick took the rare antlers and placed them on top of the cabin roof for safekeeping. The antlers stayed there until a visitor to the cabin decided that the antlers would make nice candle holders and knife handles. Dick remembered he'd had some choice words for the man who cut off all the antler's tines—and he didn't mind sharing them when he and the vandal later met up on the trail.

We stopped for lunch at Echo Bend. While the other horses grazed on grass, the pack horse managed to convince spaghetti-man to share a bite of his sandwich. After eating, Dick kneeled down on the banks of Eagle River and with his cupped hand, drew water straight from the river to drink. He never filtered his water. Never saw the need.

We were three miles from the trailhead when Bill and Sunny took the lead to slow our pack train from rushing home. It seemed our trip was far too short—we all wondered why we hadn't planned to stay longer. It would have been good to linger in a place that heightened the senses; where you could breathe a little deeper and think a little clearer. This has always been the appeal of wilderness—the distillation of life to its most basic elements. And while the cabin, like Dick, was a little hard to reach at first, once you arrived there was no place warmer or more inviting.

As we traveled back toward civilization, I thought about the countless steps Dick had taken from one end of the continent to the other. Not only how he managed to pull it off year after year, but how he would never quite answer the persistent question of "why." And having come to know this legend of the North, I came to consider this: There is something about traveling one step at a time across a wilderness. Moving under your own power becomes a way of knowing; of exploring the nuanced curves of the landscape. When you feel the earth underfoot, smell the scent of rain, touch the rough bark of a tree, you lay claim to it. As a younger man or woman the conquest may lay in the distance traveled, the heights achieved, the obstacles overcome. But with the passing of time, the claiming is no longer a matter of conquest. It becomes instead a claiming of intimacy with the land—of having and holding something that is at the same time both powerful and precious.

The footfall of the human step is roughly the same rhythm as that of a beating heart. When you look out over a vast distance—row upon row of canyons in the blue light of dusk; or frozen mountain peaks stretching from one horizon to the next; or the endless white of the Arctic plains—the expanse seems impossibly infinite. Hopelessly large in the scheme of human existence. But when you traverse that expanse, the infinite becomes finite; a quantifiable thing. It can be measured by miles, and minutes, and days. Mostly it can be measured by moments savored. And by moments when the razor-edged knife between life and death presses against the thin membrane of your own existence. Moments when everything hangs in the balance; so that when you eat your next meal, you savor each mouthful because you feel damn lucky to be alive.

And looking back at that row of canyons you've just traversed, or the expanse of ice and snow you've skied, or the mountains you've climbed—suddenly the expanse does not seem so infinite or impossible.

What feels infinite now is the soaring capacity of the human spirit. What becomes endless is *desire*. An incessant yearning to put comfort, assurances, and yes, even common sense aside to just *go*. Human existence—when done mindfully, with courage, and a good measure of luck—can be as expansive as any landscape.

A Note from Dick Griffith

THERE ARE THREE PEOPLE that had a great influence in this book: Bill Sherwonit, Craig Medred, and Kaylene Johnson. I took several writing classes from Bill and he very laboriously edited some of my diaries. Craig Medred was an outdoors writer for the *Anchorage Daily News*, a person whom I admired. It was Kaylene who persuaded me to pursue a book; without her it would have never happened.

There are hundreds of people that I should acknowledge, for each of whom I would like to write a short sentence. It would take many pages and I would likely forget some. The book is already too long so it's best that I not go there. I decided to only mention a few people who have died.

When you get to the advanced age of the mid-eighties you suddenly realize that you didn't get there alone. My parents would be the first on the list of people to acknowledge. I especially remember my father who had a third grade education but life dealt him an advanced college degree. He could read and write, add and subtract, multiply and divide. He was a cowboy and the Great Depression was very hard on my Father and Mother. After the Depression they both prospered because of hard work. My parents supported me in all my lengthy trips that took months to complete but I had to finance them with various jobs. "Any job is better than no job," my father repeated often, so I had many "any jobs." My parents and the Great Depression taught me well for I was poor only for very brief periods. In my adult years I always had money; I never had the need to borrow money from banks and always managed to buy cars and houses with cash. I was not born with a silver spoon in my mouth but I certainly intend to die with one in my mouth. My brother Bill abandoned the family to seek an easier life—a life that he never found.

I had a second family, Charlie and Fleeta Weinrich, who had a ranch high in the Colorado Mountains. In my younger years I spent many happy months with their children, one of whom died of scarlet fever. Their son, Sonny, was the same age as I. We both had scarlet fever at the same time. He died and I survived.

In my teenage years I was employed as a sheep herder on the open plains of Wyoming. I lived with a Mexican by the name of Placido Harmino; he lived in a sheep wagon and I in a tent with a band of sheep. Placido taught me Spanish and to enjoy dried chilies. On cold rainy nights he let me abandon my leaky, canvas, teepee tent and invited me into his warm dry, sheep wagon. I was very proud of my bedroll (wool blankets rolled up) that my father made for me. It was easy to carry on a horse but it became wet in rainy weather sleeping on the cold hard ground.

Isabelle Gallo, a Hungarian, made the largest impact on my life. Her Hungarian born parents wanted their only child to marry a nice Hungarian boy. They thought me to be a "ne'er do well," and I was. Isabelle worked in hospitals and I finished my degree in geology. She kept on working and fifteen years later I earned a degree in civil engineering. With the two degrees I finally made more money than Isabelle. While working, Isabelle bore three children; the first one died because of a difficult birth. Kimmer and Barney survived and were born in Alaska.

In 1959, I moved the family to Milwaukee. Isabelle wanted to be with her mother before she died. I hated the Milwaukee culture, the climate, and my Hungarian mother-in-law. Anatole and Joy Ryslinge saved my sanity. They owned a soils engineering firm where I worked for five years when not going to engineering school at Marquette University. They paid my tuition and encouraged me to finish my degree. I never quite fit in with the Milwaukee culture; drinking beer and watching football games was not for me. I was arrested just for driving a pickup truck down a boulevard. We lived in a subdivision that had no moose but I butchered five sheep every fall in my back yard. I hung them up in the many oak trees to cure for a week before putting them in the freezer. Kimmer and Barney let it be known when the sheep were to be butchered. It was an annual sporting event for all the neighbor kids but the parents were appalled at the yearly practice.

I had two very close friends who died tragic deaths, Bruce Stafford and Jerry Dixon. Bruce and I walked thousands of miles before he was killed in a light airplane accident. Jerry and I skied the Iditarod and we also did many Wilderness Classic races together. He died shortly after being diagnosed with ALS (Lou Gehrig's disease).

—Dick Griffith

Acknowledgments

Books are always a collaboration of ideas and people. I'd like to thank a handful of people for their technical assistance, editorial support, and most especially for their encouragement in the making of *Canyons and Ice*:

Family and friends of Dick Griffith who candidly shared their thoughts and memories—KIMMER GRIFFITH, BARNEY GRIFFITH, YARROW SILVERS, BOBBY SUE WOLK, ASTA SPURGIS, JILL JOHNSON, ROMAN DIAL, and BOB KAUFMAN;

LUKE WALLIN for wise counsel in helping plot the course of this book;

RICHARD GOODMAN for early feedback and always encouraging *le mot juste*;

MICHAEL CATTOGIO for helpful research on explorers of the North;

TOM MARTIN for generous and insightful fact-checking on the history of river runners on the Green and Colorado rivers;

ROCKY CONTOS for fact-checking the history of the Barranca del Cobre in Mexico—check out his website at **sierrario.org;**

GERRY and BARBARA KLOEHN for sending photos of Isabelle along with her letters, which lent insight into a remarkable woman;

JANE WILKENS for friendship and early readings of the manuscript;

MARCIA WAKELAND and HELEN CEPERO for inspiration and insights into craft;

HANNAH JOHNSON for administrative help and unwavering encouragement;

ERIK JOHNSON for illuminating ideas and website design;

MARK JOHNSON for that all-important *t-check*—thank you;

ANNE DUBUISSON ANDERSON and SUSAN SOMMER BEEMAN for their editing expertise;

LORI KEDROWSKI, JOHNNY JARNAGIN, TERI JARNAGIN, and YARROW SILVERS for their careful proofreading and attention to detail;

DAVID VAN NESS for his care and technical support;

STEVE ORF of FCI Digital for his superb color work;

JIM and LORI KEDROWSKI for kindly loaning several horses to make the trek to Raven Cabin;

NANETTE STEVENSON for artful book design, the press for excellence, and a generous dose of patience;

and to BILL SULLIVAN for the ride to Raven Cabin and beyond—with gratitude.

Kaylene Johnson is author of five books about Alaska and the people who live there. Her books include *Sarah: How a Hockey Mom Turned the Political Establishment Upside Down*; *Portrait of the Alaska Railroad*; *Trails Across Time: History of an Alaska Mountain Corridor*; and the memoir *A Tender Distance: Adventures Raising My Sons in Alaska*. Her award-winning articles and essays have appeared in the *Louisville Review, Spirit, LA Times, Alaska* magazine and other publications.